CONTENTS

A dream is always simmering
below the conventional surface
of speech and reflection.
—George Santayana

For Priscilla

THE
CHILDREN'S
WRITER'S
MARKETPLACE

by
S. F. Tomajczyk

Running Press
Philadelphia, Pennsylvania

Canadian representatives: General Publishing Co., Ltd.,
30 Lesmill Road, Don Mills, Ontario M3B 2T6.
International representatives: Worldwide Media Services, Inc.,
115 East 23rd Street, New York, NY 10010.

9 8 7 6 5 4 3 2 1
Digit on the right indicates the number of this printing

Library of Congress Cataloging-in-Publication Data
Tomajczyk, S. F.
   The children's writer's marketplace.
   Includes Index.
     1. Children's literature—Publishing—Directories.
     2. Children's literature—Marketing—Directories.
   I. Title.
   Z286.C48T65 1986   070.5 '025   86-10031
   ISBN 0-89471-421-X (pbk.)
   ISBN 0-89471-422-8 (lib. bdg.)

Printed by Port City Press.
Cover design by Toby Schmidt.
Typography: English Times, with Univers Light,
by rci, Philadelphia, Pennsylvania.

This book may be ordered by mail from the publisher. Please
include $1.00 for postage. But try your bookstore first!
Running Press Book Publishers, 125 South 22nd Street,
Philadelphia, Pennsylvania 19103.

Acknowledgments

I am humbly indebted to the hundreds of editors, publishers and their
staff members throughout North America who took time to fill out my
questionnaires and who sent me additional information concerning
their publishing programs. To one and all, thank you!

Special appreciation is due Tam Mossman, who put the proverbial bug
in my ear about this project, and who supported my work while he was
Editor for Running Press. To Nancy Steele, who nurtured this book
from rough draft to finished product, my gratitude for your perfection-
ism and expertise, not to mention your sense of humor.

My deepest thanks go to Priscilla—my biggest fan—for supporting my
late-night and early-morning writing sprees, helping to cross-reference
entries, comforting my anxiety attacks, ignoring my "caffeine highs,"
sharing my aspirations, providing constructive criticism, loving me, and
keeping me physically well: life just wouldn't be the same without you.
I guess dreams *do* come true after all.

INTRODUCTION

Let's face it: you have a lot of competition. There are some five million persons in the United States who claim to be writers. Yet, if the collective membership of the Council of Writers Organizations (CWO) accurately reflects the number of "real" writers (i.e., those who regularly publish), then there are only 25,000 of us. That's a big difference, and the odds of getting published would seem to be against you.

How can you beat those odds? With marketing!

There's an adage that a chain is only as strong as its weakest link, and writing for the children's market is no exception. Knowing how to research and write a book or article just isn't enough if you want to see your efforts in print. To compete successfully against other writers, you must know how to market your work.

What exactly *is* marketing? As a writer, you should view marketing as embracing all those activities that help sell your product. This includes researching potential markets (publishers); advertising the fact that you have a product for sale (through query letters); setting the price (negotiating royalties and fees); and supplying the finished product (the completed manuscript).

There are hundreds of individual markets for children's writers, each one a potential buyer of your product. The children's market is not one market, but a multiplicity of markets representing contrasting styles and genres, both fiction and nonfiction, each one carefully targeted to a specific age group or special interest.

This book will help you discover which of these markets is actively seeking your story, magazine article, or play. The information you'll find here also will help you to develop a marketing plan to transform your proposals into publications. In such a complex and competitive market, it makes sense to reach the proper markets as quickly as possible. This book has been designed to help you do just that.

ONE

HOW TO USE THIS BOOK

I'm going to suggest that you do something you probably haven't done since you were a child (and you may even have been spanked for it!): grab a pen and mark up this book. Put ink all over these clean, crisp sheets of paper? You bet! The number of markets in this book can make it difficult to differentiate one from another (e.g., "Is it *InSights* or *Insight* that publishes adventure fiction?"). Marking an entry lets you know at a glance.

Some authors, myself included, use markers of different colors to code entries: yellow for fiction; blue for nonfiction; green for high-paying markets. So, as you read through this book and see an entry that catches your eye, mark it! Underline the editor's name! Circle the word count! Star the payment rates! Write notes to yourself in the margins!

When you're ready to market your article or story, scan the appropriate subject indexes in this book. Using these as a guide (I hope you marked the names of publications here, too), look up the individual entries to determine which is your most-likely market, and read the information *very carefully*.

Since there are no standard guidelines for children's writers, the data in the individual listings become the rules you must follow if you want to sell your manuscript. Every market listed in this book tells you what its specific rules are: what its editors want, and often (perhaps more importantly), what they *don't* want. For the most part, it is being aware of, and following, these rules that separates published authors from unpublished writers.

The information listed here is the result of comprehensive questionnaires and interviews, and accurately reflects the current needs of each market. However, bear in mind these points:

- •Because numbers of pages, readers, and payment rates are subject to change without notice, it is best to use these figures as general guidelines as to the publication's current status.
- •Do send a self-addressed, stamped envelope (SASE) with every

submission, whether or not a publication requires it. This is the professional thing to do; publications that don't require an SASE will consider you a gem. (But be certain to either type or legibly print the SASE; "writer's scrawl" doesn't sit well with editors.)

- Estimates of response times to your query or manuscript are approximate. Holidays and editorial deadlines often extend the time period an editor needs to reply. Serious consideration of a manuscript or idea also can delay the response time; some manuscripts are circulated among the staff for reading and comments before a decision is made. If you don't get a reply within the allotted time listed, wait another 4 to 6 weeks before politely inquiring as to the status of your submission. If you do not receive a response to this effort within 3 weeks, telephone the editor.

- The needs of the publishing industry are constantly changing: companies relocate, staff positions change, publications are born and die, editorial needs are modified to meet reader demands, and so on. To keep abreast of developments, send for author guidelines, book catalogs, and sample issues once each year.

- If, after having checked the indexes, you can't find a specific market, be aware that it might not be listed because it is staff-written and doesn't accept freelance materials; because it did not wish to provide information (and thus does not welcome submissions); because it has changed its editorial slant and no longer publishes material for children; or because it is in transition or has ceased publication.

If you know of a children's market that is not listed in this edition, please send the name and address of the company to me, care of Running Press, and I will request information about it for the next edition of *The Children's Writer's Marketplace.*

TWO

WRITING FOR CHILDREN

Children are natural mythologists:
they beg to be told tales, and love not
only to invent but to enact falsehoods.

George Santayana
Dialogues in Limbo

Walk into any bookstore and you'll see just how accurate this observation continues to be; some stores dedicate more shelf space to children's books than to adult fiction. According to the Association of American Publishers (AAP), children's book sales have typically increased by 6% to 10% each year for the past decade.

The "baby boom" generation is now firmly entrenched in parenthood, and the children's market promises exponential growth. "There are lots of babies now, with two or three to a family instead of one," says Lauren Wohl, marketing director for three publishing houses, "and in a few years that's going to mean a lot of 10-year-olds." A bright outlook indeed for those of us who intend to write for this market.

Writers inspired by this positive conjecture and those who harbor a desire to capitalize on it should be aware of certain rules that a children's writer must follow:

• *Learn about children.* Sounds reasonable, but you'd be surprised by how many writers don't really understand children.

   Today's juveniles are different from the way you were when you were small, and it's important that you "rediscover" children before you attempt to write for them. Many manuscripts are rejected out-of-hand by editors simply because the plot or characters are unrealistic or too outdated for today's children.

   Spend time with children of all ages: learn what contemporary issues intrigue and/or concern them, how they perceive the world around them, what hobbies and interests they have, why they react or feel the way they do toward various situations, what goals and dreams they have, how they interrelate with peers and members of the opposite sex, what fears they have, and how they want other people to perceive them. If you learn to automatically incorporate this information into your writing, your manuscript will be right on target.

• *Research your material.* Knowledge improves all writing. As you do general research for an article or story, try to secure the most up-to-date information possible. Use a variety of sources, including interviews with authorities and experts, and then play them off one another; opposing views balance a manuscript and make it more believable. Children (as well as editors, I might add) see right through material that is not well-researched.

Even fiction is based on facts, not dreams or guesswork: writer's imagination *starts* with essential facts and *then* spirals outward into the realm of creativity. For the byproducts of imagination to be believable, the facts must be accurate.

The following character-analysis worksheet can be used by fiction writers as a guideline when outlining a story. Doing so will stabilize the character's traits so that s/he is not unintentionally transformed into another character as the story progresses, and it will help you—as you write the story—to determine an appropriate response for the character in any given situation. You can (and should!) devise similar worksheets to detail the story's setting and its major conflicts before commencing the writing. Believability and consistency are what count in fiction. These sheets can help you achieve them.

CHARACTER-ANALYSIS WORKSHEET

1. Name _____   2. Sex _____
3. Age _____   4. Height and weight _____
5. Hair color _____   6. Eye color _____
7. Date of birth _____
8. Birthplace _____
9. Physical characteristics _____
_____
10. Educational background _____
_____
11. Important past experiences _____
12. Best friends (and why) _____
_____
13. Other friends _____
14. Enemies (and why) _____
_____
15. Parents _____
16. Other family members; pets _____
_____
17. Current problem _____
18. How the problem develops in the story _____
_____
19. Strongest character traits _____
20. Weakest character traits _____
21. Perceives self as _____
22. Perceived by others as _____
23. Sense of humor (example) _____
_____
24. Unusual characteristics and abilities _____

25. Goals (short-term) _____

26. Ambitions (long-term) _____

27. Religion; personal beliefs; philosophy of life _____

28. Interests and hobbies _____
29. Favorite music, art, sports _____

30. Preferred style of dress; favorite colors _____
31. Favorite expressions and speech patterns _____
32. Favorite foods _____
33. Specific description of home environment _____

34. Specific description of location _____

35. One-line description of this character _____

36. Most important thing to know about this character _____

37. What makes this character angry? (Why?) _____
38. What makes this character sad? (Why?) _____
39. What makes this character come alive? _____
40. Why is this character worth reading about? _____

41. How is s/he different from other characters? _____

42. What do you like and dislike about this character? _____

43. Will the reader like/dislike this character for the same reasons? (Why?) _____
44. Will this character be remembered by the reader? (Why?) _____

• *Stay on your audience's level.* Target your material to the interests of a specific age group and also to its vocabulary level.

However, to "write down" to your audience is perhaps the worst sin a children's writer can commit. Successful children's writers select words that parallel the writing style of the story and challenge young readers by allowing them to grasp the meaning from context—as any page of *Winnie-the-Pooh* will confirm.

• *Remember the basics of your craft.* Many editors and agents I talk with complain not only about the choice of words they find in stories by inexperienced writers, but also about poorly-written dialogue, the lack of basic writing skills, inadequately-developed characters, and the tendency of writers to cram everything they've ever heard or thought into one story.

A lot of re-writing and self-editing can correct these problems, but that takes time—in some cases, too much time. Time isn't what a writer can afford if he or she wants to pay the bills; hence the appearance of seminars and correspondence courses in professional writing. If you are somewhat new to the children's market, you might consider taking one of these courses. Usually staffed by professional writers who have extensive publishing credits, correspondence courses teach basic technical skills (e.g., plot, theme, narration, and setting), as well as how to slant a manuscript to a specific market, and how to pace a story.

Some of the more popular writing programs include The Institute of Children's Literature (Redding Ridge, CT 06876, 800-243-9645 or 203-792-8600), Writer's Digest School (9923 Alliance Road, Cincinnati, OH 45242), and the Writers Institute (112 West Boston Post Road, Mamaroneck, NY 10543).

• *Know your market*. Since children's literature includes many styles and genres, each carefully targeted to a specific age group, you need to learn how to properly market your writing.

First, after you have generated a story idea, but before you sit down to write it, visit your local library. If you're planning a magazine article, consult the *Reader's Guide to Periodical Literature* to see what articles have been published recently on the same subject. If you plan to write a book, look in *Children's Books in Print* to see what titles currently on the market either resemble or duplicate your book idea.

If nothing similar to your idea is listed at your library, visit newsstands and bookstores to look for material similar to your own idea. (This is difficult, I know—no one enjoys learning that an idea is not original—but it's necessary!)

Finding a recent book or article identical to your own means that you will have to either significantly change your idea or replace it with another. Regardless of what you decide, you've just saved yourself valuable time by not duplicating someone else's published efforts.

Next, using this book as a guide, request the guidelines and catalogs of the publishers that interest you. Study these materials for information and clues about the publishers' specific needs, what material they currently publish, and how to submit material. Then follow these guidelines—to the letter.

Every publisher is unique and operates by its own rules. Learn and abide by these rules, and the children's marketplace will welcome you.

• *Keep at it*. Strive to make it fun, to make every word count, and to write something every day.

For the inexperienced children's writer who desires to become immersed in the industry as soon as possible, there are several possibilities. One is to apply to a local publisher as an outside manuscript reviewer. The pay probably will be low, but the benefits could be excellent. For example, you would learn exactly what kind of manuscripts are being submitted today by experienced children's writers, how successful queries are prepared, what themes are trendy, how characters are properly developed, and some of the tricks of the trade.

Another possibility is to approach a book publisher as a freelance packaging writer/editor. This job usually entails writing or editing copy to be used on the outside packaging of book series (such as Cloverdale's *Sweet Dreams* series for teens). Payment typically ranges from a flat fee to a royalty of 4%, both with varying advances. This position offers the same advantages as an outside reviewer position, plus one more: you are immersed in the marketing strategy of a book. This will help you learn to recognize the marketing potential of any book you produce and to discuss it knowledgeably with your publisher. Such knowledge also will be warmly welcomed by any editor; after all, editors and publishers want to sell as many of your books as possible!

Being the author of children's literature can be fun and rewarding. You have the opportunity to shape the ideals and aspirations of millions of children who will cherish throughout their lives what you've taught, shared and shown them. Good children's stories are universal and are handed down from generation to generation. (Remember *How the Grinch Stole Christmas, Charlotte's Web, The Ugly Duckling,* and *The Little Engine That Could*?)

If you believe you possess the ability to teach and captivate young readers, pursue your writing dreams: paint the pictures you see inside your head with words, and share them with the world. Your words and ideas *can* make a difference.

THREE

MAGAZINES

If you were to group all the children's magazines into stacks (as I did one rainy afternoon), you probably would organize them into three towering stacks: religious, special interest, and general interest.

The first stack consists of magazines published by religious organizations whose goal is to teach children the ethics, morals, and doctrine decreed by their faiths, with Christian themes predominating. The orientation of these publications doesn't mean, however, that their articles and stories are "preachy"; to the contrary. Again and again, editors tell me that they prefer articles and stories with subtle contemporary teachings that entertain and challenge their readers. Manuscripts with tacked-on morals don't make it in this market.

Religious magazines offer new writers a way to establish their credentials in publishing both fiction and nonfiction, and if you have the knack of catching and holding a child's interest while reinforcing religious ideals, this abundant market might be just the one for you.

The second stack of magazines consists of publications that teach and entertain children about a wide variety of topics, ranging from crafts to cooking and from math to foreign cultures. These publications include *Children's Digest* and *Highlights for Children,* for example.

For the widest exposure and the greatest financial rewards, turn to those glossy special-interest magazines in the third stack. Here you'll find some of the best-known children's magazines: *Ranger Rick* (nature), *Tiger Beat* (entertainment), and *Boy's Life* (scouting). It goes without saying that these are extremely competitive markets. To gain acceptance, you must 1) be able to find new approaches to topics of wide appeal and 2) possess excellent writing skills.

In this chapter, you'll find specific information about the exact needs of all types of children's magazines, arranged by title in alphabetical order. But before you rush to the mailbox with your manuscript, ask yourself these questions:

•Is my article or story written for *children* (not the editor)?
•Is it well organized?
•Is it interesting?
•Is it appropriate to the audience of the magazine to which it's being submitted?
•Are the characters, situations, and dialogue believable?
•If the article is nonfiction, is the research complete? Are experts and authorities quoted wherever appropriate, and is there available for the editor's reference a list of research material used to prepare the article?

If your manuscript meets these minimum requirements, go ahead and submit it to the magazine of your choice. In passing this simple review, your article or story has greatly bettered its chances of acceptance.

It's important, however, to pay close attention to each magazine's procedures. Editors *do* fantasize about discovering the next Dr. Seuss, Judy Blume, or E.B. White, but they have little patience for writers who don't do their homework or abide by the magazine's editorial rules.

Unless they state otherwise, most magazine editors prefer to receive a double-spaced manuscript accompanied by a cover letter outlining word count (an average of 250 words per page), topic, your writing credentials, and the intended readership. Such a letter should be no longer than two pages. Fiction requires an additional page: a synopsis of the story.

For manuscripts of considerable length, editors prefer that you query them with a short letter explaining your article/story and asking them whether they would like to see it. (Not surprisingly, magazine editors don't smile when a 100-page manuscript unexpectedly arrives.)

As for proposals, you'd be surprised by the number of editors who prefer them to a manuscript; a proposal allows the editor to control an article's development. If you have a marketable idea for a nonfiction article and do not want to commit your time, money, and effort to pursuing it on speculation, send a query letter to the editor describing the article's slant, its intended length, the availability of photographs or illustrations that can accompany it, and explain what specifically qualifies you to write the article.

Whether you send a complete manuscript or a query letter, *always* make certain to include an SASE for editorial correspondence and proper postage for the return of your material in the event it is rejected.

If you are trying to make a living from your writing, you might consider using the simultaneous submissions process. This simply means sending the same query or manuscript to two or more competing markets (e.g., sending "How to Preserve Animal Tracks in Plaster" to *Ranger Rick* and *Boy's Life* magazines). But be forewarned that most editors dislike this marketing method because it pressures them to make a quick decision and because a simultaneous submission is less apt to be perfectly suited to a specific publication. The implied haste of a simultaneous submission can backfire on the author: because of the need for a fast turnaround, many editors will consider your manuscript only for the magazine's immediate use, not for its long-term needs. Hence a rejection may be more likely.

If a fast decision is what you need, be certain to check the entry in this book for the magazine that interests you to see whether it accepts simultaneous submissions. If not, you can always try the safer, multiple submissions process: send manuscripts on the same subject, *but with different slants,* to two or more *non*-competing markets (e.g., "Swimming Games for Your Summer Party" for *Teenage Magazine,* and "How to Make Swimming Drills More Fun" for *Sharing the Victory*).

One fine day, several weeks after having submitted your manuscript/query to a magazine, you will remove from your mailbox a response from a magazine editor who has used your SASE. If it is an acceptance letter, you may also receive a contract from the magazine, especially if you are assigned a story.

A typical contract states the payment for an acceptable manuscript; the kill fee for unacceptable material (usually 1/3 of the regular payment); when you will be paid (on acceptance or on publication); the deadline for arrival of the manuscript in the editorial office; any restrictions on manuscript length (avoid going 10% over the specified length); what rights are being purchased (e.g., all rights or first serial rights); and illustration or photo requirements.

If you disagree with any term within the publication's contract, don't hesitate to present either a counterproposal or your own contract (but be prepared to have your attorney or agent step in if the red tape gets too thick).

Most periodicals offer contracts, but there are still some who do not confirm an oral agreement with the written word. In these cases you will want to send your confirmation of the oral terms/conditions to the editor as soon as possible; this will save time and money on both sides. The easiest method of confirmation is to mail the publication a contract letter, or facsimile. For example:

SAMPLE CONTRACT LETTER

Dear _____:

I am pleased to learn that you are interested in publishing my (article/story), tentatively titled "_____." This is to confirm that I will research and write an article of approximately _____ words on the topic _____ in accordance with our (discussion/letter) of (date). The deadline for delivery of this to your editorial office is (date).

It is understood that I will be paid $_____ on (acceptance/publication) for _____ rights. It is further understood that I will be paid a $_____ kill fee within _____ weeks after submission should this manuscript be considered unacceptable for publication or be withheld from publication for other reasons.

It is also agreed that you will reimburse me for routine expenses incurred in the researching and writing of the article, (including/excluding) long-distance telephone calls, and that any unusual expenses will be approved by you before they are incurred.

We further agree that I shall be given an opportunity to examine and correct production proofs of the article before it goes to press.

Please sign and return the attached copy of this letter to indicate your agreement to the terms and conditions of this contract. Thank you.

Sincerely yours,

When reviewing your contract, or offering a counterproposal to your editor, you will want to carefully note what publishing rights you are, in effect, selling to the publisher. As a rule of thumb, you want to retain as many rights to your works as possible so that you can resell them to other markets. There are essentially nine categories of publishing rights that periodicals consider buying from you:

First serial rights: the right to publish an article, story, or related material for the first time.

First North American serial rights: the right to first publication in both the U.S. and Canada.

One-time rights: the right to publish the material once; the buyer has no guarantee of being the first to publish the material.

Second serial rights: the right to publish an article, story, or related material after it has appeared in the same form in another publication. (These rights also may be called reprint rights.)

All rights: the unrestricted right to publish or sell the reprint rights to other publications. In general it's best to avoid selling all rights to your material; but top magazines such as *National Geographic World* usually insist upon purchasing all rights.

Simultaneous rights: the nonexclusive right to publish within two or more publications with non-overlapping markets and circulation. (Always inform the editor when you're offering simultaneous rights; some do not approve of this practice.)

Foreign serial rights: like first serial rights, purchased by a foreign publication. (To sell material published in the U.S. to foreign publications, you must specifically reserve foreign rights when you sell U.S. serial rights to an American publication.)

Motion picture rights (also extend to stage and television): the right to adapt and market material for TV or motion pictures (usually, via a 1-year "option" that is renegotiated year by year).

Syndication rights: the right to distribute material to many newspapers or magazines through a syndicate.

While we're on the topic of contracts, I'd like to bring to your attention a current trend among magazines that also requires an occasional contract: a preference of periodicals to contract work with writer/illustrator and writer/photographer teams. Many editors feel that photos and illustrations submitted by these teams are of far better quality than unsolicited material. As a freelance writer, you can capitalize on this trend by teaming up with a professional illustrator/photographer or even learning to illustrate your own work. Doing so will pay off over the long term; most magazines pay significantly more for all-inclusive manuscript packages.

If you or your photographer teammate submit photographs to a magazine to illustrate a manuscript, you also must submit a model release form (MRF) with every slide/negative in which a person is featured or prominently shown. This form is signed by the model, allowing the writer or photographer (and, eventually, the magazine) to publish the photograph. You can make your own model release form by following this sample.

SAMPLE MODEL RELEASE FORM

Name of Photographer _____
Description of the photograph(s) _____
Date of the photograph(s) _____
Location _____
    For consideration received, I give _____ (hereafter Photographer) the absolute right to copyright and use the photograph(s) described above, in whole or in part,

alone or in composite or altered form, or in conjunction with any wording, for advertising, editorial, publicity, or any other purpose.

I understand that I do not own the copyright in the photograph(s), and I waive any right to inspect or approve the finished use of the photograph(s).

I also hereby release the Photographer and all licensees from any liability whatsoever by reason of any distortion or alteration, whether intentional or not, which may occur in the making or use of the photograph(s)

I have read and fully understand this release and agree to abide by the conditions outlined in it.

Name _____

Signature _____

Address _____

Parent's or guardian's signature _____

(if model is under the age of consent)

Once your magazine contract has been agreed upon by both parties, you can sit back and enjoy the creative role reserved for you: writing.

Whether you are writing a nonfiction article or creating an original story, there is a commonality among them, and that is research. Every children's writer has a preference as to what books occupy his or her limited desktop space. Here is my own suggested (and subjective) list of reference books that you should consider having within easy reach of your typewriter or word processor.

- *The Address Book: How to Reach Anyone Who's Anyone* (Facts on File, hardcover; Putnam, paperback)
- *The Random House College Dictionary* (Random House)
- *The International Thesaurus of Quotations* (Harper & Row, hardcover; T.Y. Crowell, paperback)
- *National Directory of Addresses and Phone Numbers* (Concord Reference Books)
- *The Oxford Companion to Children's Literature* (Oxford University Press)
- *Roget's International Thesaurus* (Harper & Row, hardcover; T.Y. Crowell, paperback)
- *Subject Guide to Children's Books in Print* (R.R. Bowker Co., hardcover)
- *UPI Stylebook* (United Press International)
- *Webster's Instant Word Guide;* lists 35,000 spelled and divided words (Merriam-Webster, Inc.)
- *World Almanac,* current edition (World Almanac)
- A Zip Code directory

The following section includes vital information about magazines that actively solicit juvenile material. If you are relatively new to the children's market, it's important to remember that nonfiction articles and fiction stories are not the only material that children's magazines publish; editors also look for high-quality puzzles, quizzes, filler material, poetry, humor, games, and riddles.

To enter the top, competitive markets such as *Highlights* and *National Geographic World,* you might want to initially submit some shorter pieces like the ones listed above. After a while your name and performance may become so well-known that the editors will approach *you* with an assignment.

If you follow the rules established by these publications, make the editor's job easier, remember your SASEs, and write material that children enjoy and can learn from, you'll always be in demand as a writer for children's magazines.

AGLOW MAGAZINE, PO Box 1, Lynnwood, WA 98046–1557. (206) 775–7282. First published 1969. Printed by Aglow Publications, a Ministry of Women's Aglow Fellowship International. Gwen Weising, Managing Editor. Gloria Chisholm, submissions editor. Candy Paull, Editorial Assistant. National bimonthy, non-denominational magazine with 30,000 readers. Target audience: "fundamental, charismatic Christian women of all ages." Average issue length: 26 pages.

□A Christian periodical, *Aglow* specializes in "women's personal experiences and teaching articles on salvation, baptism in the Holy Spirit, and Christian life." The editors seek profiles of women who make a difference; interviews with influential women; and self-help and how-to articles about personal experiences, teachings, and personal growth; 1,500 to 2,000 words. Well-received articles: "When God Seems to Have Failed You" and "Opening the Prison Doors" (overcoming eating disorders).

□*Aglow* seeks "more articles on how to handle women's internal needs: loneliness, anger, jealousy, despair," comments Paull.

□Pays on acceptance: $.08 to $.10 per word. Buys first rights only (not negotiable). Prefers to receive query. Interested in reprints. Simultaneous submissions and photocopies acceptable. Replies in 6 weeks. Author guidelines and sample issues available. Send SASE.

AIM MAGAZINE, 7308 S. Eberhart Ave., Chicago, IL 60619. (312) 874–6184. First published 1974. Printed by AIM Publishing Company. Dr. Myron Apilado, Managing Editor. Ruth Apilado, Editor/Publisher. Henry Blakely and Mark Boone, submissions editors. National quarterly magazine with 7,000 readers. Target audience: "high-school students and teachers, college students and teachers, general public." Average issue length: 48 pages.

□Brotherhood is the focus of *AIM,* which publishes nonfiction articles and interviews (one per issue) about people who are making contributions to their communities, and fiction stories emphasizing that people are more alike than different; 1,500 words or less. The editors also seek humor and fillers (100 to 500 words) as well as poems (2 or 3 per issue) and some puzzles. Criteria: "social significance." *Aim* considers illustrations for its short stories, and photos for its interviews and articles. Well-received articles: "The South African Struggle," "Freeing of Nelson Mandela," "Tutu's Winning Nobel Peace Prize," and "Plight of the American Indian."

□"Because of the possibility of nuclear war, people are seeking out ways for survival," says Ruth Apilado. "They are feeling more alienated from society and are more conscious of the importance of getting together. Submissions should reflect this concern."

□Pays on publication: $25 maximum for articles and stories ("unless for a contest"); $5 for cartoons; $100 for winning short stories. Buys first serial rights (negotiable). Prefers to receive entire manuscript. Not interested in reprints. Simultaneous submissions and photocopies acceptable. Replies in 4 weeks. Author guidelines and sample issue available for $3. Send SASE.

THE AMERICAN NEWSPAPER CARRIER, PO Box 15300, Winston–Salem, NC 27103. Monthly magazine. Target audience: preteen and teenage newspaper carriers in the United States.

☐ The magazine is looking for "upbeat articles and light fiction, including humor, adventure, mystery, and inspirational." Preferred article length: 1,000 words.

☐ Pays on publication: $25 for articles and stories. No kill fee. Buys all rights. Prefers to receive entire manuscript. Not interested in reprints. Simultaneous submissions acceptable if editor is so informed. Responds in 4 to 6 weeks. Send SASE.

AMERICAN POETRY ANTHOLOGY, Dept. JY–86, 1620 Seabright Ave., PO Box 2279, Santa Cruz, CA 95063. (408) 429-1122. First published 1981. Printed by American Poetry Association. John Frost, Managing Editor. Richard Elliot, submissions editor. Jennifer Manes, Outreach Manager. National quarterly hardback anthology with 10,000 readers. Target audience: young adults and adults from all walks of life. Average issue length: 325 pages.

☐ Publishing poetry of all styles, *American Poetry Anthology* considers poems on any subject for adults and young adults ("whatever the author's age"); 20 lines maximum. Every contributor receives, free, "The Poet's Guide to Getting Published," a handbook of practical ideas and suggestions.

☐ "We are interested in seeing work from poets of all levels of skill and experience, especially those who are new or little known," says Manes.

☐ Awards annual prizes on November 15: $1,000 grand prize; 140 lesser prizes with a combined value of $3,200. Author retains rights (not negotiable). Prefers to receive entire manuscript; one poem per poet. Simultaneous submissions and photocopies acceptable. Replies in 2 to 3 weeks. No author guidelines or sample issue available. SASE not required.

THE BLACK COLLEGIAN, 1240 S. Broad St., New Orleans, LA 70125. (504) 821–5694. First published 1970. Printed by Black Collegiate Services, Inc. James Borders, Editor. National bimonthly (4 times during school year) magazine with 131,000 readers (BPA-audited). Target audience: "college students interested in career development/guidance and in black socioeconomic-cultural issues." Average issue length: 160 pages.

☐ Publishes a variety of nonfiction articles regarding career opportunity, black history, how-to, and sports; 1,000 to 2,500 words. The editors are especially interested in receiving profiles of outstanding black professionals in technical fields (2,500 words maximum). Theme issues: Engineering and Travel; Job Market; Medicine; Science Careers; Computers/Graduate Schools. Will consider illustrations and photos as part of the manuscript package. Well-received articles: "The Next Era of Technology: People Dealing With People" and "Career Opportunities in Communications."

☐ Pays on publication: $25 to $350 per article; $35 per B&W photo; $50 per color photo. Offers kill fee. Buys one-time and first rights (negotiable). Prefers to receive entire manuscript. Not interested in reprints. Simultaneous submissions acceptable. Replies in 2 weeks. Author guidelines and sample issue available. Send SASE.

BLUEGRASS UNLIMITED, PO Box 111, Broad Run, VA 22014. (703) 361-8992. First published 1966. Printed by Bluegrass Unlimited, Inc. Peter V.

Kuykendall, Editor. National monthly magazine with 84,280 readers. Target audience: "devotees of bluegrass and old-time country music." Average issue length: 72 pages.

□Although not dedicated to children and young adult readers, *Bluegrass Unlimited* does publish some children's material each month within the magazine's focus. The editors seek artist interviews and profiles; feature articles; and book and record reviews that pertain to bluegrass, old-time, and traditional country music; length varies. How-to articles should focus on songwriting, playing techniques, and repairing instruments. *Bluegrass Unlimited* is also interested in some fiction, puzzles, news, humor, and photos and illustrations. Seldom uses poetry or fillers. Well-received articles: profiles on Jimmy Martin and Jim & Jesse, and Festival List.

□Pays on publication: $.06 to $.08 per word. Buys first serial rights (negotiable). Prefers to receive query. Not interested in reprints. Simultaneous submissions not acceptable. Photocopies acceptable. Replies in 3 to 4 weeks. Author guidelines and sample issue available. SASE preferred.

BOY'S LIFE, 1325 Walnut Hill La., Irving, TX 75038-3096. (214) 659-2360. First published 1911. Printed by The Boy Scouts of America. William B. McMorris, Managing Editor. W.E. Butterworth, IV, Fiction and Features Editor. Scott Stuckey, Special Features Editor. Gene Daniels, Photography Editor. Leslie Jackson, Editorial Assistant. National monthly magazine with 1.4 million subscribers and 7.2 million readers (ABC-audited). Target audience: "Boy Scouts and Cub Scouts, ages 8 to 18." Average issue length: 76 pages.

□Accepts fiction (adventure, humor, outdoor adventure, science fiction, suspense, mystery, and westerns) of 1,000 to 3,000 words, and nonfiction: how-to, 200 to 300 words; columns about sports, pets, and other subjects, 750 words; major articles on any topic, 1,500 words; and photo features (2-page spread with up to 750 words). Will also consider puzzles, jokes, professional cartoons, profiles, interviews, photos, and illustrations. "We look for stories of high quality, preferably from experienced authors." Well-received articles include stories on aviation, computers, space, nature, sports, nonfiction war stories, and detective stories.

□Pays on acceptance: $150 to $1,500 per article, depending on length; $5 for fillers. Buys first rights (negotiable). Prefers to receive query for nonfiction and entire manuscript for fiction. Interested in reprints. Simultaneous submissions and photocopied manuscripts are *not* accepted. Replies in 2 to 4 weeks. No author guidelines or sample issues available. Send SASE.

BREAD, 6401 The Paseo, Kansas City, MO 64131. (816) 333-7000. First published 1939. Printed by the Nazarene Publishing House (PO Box 527, Kansas City, MO 64141). Karen DeSollar, Editor. National monthly magazine with 26,000 readers. Target audience: "junior- and senior high-school aged teens in the Church of the Nazarene." Average issue length: 34 pages.

□Seeks a variety of material for young adults and older teens that will develop and enrich their Christian lives. The editors are interested in nonfiction and first-person articles that deal with witnessing, church doctrine, secular issues, Christian living, and concerns afflicting teens today; 1,200 to 1,500 words. Occasionally buys poetry (traditional, free verse); up to 25 lines. The editors are also looking for fictional stories (1,500 words maximum) in which charac-

ters must put Christian principles into action (e.g., situations involving relationships with family and friends, moral and ethical decisions). No interviews,
profiles, humor, or puzzles.

□Professional-quality B&W photos of teens in groups ("especially close-ups
of individual kids in a variety of mood poses") are considered for publication
with or without accompanying manuscript (but make certain that dress and
styles are current). Illustrations are done by assignment only. Contact the
editorial staff to be considered for future assignments.

□Pays on acceptance: $.03 per word for articles and stories (less for second
rights); $15 minimum for B&W photos; $.25 per line for poetry. Buys first
rights (negotiable). Prefers to receive entire manuscript. Interested in reprints.
Simultaneous submissions acceptable. Replies in 6 to 8 weeks. Author guidelines and sample issues both available. Send SASE.

CAMPUS LIFE, 465 Gunderson Dr., Carol Stream, IL 60188. (312)
260–6200. Printed by Christianity Today, Inc. James Long, Senior
Editor/Creative Director. Gregg Lewis, Senior Editor (submissions editor).
National monthly magazine with 200,000 subscribers and 600,000 readers.
Target audience: high-school and college-age youth with traditional values
and Christian orientation. Average issue length: 80 pages.

□Publishes fictional stories about real-life situations (but no romance!); and
nonfiction articles of 500 to 3,000 words in the following areas: general interest; youth needs and values; interviews and profiles (most of which are staff-
written); sports; travel and personal experiences. The editors also will consider
humor ("all styles but cute"); poetry "that doesn't read like a greeting card";
illustrations and photos. Well-received article: "Me and My C.M." (a humorous story about a girl falling in love with a talking Coke machine).

□ "We're always looking for excellent thematic first-person stories that utilize
the techniques of fiction. As a Christian magazine that presents a balanced
view of all of life, we are not interested in 'religious' material in a traditional
sense. . . however, stories must reflect a Christian world-life view. If you are a
freelancer who can produce powerful writing for the youth audience, we want
to hear from you."

□Pays on acceptance: $200 and up per article, depending on length, author's
experience and quality of writing; $50 for B&W photos; $100 for color photos;
$250 for cover photos. Buys first serial rights (negotiable). Prefers to receive
query, "but we need to see more if you're a new author." Simultaneous submissions OK. Will consider reprints on an individual basis. Replies in 4 weeks.
Author guidelines available; sample issues: $2. Send SASE.

CAMPUS VOICE, 505 Market St., Knoxville, TN 37902. (800) 251–5002.
First published 1984. Printed by Whittle Communications. Keith Bellows,
VP/Executive Editor. Elise Nakhnikian, Senior Editor (submissions editor).
National quarterly magazine. Target audience: graduating high-school seniors
and college students.

□*Campus Voice* publishes 3 issues for college students and 1 issue for graduating high-school seniors each year. The editors seek fiction (2,500 to 4,000
words), nonfiction (1,500 to 3,500 words), profiles (2,000 to 3,500 words),
interviews (1,500 to 4,000 words), and humor (1,000 to 2,000 words). Looking
for "well-written, witty or well-researched, incisive prose about subjects of
interest to intelligent young adults." Considers photos and illustrations. Well-

received articles: "Inside MTV," "The Dawn of the New Fraternity," and "Abortion: The Toughest Choice."
□ "A lively voice is of the essence," stresses Nakhnikian.
□ Pays on acceptance: $300 to $1,000 per article. Buys first North American rights (not negotiable). Prefers to receive query. Not interested in reprints. Simultaneous submissions not accepted. Photocopies acceptable. Replies in 8 weeks. Author guidelines and sample issue available. SASE preferred.

CARTOON WORLD, PO Box 30367, Lincoln, NE 68503. (402) 435-3191. Printed by Hartman Publishing Company. George Hartman, Editor/Publisher. Monthly newsletter with up to 1,000 readers. Target audience: cartoonists, artists, and humor writers. Average issue length: 26 to 28 pages.
□ Pays on acceptance: $5 per 8½″ × 11″ ms. page. Buys first serial rights (negotiable). Prefers to receive query. Interested in reprints. Photocopies acceptable. Replies in 2 weeks. Author guidelines available; sample issue: $5. Send SASE.

CATHOLIC TWIN CIRCLE, 6404 Wilshire Blvd., Suite 900, Los Angeles, CA 90048. (213) 653-2200. First published 1965. Printed by Twin Circle Publishing. Mary Louise Frawley, Executive Editor. Loretta G. Seyer, Foreign Editor (submissions editor). National weekly tabloid with 50,000 readers (Alcor-audited). Target audience: "Catholic and Christian families interested in issues that affect them personally and generally; people who want information and inspiration." Average issue length: 20 to 24 pages.
□ This religious periodical publishes feature articles for Christian families and young adults. Sporadically publishes material for children depending upon the submission's quality. The editors seek nonfiction articles, profiles, interviews, and selected humor: 1,000 to 2,000 words. No fiction, poetry, puzzles, or fillers. Will consider photos and illustrations. Well-received articles: series on Catholic annulments and "The Problem of Being a Single Male." and teen series.
□ The editors are "always looking for well-researched articles on topics of religious and general interest," reports Seyer.
□ Pays on publication: $.10 per word. Buys general rights (negotiable). Prefers to receive query or entire manuscript. Interested in reprints that have appeared in non-Catholic publications. No simultaneous submissions; photocopies acceptable. Replies in 6 to 8 weeks. Author guidelines and sample issue: $1. Send SASE.

CHICKADEE, 56 The Esplanade, Ste. 306, Toronto, Ontario Canada, M5E 1A7. (416) 868-6001. First published 1979. Printed by The Young Naturalist Foundation. Janis Nostbakken, Editor. Catherine Ripley, Managing Editor. National magazine published 10 times annually (July and August excluded); 100,000 readers in Canada; 50,000 in the U.S. Target audience: children ages 4 to 9. Average issue length: 32 pages.
□ Interested in adventure and "Read-to-Me" stories (child-centered or animal stories); 200 to 800 words. Acceptable nonfiction topics: animal traits and habits, crafts ("easy to make—without parental supervision—from things around the house"), how-to, and unusual wildlife stories; length varies. The editors also will consider fillers of amazing animal facts (10 to 25 words),

poems (4 to 25 lines), high-quality environmental and wildlife photographs and illustrations (commissioned only).

☐ "Quality is the main thing we look for. . . also imaginative twists on the ordinary." Well-received articles: "Emma's Valentine" and "Country Summer/City Summer."

☐ Pays on publication: $150 to $300 per story; $15 to $50 per idea. Buys all rights (negotiable). Prefers to receive entire manuscript. Interested in reprints. Simultaneous submissions acceptable if editor is so informed. Replies in 6 weeks. Author guidelines available for SASE; sample issue: $1.50 and SASE. Send SASE with all submissions (U.S. authors should use international postal coupons).

CHILD LIFE, 1100 Waterway Blvd., PO Box 567, Indianapolis, IN 46206. (317) 636-8881. Printed by Children's Better Health Institute, Benjamin Franklin Literary & Medical Society Inc. Steve Charles, Editor. Florence Kramer and Kathleen B. Mosher, Associate Editors. National magazine published monthly (bimonthly in February/March, April/May, June/July, and August/September). Target audience: children ages 7 to 9. Average issue length: 48 pages.

☐ Wants quality fiction and nonfiction, primarily about good health—articles that not only entertain but also educate. Desired fiction: realistic stories, adventure, humor, mysteries, and science fiction; 500 to 1,800 words. "Stories that deal with a health theme need not have health as a primary subject, but should include it in some way in the course of events. Main characters should adhere to good health practices, unless failure to do so is necessary to a story's plot." The editors also are looking for nonfiction articles of 500 to 1,200 words on general interest, nature, science, history, biography, health, and nutrition, and photo features (6-8 photos). Make certain to include a list of sources. Photos and illustrations are considered when they accompany a manuscript; single photos are not purchased.

☐ "When writing, avoid an encyclopedic or 'preachy' approach. We try to present our health material in a positive manner, incorporating humor and a light approach wherever possible without minimizing the seriousness of what we are saying." Holiday and seasonal material—stories, articles and activities —are the best bet for a new author. Submit material at least 8 months in advance. Well-received article: "The Lost Goblin" by Frances B. Watts.

☐ Pays on publication: $.06 per word for stories and articles; $7 per poem; $7 minimum per photo; variable rate for puzzles and games; plus 2 complimentary copies upon publication of author's material. Buys all rights (negotiable). Prefers to receive entire manuscript. Interested in reprints. No simultaneous submissions. Replies in 8 to 10 weeks. Note: Submissions are considered for publication in all 6 of this publisher's magazines, so do not resubmit material to another publication at this address (see listing for *Children's Better Health Institute*). Author guidelines available. Sample issue: $.75. Send SASE.

CHILDREN'S BETTER HEALTH INSTITUTE, BENJAMIN FRANKLIN LITERARY & MEDICAL SOCIETY, INC. Publishes *Child Life*; *Children's Digest*; *Children's Playmate*; *Humpty Dumpty's Magazine*; *Jack and Jill*; and *Turtle Magazine for Preschool Kids*.

CHILDREN'S DIGEST, 1100 Waterway Blvd., PO Box 567, Indianapolis, IN 46206. (317) 636-8881. Printed by Children's Better Health Institute,

Benjamin Franklin Literary & Medical Society, Inc. Elizabeth Rinck, Editor. National magazine published monthly (bimonthly in February/March, April/May, June/July, and August/September). Target audience: children ages 8 to 10. Average issue length: 48 pages.

□Desired fiction includes realistic stories, adventure, humor, mysteries, and science fiction of 500 to 1,800 words. "Remember, characters in realistic stories should be up-to-date. Many of our readers have working mothers and/or come from single-parent homes. We need more stories that reflect these changing times while communicating good, wholesome values." The editors also are looking for nonfiction articles of 500 to 1,200 words on nature, science, history, biography, health and nutrition, and photo features. Photos and illustrations are considered for publication when they accompany a manuscript. Well-received articles include: "The Witch Who Switched" by Jean Leedale Hobson.

□Pays on publication: $.06 per word for stories and articles; $10 minimum per poem; $7 minimum per photo; variable rate for puzzles and games; plus 2 complimentary copies upon publication of author's material. Buys all rights. Prefers to receive entire manuscript. Interested in reprints. No simultaneous submissions. Replies in 8 to 10 weeks. Note: submissions are considered for publication in all 6 of this publisher's magazines, so do not resubmit material to another publication at this address (see listing for *Children's Better Health Institute*). Author guidelines available; sample issue: $.75. Send SASE.

CHILDREN'S PLAYMATE, 1100 Waterway Blvd., PO Box 567, Indianapolis, IN 46206. (317) 636–8881. Printed by Children's Better Health Institute, Benjamin Franklin Literary & Medical Society, Inc. Elizabeth Rinck, Editor. National magazine published monthly (bimonthly in February/March, April/May, June/July, and August/September). Target audience: children, ages 5 to 7. Average issue length: 48 pages.

□Seeks easy-to-read fiction for the beginning reader. Topics of interest: adventure, humor, mysteries and science fiction of 500 to 800 words. Publishes nonfiction of 300 to 600 words that introduces rather than explains a specific aspect (i.e., the "All About..." approach) of interest to young children: animals, nature, science, places, events, health, and people. "We are also looking for short, simple poems or stories in rhyme." Editors will consider photographs and illustrations that accompany a manuscript.

□Suggestion: Seasonal stories with holiday themes are a new author's best chance for publication. Submit manuscripts at least 8 months in advance. Well-received articles include: "The Dumbest Dog in the World" by Susanne Shaphren.

□Pays on publication: $.06 per word for stories and articles; $10 minimum per poem; $7 minimum per photo; variable rate for puzzles and games; plus 2 complimentary copies upon publication of author's material. Buys all rights. Prefers to receive entire manuscript. Interested in reprints. No simultaneous submissions. Replies in 8 to 10 weeks. Note: Submissions are considered for publication in all 6 of this publisher's magazines, so do not resubmit material to another publication at this address (see listing for *Children's Better Health Institute*). Author guidelines available; sample issue: $.75. Send SASE.

CHOICES, 730 Broadway, New York, NY 10003. (212) 505–3132. First published 1985. Printed by Scholastic, Inc. Vicky Chapman, Editorial Director.

National magazine published 9 times annually during school calendar. Target audience: junior-high and high-school students, ages 12 to 15.

☐ Geared toward young teens in home economics classes, *Choices* publishes how-to, feature, and service articles about food and nutrition, clothing, family issues, personal grooming, careers, child development, and consumer concerns; 1,200 words maximum. The editors also will consider shorter articles (400 words) for the magazine's "Hands-On" feature. Well-written fiction also is encouraged.

☐ Pays on acceptance: $100 to $400 for articles and stories. No kill fee. Buys all rights (negotiable). Prefers to receive entire manuscript. Not interested in reprints. Simultaneous submissions acceptable if editors are so informed. Responds in 4 to 6 weeks. Author guidelines available. Send SASE.

CHRISTIAN ADVENTURER, PO Box 850, Joplin, MO 64802. (417) 624-7050. Printed by Messenger Publishing House. Rosmarie Foreman, Managing Editor. Billie Blevins, Assistant Editor. National weekly magazine. Target audience: teens, ages 12 to 19, who participate in Sunday school education. Average issue length: 8 pages.

☐ *Christian Adventurer* publishes articles of 1,500 to 1,800 words for teens involved in religious education: contemporary issues, social concerns, inspirational, profiles of historical figures, and substance abuse. The editors seek stories written by young adult students, and "short fiction with a spiritual or moral lesson involved." No occult material, vulgar language, unacceptable alternative lifestyles, or material that doesn't present Christian or doctrinal viewpoint.

☐ Pays on publication: $.015 per word for articles and stories. Buys first serial rights; not negotiable. Prefers to receive entire manuscript. Interested in reprints. Simultaneous submissions and photocopies acceptable. Replies in 4 weeks. Author guidelines and sample issues available. Send SASE.

CHRISTIAN HOME & SCHOOL, 3350 E. Paris S.E., PO Box 8709, Grand Rapids, MI 49518-8709. (616) 957-1070. First published 1922. Printed by Christian Schools International. Gordon L. Bordewyk, Editor. Judy Zylstra, Associate Editor. International magazine published 8 times each year; circulation: 13,500. Readership: 28,000. Target audience: "Contemporary Christian families." Two-thirds of family readership have 2 children living at home. Average issue length: 36 pages.

☐ Designed for parents who support Christian education, *Christian Home & School* publishes very little material for children ("perhaps a Christmas story or two"). Articles primarily deal with issues that confront Christian parents. Photos and illustrations welcome. Well-received articles: "Children and Death," "The Homework Blues," "Children and Fantasy."

☐ Pays on publication: $40 to $75 per article, depending upon length. Buys first serial rights. Prefers to receive query or entire manuscript ("include a sentence or two about yourself for us to use as a contributor's note"). Rarely publishes reprints. Simultaneous submissions acceptable if editor is so informed; photocopies acceptable. Replies in 3 to 4 weeks. Author guidelines and sample issue available. Send SASE.

CHURCH HERALD, 1324 Lake Drive S.E., Grand Rapids, MI 49506-1692. (616) 458-5156. First published 1826. Printed by The Church Herald, Inc. Kim

N. Baker, Managing Editor. Rev. Dr. John C. Stapert, Editor. National biweekly magazine with 127,000 readers. Target audience: "general interest, Reformed Church in America. Approximately equal distribution from ages 15 to 65." Average issue length: 32 pages.

☐A religious periodical, the *Church Herald* publishes fiction (1,500 words), nonfiction (2,000 words maximum), and poetry (30 line limit) for young adults and adults ages 15 to 65. Publishes approximately 6 articles slanted for young children each year. No puzzles, profiles, fillers, or humor. Illustrations and interviews are staff produced. Well-received article topics: farm crisis, ethics, alcoholism, depression, and healing.

☐Pays on acceptance: $30 to $125 for articles and stories depending upon length. Buys all rights (negotiable). Prefers to receive entire manuscript. Not interested in reprints. Simultaneous submissions and photocopies acceptable. Replies in 3 to 4 weeks. Author guidelines and sample issue available. Send SASE.

CLUBHOUSE (formerly *The Good Deeder*), PO Box 15, Berrien Springs, MI 49103. (616) 471-9009. First published 1951. Printed by Your Story Hour. Elaine Meseraull, Editor. National digest published 10 times each year; 15,000 subscribers. Target audience: children, ages 9 to 14. Average issue length: 32 pages.

☐Publishes articles and stories that support Christian principles for young children. The editors seek fiction in which characters serve as role models. Acceptable topics: adventure, humor, and historical slants; 800 to 1,200 words. Acceptable nonfiction topics: health, exercise, substance abuse, smoking, fitness, and dieting; 500 to 600 words. No romance, science fiction, mystery, or fantasy. The editors also consider humorous or mood poetry (4 to 24 lines); puzzles (word search, hidden pictures, brainteasers); and cartoons (vertical format). Illustrations are done by assignment only. Well-received articles: "Cinderfella Pink," "She Can Drive You Crazy," "The Babysitting Incident," "Harvest of Love," "Mom, Why is There a Skunk in the Bathroom?" and "The Gold Coin."

☐"Articles should capture a child's innocence, intelligence, and mischievousness and teach important issues or ethics without being preachy," says Meseraull. "Stories must have action or strong emotional appeal, of interest to both boys and girls, and give the underlying message that kids are O.K., smart, good, or kind."

☐Pays 6 to 8 weeks after acceptance: $35 for lead stories, $30 for regular stories, $25 for stories less than 800 words, $12 for cartoons, $10 minimum for poetry, and $10 for puzzles. Buys first North American serial rights (negotiable). Prefers to receive entire manuscript. Interested in reprints. Simultaneous submissions and photocopies acceptable. Replies in 4 weeks. Author guidelines and sample issue available for SASE with 3 first-class stamps. Send SASE.

COBBLESTONE: THE HISTORY MAGAZINE FOR YOUNG PEOPLE, 20 Grove St., Peterborough, NH 03458. (603) 924-7209. First published 1980. Printed by Cobblestone Publishing, Inc. Carolyn P. Yoder, Editor-in-Chief. Audrey W. Sweeney, Managing Editor. National monthly magazine with 40,000 readers. Target audience: children, ages 8 to 14, interested in American history. Average issue length: 48 pages.

☐Presents one specific historically-related theme in each issue (e.g., natural disasters, American fads, Eleanor Roosevelt), and all articles appearing in that issue support the theme. The editors are seeking feature articles, including in-depth nonfiction, plays and biographies (800 to 1,200 words); supplemental nonfiction that includes subjects directly or indirectly related to the theme (200 to 800 words); activities such as crafts, recipes, and other projects that can be done alone or with adult supervision (1,000 words maximum); fictional stories of adventure, history, biography, and topics relating to the issue's theme (1,500 words maximum); poetry with objective imagery (100-line limit); and theme-related puzzles, crosswords and games (no wordfinds).

☐"Historical accuracy and lively, original approaches are the primary concerns of the editors in choosing material for publication." Suggestion: request *Cobblestone*'s guidelines to see its editorial calendar with upcoming themes and deadlines. Pick an issue and submit your query as soon as possible.

☐Pays on publication: $.13 to $.15 per printed word for feature articles; $.10 to $.12 per printed word for supplemental nonfiction; $.10 to $.15 per printed word for fiction; variable rates for poetry, puzzles, games, and activities. Buys all rights (negotiable). Prefers to receive query with an outline, proposed bibliography, and short writing sample. Interested in reprints. Simultaneous submissions acceptable if editors are so informed. Replies in 10 to 12 weeks, longer depending on issue's deadline. (Queries are filed and considered in the order in which they are received.) Author guidelines available for SASE; sample issue: $2.95. Send SASE.

CONFIDENT LIVING, PO Box 82808, Lincoln, NE 68501. (402) 474–4567. First published 1944. Printed by Good News Broadcasting Association, Inc. Norman A. Olson, Managing Editor. National magazine published monthly (except for July/August issue); about 125,000 subscribers. Target audience: "evangelical Christians of all ages, 4 years old and up." Average issue length: 64 pages.

☐An interdenominational magazine that promotes Biblical teachings, *Confident Living* is looking for articles of 1,500 words that teach the word of God from a conservative, evangelical position and show how it applies to everyday life. The editors also will consider interviews, newsworthy reports, profiles, first-person stories, and family issues having a Biblical basis. Where applicable, make certain to support your article with correct Bible references.

☐Photos, more than ever before, are playing a major role in determining an article's acceptance for publication. Photos or illustrations should be submitted with manuscript.

☐Pays on acceptance: up to $.10 per word for articles; up to $25 for B&W photos; $25 to $75 for color slides. Occasionally pays expenses for special assignments. Buys first serial rights (not negotiable). Prefers to receive entire manuscript. Not interested in reprints. No simultaneous submissions or photocopied manuscripts. Responds in 16 working days. Author guidelines and sample issue available. SASE required.

THE COVENANT COMPANION, 5101 N. Francisco Ave., Chicago, IL 60625. (312) 784–3000. First published 1921. Printed by Covenant Press, 3200 W. Foster Ave., Chicago, IL 60625. Jane Swanson-Nystrom, Managing Editor. James R. Hawkinson, Editor. National monthly magazine with 26,000 subscribers and 60,000 to 65,000 readers (Touche Ross-audited). Target audience: "members and friends of The Evangelical Covenant Church." Readers have higher than average income and educational level. Average issue length: 48 pages plus inserts.

☐Publishes material with Christian orientation and an evangelical perspective for young adult and adult readers. Occasionally publishes articles and stories slanted for young children ("hope to move to monthly or bimonthly inclusion"). The editors seek fiction and nonfiction (1,000 words) as well as some poetry and puzzles (length varies). Photos also are considered. Well-received article: "Poems and Prayers from the Ark" (by children).

☐Pays one month after publication: $15 to $35 for articles and stories, depending upon length ("children might be less, in view of 'recognition' value to budding writers"). Buys first serial rights (negotiable). Prefers to receive entire manuscript. Interested in reprints. Simultaneous submissions and photocopies acceptable. Replies in 8 to 10 weeks. Author guidelines available; sample issue: $1.50. Send SASE.

CRICKET MAGAZINE, PO Box 300, Peru, IL 61354. Marianne Carus, Editor. National monthly magazine. Target audience: children ages 6 to 12.

☐Primarily publishes fantasy, fiction, nature, and science articles; 400 to 1,250 words. The editors are looking for lively writing that shows respect for the readers, and does not talk down. Stories that weave together biography and historical fiction are in high demand. Stories with talking animals are not accepted. Seasonal material should be submitted at least 6 months in advance.

☐Pays on publication: $.25 per word for first rights; $.12 per word for reprint rights. No kill fee. Buys first North American serial rights. Prefers to receive entire manuscript. Occasionally interested in reprints. Simultaneous submissions undesirable. Responds in 6 to 8 weeks. Author guidelines available for SASE; sample issue: $2. SASE required.

CRUSADER, PO Box 7259, Grand Rapids, MI 49510. (616) 241-5616. First published 1958. Printed by Calvinist Cadet Corps. G. Richard Broene, Editor. International magazine published 7 times annually (October through April) with 13,000 readers. Target audience: "boys, ages 9 to 14, who are members of the Calvinist Cadet Corps, church members or not." Average issue length: 24 pages.

☐A religious magazine for young men, *Crusader* is interested in publishing articles with Christian perspectives: nonfiction of 600 to 900 words about nature, profiles, humor, sports, science, crafts, outdoor recreation, and general interest; fiction of 800 to 1,500 words, with fast-moving action that doesn't oversimplify situations and solutions.

☐"We look for fiction that will fit into one of 7 themes (1 per issue) that we have pre-selected for the year. An author who avoids long dialogue and who can write believable action and characters will find a warm welcome with us." Themes are selected in January; manuscripts requested in February and March. The editors also are interested in word puzzles and mazes (½-page). Well-received articles: "Letter to Grandma" (a series of letters about giving).

☐Pays on acceptance: up to $.05 per word for articles; $.03 per word for article reprints; $5 to $25 for photos. Buys one-time rights (not negotiable). Prefers to receive entire manuscript. Interested in reprints. Simultaneous submissions acceptable. Replies in 2 to 3 weeks. Author guidelines and sample issue available. Send SASE.

DISCOVERIES, 6401 The Paseo, Kansas City, MO 64131. (816) 333–7000. First published in the 1920s. Printed by the Nazarene Publishing House, PO Box 527, Kansas City, MO 64141. Libby Huffman, Editor. International weekly magazine with 75,000 readers. Target audience: "children, ages 8 to 12, from church or non-church families." *Discoveries* is distributed during the Sunday School hour." Average issue length: 8 pages.

☐The editors use stories that correspond to the teachings of the Nazarene church: obedience to God, trust in God, kindness to others, and Bible appreciation; 800 to 1,000 words. Manuscripts should not be "preachy." *Discoveries* will also consider poetry written by children (any length), puzzles (½-page to full page), cartoons (½-page), and devotional material. Illustrations are needed for each story; B&W photos for cover only.

☐Pays on acceptance: $20 to $35 average for stories; $.02 per printed word for second rights; $15 to $25 for B&W photos; up to $40 for commissioned illustrations. Buys all rights but allows authors to reprint their own articles. Prefers to receive entire manuscript. Interested in reprints. Simultaneous submissions acceptable. Responds in 3 to 4 weeks. Author guidelines and sample issue available. SASE required.

DOLLY MAGAZINE, 140 Joynton Ave., Waterloo, New South Wales 2008, Australia. Published by Fairfax Magazines. Deborah Bibby, Editor. National monthly magazine with 230,000 circulation. Target audience: "female teenagers, ages 13 to 18." Average issue length: 162 pages.

☐Caters to the diverse interests of teenage girls: beauty, decorating, photos and stories, music, successful teenage actors, and hints on everything a teenager is interested in. The editors seek fiction (2,000 words); profiles and interviews (1,500 words); general nonfiction (2,000 words); fillers and humor (1,200 words); and poetry (200 words). *Dolly* also considers photos and illustrations. Well-received articles: "Things Your Mother Should Have Told You But Didn't," "Beauty Makeovers," and "Survey on Sex, Drugs, and Rock 'n Roll."

☐Pays on publication: $120 to $180 per 1,000 words. Buys all Australian rights (negotiable). Prefers to receive entire manuscript. Interested in reprints. Simultaneous submissions and photocopies acceptable. Replies in 6 weeks. Author guidelines and sample issue available. Send SASE.

THE DOLPHIN LOG, 8440 Santa Monica Blvd., Los Angeles, CA 90069. (213) 656–4422. Printed by The Cousteau Society. Pamela Stacey, Editor. National quarterly magazine with 60,000 readers. Target audience: "children, ages 7 to 15, who are intrigued by the oceans and marine life." Average issue length: 16 pages.

☐An educational publication for children about the environment, marine biology, ecology and environmental concerns. The editors are looking for factual articles on all aspects of the aquatic environment; 1,000 to 1,200 words. Profiles and interviews of well-known scientists or youths involved in oceanography are also welcome; 1,500 words maximum. Stories should have an ecological message or show environmental interactions. Games, puzzles, filler material, poetry and short humor are considered. Photos (B&W and color) of undersea action (especially if it involves children) are reviewed with or without an accompanying manuscript (send duplicates only).

☐"Give us a new approach on common topics," stress the editors. "Use a well-written, factual style that not only educates and entertains children but also challenges them to think.''

☐Pays on publication: up to $125 for articles; $25 for B&W photos; $25 minimum for color slides. Replies in 6 to 8 weeks. Writer's guidelines available for SASE; sample issue: $2. Send SASE.

DRAMATICS MAGAZINE, 3368 Central Pkwy., Cincinnati, OH 45225. (513) 559–1996. First published 1929. Printed by The International Thespian Society. Don Corathers, Editor. National magazine published monthly during school year; 32,000 readers (SRDS-audited). Target audience: "high school and college theater students and teachers." Average issue length: 48 pages.

☐Publishes practical articles about various aspects of theater for high-school and college students and teachers. The editors seek plays (1 act to full-length), profiles and interviews of people involved in theater (2,000 to 4,000 words), humor, and nonfiction articles on actor training and theater (2,000 to 4,000 words). Photos and illustrations accompanying manuscripts also are welcome. No puzzles, poetry, or filler material.

☐Pays on acceptance: $25 to $250 for plays and articles. Buys first North American serial rights (negotiable). Prefers to receive entire manuscript. Interested in reprints. Simultaneous submissions and photocopies acceptable. No dot-matrix print. Replies in 3 to 6 weeks. Author guidelines and sample issue available. Send SASE.

ECLIPSE COMICS, INC., PO Box 199, Guerneville, CA 95446. (707) 869–9401. Founded 1977. Catherine Yronwode, Editor-in-Chief. Dean Mullaney, Publisher. Comics trademarked under Eclipse Comics, Inc. and Eclipse Enterprises, Inc. include *Airboy, Alien Encounters, Tales of Terror,* and *Zot.* National monthly "comic" books, each with 30,000 to 80,000 readers. Target audience: teens and young adults (mostly male) interested in adventure, super-heroes, horror, and science fiction comics. Average issue length: 32 pages (26 pages editorial; 6 pages of columns, letters and ads).

☐"We publish 20 comic books per month," reports Yronwode, "but only 2 anthology titles (i.e., *Tales of Terror, Alien Encounters)* are routinely open to freelancers."

☐*Tales of Terror* (horror slant) and *Alien Encounters* (science fiction) are alternating bimonthly comic books. Both feature 3- to 8-page graphic narratives with "twisted endings." The editors buy 4 stories per month ("We're always buying from freelancers"). They seek full scripts for alien "first contact" stories and tragic vampire romance stories: acceptable length varies. Well-received horror stories: "Bear-Bear," "Every Evening Billy Comes Home," and "Remembering Rene." Well-received science fiction stories: "Picture Me and You," "Freefall," and "Night of the Monkey."

☐"We select artists to illustrate scripts we've purchased from freelancers," says Yronwode.

☐Pays 30 days after acceptance: $30 to $35 per page for scripts (as drawn, not as typed manuscript); $125 per page for artwork (pencils plus ink); $12 to $15 per page for lettering; $25 per page for coloring; and $200 to $300 for cover paintings. Buys first publishing rights, foreign syndication rights (with additional payment to author/artist), and 5-year reprint/repackaging rights, with additional payment, (negotiable). Prefers to receive entire manuscript. Interested in reprints, but only in "first time comic art adaptations of well-known science fiction/horror author's works in the short story genre." Simultaneous submissions acceptable if editor is so notified; photocopies acceptable. Replies in 6 to 8 weeks. Author guidelines available for SASE; sample issue: $1.75. Send SASE.

ELECTRIC COMPANY, 1 Lincoln Plaza, New York, NY 10023. (212) 595-3456. First published 1977. Printed by the Children's Television Workshop. Aura Marrero, Managing Editor. Randi Hacker, Editor (submissions editor). National magazine published 10 times each year; 300,000 readers (ABC-audited). Target audience: "upper-middle class children, ages 6 to 10." Average issue length: 32 pages.
☐Publishes fiction (1,000 words) and nonfiction (500 words) on various topics. Seeks "factual pieces with a light touch on animals, the world, other children." The editors also use puzzles (e.g., wordhunts, crosswords, and mazes). Well-received articles: "Penguins," "Bugs Bunny," "Back to School with Snoopy," and "Career Dogs."
☐Pays on acceptance: $50 to $75 for articles and stories. Buys all rights (not negotiable). Prefers to receive entire manuscript. Not interested in reprints. Simultaneous submissions not accepted; photocopies acceptable. Replies in 4 to 6 weeks. Sample issues available. Send SASE.

THE EXCEPTIONAL PARENT, 605 Commonwealth Ave., Boston, MA 02215. (617) 536-8961. First published 1971. Published by Psy-Ed Corporation. Maxwell J. Schleifer, Ph. D., Editor-in-Chief. Stanley D. Klein, Ph. D., Editor. Christine Sandulli, Managing Editor. National monthly magazine with 35,000 readers. Target audience: "parents with children, from infancy to age 18, who have mental and/or physical disabilities." Average issue length: 68 pages.
☐Although *The Exceptional Parent* primarily publishes non-technical articles for parents of disabled children, it also publishes children's and young adult's submissions within a special section of the magazine; acceptable length varies. No fiction, fillers, poetry, or puzzles. Will consider humor, but "only if in good taste." All photo submissions should be accompanied by a model release form, as required by law.
☐Pays on publication: $50 minimum for articles, depending upon topic, amount of research, and author's reputation. Buys first serial rights (negotiable). Prefers to receive query. Interested in reprints. Simultaneous submissions not accepted; photocopies acceptable. Replies in 4 to 8 weeks. Author guidelines available. Send SASE.

EXPLORING MAGAZINE, 1325 Walnut Hill La., Irving, TX 75038. (214) 659-2365. Printed by the Boy Scouts of America. Scott Daniels, Executive Editor. National quarterly magazine with 400,000 readers. Target audience: young men and women, ages 14 to 21, who are involved in the Explorer program.
☐Publishes how-to and general-interest articles: camping skills, outdoor recreation, contemporary teen issues, and travel; 1,500 words. The editors also seek profiles of unusual or outstanding Explorer Scouts. Suggestion: send for the Explorer fact sheet, and become acquainted with a local Explorer post.
☐"Write stories that lend themselves to good photography," says one editor.
☐Pays on acceptance: $300 and up for feature articles. Buys first serial rights.

Prefers to receive query with writing sample. Interested in reprints. Simultaneous submissions acceptable. Replies in 4 weeks. Author guidelines and sample issues available for SASE and $1. Send SASE.

FAMILY CIRCLE MAGAZINE, 488 Madison Ave., New York, NY 10022. (212) 593–8000. Printed by *The New York Times,* 229 W. 43rd St., New York, NY. Barbara Blakemore, Managing Editor. Susan Ungard, submissions editor. Linda Oliveri, Executive Assistant to the Editor-in-Chief and President. National magazine/digest published 17 times each year; 7 million readers. Target audience: working and non-working women of all ages, many with families. Average issue length: 140 pages.
□Publishes various materials slanted for children "a couple of times a year." *Family Circle* specializes in fiction and nonfiction for a largely female readership; length varies. The editors also consider short poetry, fillers, 1-page puzzles, cartoons, and short humor pieces. Photos and illustrations welcome.
□Pays on acceptance: varying rate depending upon article's topic, timeliness, and length. Buys all rights (negotiable). Prefers to receive entire manuscript. Interested in reprints. Simultaneous submissions, photocopies acceptable. Replies in 6 to 8 weeks. Author guidelines and sample issues available. Send SASE.

FANTASY BOOK, PO Box 60126, Pasadena, CA 91106. First published 1981. Printed by Fantasy Book Enterprises. Dennis Mallonee, Publisher. Nick Smith, Editor. National quarterly magazine with 5,000 readers. Target audience: young adults and older adults who enjoy science fiction. Average issue length: 64 pages. *Fantasy Book* is not buying new fiction until January, 1988.

FIRST COMICS, INC. 435 N. LaSalle, Chicago, IL 60610. (312) 670–6770. First published 1982. Richard Obadiah, Publisher. Rick Oliver, Managing Editor. Laurel Fitch, Editor. National magazines published monthly, bimonthly, and annually; 500,000 readers. Target audience: males ages 15 to 25 with an interest in science fiction, fantasy, and adventure. Average issue length: 28 editorial pages.
□Publishes comic books (e.g., *American Flagg!, Grimjack, Badger, Nexus, Whisper, Beowulf, Elric, Hawkmoon, Corum, Jon Sable, Time Beavers, The Enchanted Apples of Oz,* and others) with adventure, fantasy, and science fiction themes. The editors consider humor, interviews, scripts, and illustrations. Lettering, inking, and coloring also welcome. No poetry, puzzles, photos, profiles, or fillers.
□Pays on acceptance/publication: variable page rate and royalty. Buys all rights (negotiable). Prefers to receive outline. Interested in reprints. Simultaneous submissions and photocopies acceptable. Replies in 12 to 36 weeks. No author guidelines or sample issues available. SASE preferred.

FREEWAY, PO Box 632, Glen Ellyn, IL 60138. (312) 668–6000. Printed by Scripture Press. Billie Sue Thompson, Editor. National quarterly magazine with 70,000 readers. Target audience: "evangelical Christians, ages 13 to 21." Average issue length: 4 pages.
□The editors are looking for true stories and personal experiences with Christian themes (especially about how God has worked in teens' lives); 1,000 words. Also interested in how-to and self-help articles offering Christian ad-

vice on dealing with a variety of secular issues; 750 words. No fiction, poetry or puzzles. Photos and illustrations are considered when accompanied by a manuscript.

☐Fillers must include Christian themes and ideas!

☐Pays on acceptance: $.04 to $.07 per word for articles; $5 to $30 for B&W photos. Buys first rights (negotiable). Prefers to receive entire manuscript. Interested in reprints. Simultaneous submissions acceptable. Responds in 4 weeks. Author guidelines and sample issue available. SASE required.

THE FRIEND MAGAZINE, 50 E. North Temple, Salt Lake City, UT 84150. (801) 531-2210. First published 1971. Printed by the Church of Jesus Christ of Latter Day Saints. Vivian Paulsen, Editor. Carrie Kasten, Secretary. International monthly magazine with more than 200,000 readers. Target audience: "boys and girls, ages 3 to 11." Average issue length: 48 pages.

☐Interested in stories and articles with universal settings, conflicts, and characters; up to 1,000 words. Stories about boys and girls resolving conflicts are particularly in demand. Other topics: picture, holiday, sports, science, and photo stories, as well as manuscripts that portray various cultures. Very short fiction and nonfiction pieces are also needed for young readers and preschool children; up to 250 words. The editors consider humor, nature and picture poetry, cartoons, games and puzzles about pets, nature, history and religion, and crafts and projects of all types. No freelance illustrations; commissioned work only. Submit seasonal material at least 8 months in advance.

☐"Stories should focus on character-building qualities and should be wholesome without moralizing or preaching. Poems should be uplifting and of substance, evoking positive emotions and worthy aspirations without over-attention to rhyme."

☐Pays on acceptance: $.08 per word and up for articles; $15 minimum for poetry; $10 minimum for games and activities; plus 2 complimentary copies upon publication. No payment for children's contributions. Buys all rights (not negotiable), but authors may request rights to have their work reprinted after their manuscript is published. Prefers to receive entire manuscript; query letters not encouraged. Not interested in reprints. No simultaneous submissions. Responds in 8 weeks. Author guidelines and sample issue available. SASE required.

GREYLORE, PO Box 8212, Woodside, MY 11377. (718) 721-6478. Printed by Sirius Comics. Juan Collado, Publisher. National bimonthly magazine. Target audience: children and young adults, ages 14 and up.

☐*Greylore* is a "swashbuckling" comic book that eliminates the super-hero image found in traditional comic books. The editors look for authors who can "appeal to both teenagers and adults with their stylistic writing and creativity."

☐Pays on publication: $35 minimum per published page plus 8% royalty on cover price. No kill fee. Buys all rights (not negotiable). Prefers to receive query. (Note: the editor seeks synopses and scripts for new 25-page stories; submit entire manuscript.) Not interested in reprints. Simultaneous submissions accepted if editor is so informed. Replies in 6 to 8 weeks. Author guidelines available; sample issue: $2. Send SASE.

GROUP MEMBERS ONLY, PO Box 481, 2890 N. Monroe Ave., Loveland, CO 80539. (303) 669-3836. First published in 1983. Printed by Thom Schultz

Publications, Inc. Thom Schultz, Publisher. Barbara Beach, Editorial Assistant. National magazine published 8 times each year (January, February, March, May, June, September, October, November); 27,500 readers. Target audience: "high-school-age Christian young people and their youth group leaders—interdenominational." Average issue length: 16 pages.

□Primarily publishes how-to articles for high-school teens on improving self-image and relationships with others (i.e., family, friends), and articles on strengthening faith and applying it to daily life; 800 to 1,000 words. The editors also consider cartoons and photos (B&W and color of teenage individuals and couples, families and groups of people—all races). Well-received articles: "The Love Secret: Friends Forever," "Sexual Abuse: The Secret You Don't Keep," and "Are You a Christian Snob?"

□"Write for high-school age young people in a non-preachy way," says Beach.

□Pays on acceptance: up to $150 for 800 to 1,000 words. Buys all rights (negotiable). Prefers to receive query. Not interested in reprints. No simultaneous submissions; photocopies acceptable. Replies in 2 to 4 weeks. Author guidelines and sample issue available. SASE preferred.

GUIDE, 55 W. Oak Ridge Drive, Hagerstown, MD 21740. (301) 791-7000. First published 1953. Printed by Review & Herald Publishing Association. Jeannette Johnson, Editor. National weekly magazine with 50,000 readers. Target audience: "juniors and early teens, ages 10 to 14." Average issue length: 32 pages.

□Publishes nonfiction only. The editors are looking for stories dealing with the problems that today's Christian youth meet in a "normal" life; 800 to 2,000 words. Occasionally will buy serialized true stories (10 chapters maximum), poetry (up to 12 lines), and adventure "just-for-fun" stories (1,000 words). "We're looking for top quality writing—writing with depth. We touch on family problems such as divorce or changes such as grandparents moving into the home; latchkey children; and how Christians relate to and solve problems."

□Pays on acceptance: $.03 to $.04 per word for articles; $.50 to $1 a line for poetry. ("It takes from 4 to 6 weeks to process and pay acceptances.") Buys first and/or one-time rights (not negotiable). Prefers to receive entire manuscript. Interested in reprints. Simultaneous submissions acceptable if editor is so notified. Responds in 6 weeks. Author guidelines and sample issue available. SASE required.

HICALL, 1445 Boonville Ave., Springfield, MO 65802. (417) 862-2781. First published 1954. Printed by Gospel Publishing House. Rick Knoth, Youth Editor. Don Bailey, Editorial Assistant. National weekly magazine with 120,000 readers. Target audience: young people, ages 12 to 17, enrolled in junior-high and high-school. Average issue length: 8 pages.

□A Christian periodical, *HiCall* publishes articles for teenagers on various aspects of Christian living; 500 to 1,000 words. Nonfiction needs: missionary material and scientific, historical, and nature articles with a spiritual message or lesson. Acceptable fiction should present "believable characters working out problems according to Bible principles"; 1,200 to 1,800 words. The editors also seek meaningful poetry with spiritual emphasis; 10 to 30 lines, puzzles that either incorporate Scripture verses or ask questions about the Bible (length varies), and filler material with an evangelical emphasis (up to 300 words). Criteria: "realistic plot (if fiction), strong spiritual emphasis, element of conflict, relates well to teenagers." Well-received article topics: peer pressure, dating, practical information on living the Christian life, and articles on emotions (e.g., doubting).

☐ "Characters, setting, plot, and action should be realistic," stress the editors. "Construct your plot carefully so each incident moves naturally and sensibly toward crisis and conclusion."

☐ Pays on acceptance: $.03 per word for first rights; $.02 per word for reprint rights. Buys first or second serial rights. Prefers to receive entire manuscript. Send seasonal material one year in advance. Interested in reprints. Simultaneous submissions and photocopies acceptable. Replies in 12 weeks. Author guidelines and sample issue available. Send SASE.

HIGH ADVENTURE, 1445 Boonville Ave., Springfield, MO 65802. (417) 862-2781. First published 1972. Printed by the Assemblies of God. Johnnie Barnes, submissions editor. Donna Jester, Editorial Assistant. National quarterly magazine with 70,000 readers. Target audience: "adolescent boys of the Royal Rangers." Average issue length: 16 pages.

☐ Designed to "provide boys with worthwhile, enjoyable, leisure reading, to challenge them to higher ideals and greater spiritual dedication, and to perpetuate the spirit of the Royal Rangers program through stories, ideas and illustrations." The editors are looking for nonfiction features and articles (Christian living, devotional, salvation, self-help, historical); biographies, how-to, news items, missionary stories, and testimonials dealing with adolescent themes; varying length. Fiction themes include adventure, nature, westerns, and humor; 1,200 words. Editors also will consider puzzles, games, cartoons, jokes, and fillers; varying length. Color slides are also purchased, with or without accompanying manuscript.

☐ "Avoid long, involved sentences—shoot for an average of 15 words. Also, beware of clichés and hackneyed expressions. And if scripture passages are quoted from a version other than King James, identify the version."

☐ Pays on acceptance: $.02 per word for articles and stories; $7.50 for cartoons; $1 to $2 for jokes; $10 for puzzles. Buys either first or all rights (negotiable). Prefers to receive entire manuscript. "New writers should send a letter of introduction giving personal background, etc." Interested in reprints. Simultaneous submissions OK. Responds in 6 to 8 weeks. Author guidelines and sample issue available. SASE preferred.

HIGHLIGHTS FOR CHILDREN, 803 Church St., Honesdale, PA 18431. (717) 253-1080. First published 1946. Printed by Highlights for Children, Inc., 2300 W. Fifth Ave., Columbus, OH 43272-0002. Kent L. Brown, Jr., Editor. National magazine published 11 times annually; more than 2 million readers. Target audience: children ages 2 to 12. Average issue length: 40 pages.

☐ Publishes fiction and nonfiction of interest to children. Nonfiction topics: history, nature, science, sports, biographies; up to 900 words. As for fiction, the editors are looking for humor, suspense, adventure (no violence), horse stories, rebuses, and mysteries; up to 900 words. The editors also are interested in fillers such as craft ideas, party plans, and fingerplays; 10 to 250 words. Puzzles and games ("must not require marking page") also are welcome. Poetry is seldom published in *Highlights*.

☐In fiction, "The main character should overcome difficulties and frustrations through his or her own efforts. Leave a strong emotional residue for the reader to learn from."

☐Pays on acceptance: $.10 minimum per word for articles and stories (more for short pieces); $15 to $30 for crafts ideas. Buys all rights (not negotiable). Prefers to receive entire manuscript for fiction; for nonfiction, prefers query from established authors only. No simultaneous submissions. Responds in 6 to 8 weeks. Author guidelines available for SASE; sample issue: $2.25 and SASE. SASE required with all submissions.

HUMPTY DUMPTY'S MAGAZINE, 1100 Waterway Blvd., PO Box 567, Indianapolis, IN 46206. (317) 636–8881. Printed by Children's Better Health Institute, Benjamin Franklin Literary & Medical Society Inc. Christine French Clark, Editor. Florence Kramer, Associate Editor. National magazine published monthly (bimonthly in February/March, April/May, June/July, and August/September); Target audience: children ages 1 to 6. Average issue length: 48 pages.

☐Publishes easy-to-read fiction and nonfiction stories for beginning readers. Fictional topics of interest: adventure, humor, mysteries and science fiction; 500 to 800 words. Short nonfiction articles (600 words maximum) are published about exercise, health, simple crafts, animals, simple word games, puzzles, and science. Humorous stories and poems that rhyme, and healthful recipes requiring little or no need for the stove, are eagerly sought. "In devising recipes, keep the ingredients healthful. Avoid sugar, salt, chocolate, red meat and fats." The editors consider photos only if captioned and accompanied by a manuscript. Well-received articles include "Katie's Marching Band" by Judy Mason.

☐Pays on publication: $.06 per word for stories and articles; $10 per poem; $7 per photo minimum; variable rate for puzzles and games; plus 2 complimentary copies upon publication. Buys all rights. Prefers to receive entire manuscript. Interested in reprints. No simultaneous submissions. Replies in 8 to 10 weeks. Note: Submissions are considered for publication in all 6 of this publisher's magazines, so do not resubmit material to another publication at this address (see listing for *Children's Better Health Institute).* Author guidelines available; sample issue: $.75. Send SASE.

INSIGHTS, 1600 Rhode Island Ave., N.W., Washington, D.C. 20036. (202) 828–6059. Printed by the National Rifle Association of America. Marsha Beasley, Editor. National monthly magazine. Audience: male and female junior members, ages 20 and under, of the National Rifle Association.

☐*InSights* caters to youths involved in hunting, competitive shooting, or gun collecting. The editors seek fiction—adventure (e.g., wilderness survival), humor, history—and nonfiction; 1,200 words. Submit seasonal material 6 months in advance. Suggestion: remember that the reader is 20 years old or younger; address the story appropriately.

☐"All stories must relate to one of the shooting sports, and if your story teaches the reader a skill or lesson in the process of entertaining, so much the better."

☐Pays on acceptance: up to $150 for stories with photographs. No kill fee. Buys first North American serial rights. Prefers to receive query with synopsis, though unsolicited manuscripts are considered. Not interested in reprints. No simultaneous submissions. Replies in 4 to 6 weeks. Author guidelines and sample issues available. Send SASE.

INSTRUCTOR MAGAZINE, 545 Fifth Ave., New York NY 10017. (212) 503-2888. First published 1890. Marge Scherer, Managing Editor. Mary Harbaugh, Associate Editor. National monthly magazine with 250,000 subscribers and 700,000 readers (ABC-audited). Target audience: "elementary school teachers." Average issue length: 120 to 200 pages.
☐Although not dedicated to juvenile readers, *Instructor Magazine* often publishes holiday stories, plays, songs, and poems appropriate for public-school children. Nonfiction articles must be curriculum-related (e.g., how-to); 1,000 to 2,500 words. For fiction, the editors seek "read-along" stories that focus on either a specific holiday season or a special event; 1,000 to 1,500 words.
☐"Stories and articles must be appropriate for public schools and sensitive to children. Avoid sexist, derogatory and questionable material."
☐Pays on acceptance: up to $350 for an article; $100-$250 for short features. Buys all rights, first rights, and one-time rights (negotiable). Prefers to receive entire manuscript. Rarely interested in reprints. No simultaneous submissions. Responds in 6 to 8 weeks. Author guidelines available for SASE; no sample issues available. SASE preferred.

THE INSTRUMENTALIST, 200 Northfield Rd. Northfield, IL 60093. (312) 446-5000. First published 1946. Printed by James T. Rohner. Anne Driscoll, Managing Editor. National monthly magazine with 19,000 readers. Target audience: "band and orchestra players and educators." Average issue length: 100 pages.
☐Primarily publishes nonfiction, nontechnical articles about music (e.g., what it's like to play an instrument and participate in a musical ensemble). Editors will consider profiles of memorable musicians, photo features, techniques, how-to, philosophy, newsworthy reports, and trends analysis; up to 1,500 words. The magazine features 4 theme issues: Back to School; Marching Bands; Summer Camps, Clinics and Workshops; New Products. Inquire about the editorial calendar each year to learn about any theme changes.
☐Pays on publication: $25 to $40 per printed page for articles; $10 for B&W photos; $50 minimum for color cover shots; plus 2 copies upon publication. Buys all rights (negotiable). Prefers to receive entire manuscript; query about articles you anticipate to exceed 1,000 words. Not interested in reprints. Simultaneous submissions acceptable. Replies in 2 to 4 weeks. Author guidelines and sample issue available. SASE not required.

INTERACTION, 1333 S. Kirkwood Road, St. Louis, MO 63122. (314) 965-9000. First published 1961. Printed by The Lutheran Church–Missouri Synod. Martha S. Jander, Editor. National bimonthly magazine and monthly newsletter with 16,000 readers. Target audience: Sunday school teachers and superintendents of the Lutheran Church, ages 16 to 80. Average issue length: magazine, 16 pages; newsletter, 8 pages.
☐Publishes religion-oriented articles for students and teachers of the Lutheran Church–Missouri Synod. Acceptable nonfiction topics: inspirational, how-to, educational, and theological; 1,500 words maximum. "Must be doctrinally sound and meet Sunday-school teacher's needs." The editors

also consider puzzles (crossword, word search, dot-to-dot) for their New Life in Christ Sunday School material; 1 page. *Interaction* publishes a variety of materials slanted for teachers of children on a monthly basis. Some fiction is published, but primarily for "teachers to share with their classes for discussion." Well-received articles: "Molly Finds Out," "Helping Sunday School Children Witness," "We Are The Church Together," "All About Stewardship," and "VBS, Reach In, Reach Out!"

☐Pays on publication: $5 to $35 for articles and stories. Buys all rights (negotiable). Prefers to receive query. Not interested in reprints; no simultaneous submissions. Photocopies acceptable. Replies in 12 weeks. Author guidelines and sample issues available. Send SASE.

IN TOUCH, PO Box 2000, Marion, IN 46952. (317) 674-3301. First published 1970. Printed by Wesley Press. James Watkins, Editor. David Holdren, Executive Editor. National monthly magazine with 50,000 readers. Target audience: "boys and girls, ages 13 to 19, and parents." Average issue length: 32 pages.

☐The editors are looking for nonfiction testimonies, articles about contemporary issues, how-to, humor, interviews of well-known Christians, profiles, and book excerpts; 500 to 1,500 words. Acceptable fiction includes true experiences written in fiction form, humorous fiction, or C.S. Lewis-type allegory; 500 to 1,500 words. No poetry, cartoons or puzzles. Seasonal material should be submitted at least 9 months in advance. Photos are considered with or without accompanying manuscript. "We need *Seventeen* and *Campus Life*-type cover shots and candid close-ups of faces; not teens sitting in meadows reading Bibles in soft focus."

☐*In Touch's* official password is: "Wesleyan-Arminian-evangelical-holiness manuscript." According to editor James Watkins, this means that "articles should reflect a joy and excitement in a personal relationship with God, a transformed life, holiness of heart and effective Christian service."

☐"We attempt to encourage a biblical lifestyle; witnessing, sexual purity and abstinence from all things harmful to the body and soul, without being preachy."

☐Pays on acceptance: $.02 to $.03 per word for articles and stories; $.02 per word for reprints; $15 to $25 for B&W photos. Occasionally pays expenses of authors on special assignment. Buys first, second, and reprint rights (negotiable). Prefers to receive entire manuscript. Interested in reprints. Simultaneous submissions acceptable. Replies in 4 to 6 weeks. Author guidelines available; no sample issues. SASE required.

JACK AND JILL, 1100 Waterway Blvd., PO Box 567, Indianapolis, IN 46206. (317) 636-8881. Printed by Children's Better Health Institute, Benjamin Franklin Literary & Medical Society, Inc. Christine French Clark, Editor. National magazine published monthly (bimonthly in February/March, April/May, June/July, and August/September). Target audience: children ages 6 to 8. Average issue length: 48 pages.

☐Publishes fiction and nonfiction that deal with health issues, directly and indirectly; 500 to 1,800 words. Preferred fiction includes realistic stories, adventure, fantasy (past and future), biographical fiction, humor, mysteries, and science fiction. Characters must be real, contemporary and easy for children to relate to. Acceptable nonfiction topics: science, sports, crafts, exercise, nature, history and biographies of famous people who are children's heroes; 500 to 1,200 words. Puzzles and word games appropriate for elementary-school children are also welcome if you know the vocabulary level for children 6 to 8. The editors consider photos only if captioned and accompanied by a manuscript. Well-received article: "Night Pilots" by Linda G. Shail (a factual account of how bats can "see" in the dark).

☐Pays on publication: $.06 per word for stories and articles; $10 per poem; $7 minimum per photo; variable rate for puzzles and games; plus 2 complimentary copies upon publication of author's material. Buys all rights. Prefers to receive entire manuscript.

☐Interested in reprints. No simultaneous submissions. Replies in 8 to 10 weeks. Note: Submissions are considered for publication in all 6 of this publisher's magazines, so do not resubmit material to another publication at this address (see listing for *Children's Better Health Institute*). Author guidelines available. Sample issues: $.75. Send SASE.

JUNIOR LIFE, PO Box 850, Joplin, MO 64802. (417) 624-7050. First published 1962. Printed by Messenger Publishing House. Rosmarie Foreman, Managing Editor. Billie Blevins, Assistant Editor. National weekly magazine. Target audience: children, ages 9 to 11, who are in Sunday school. Average issue length: 8 pages.

☐Publishes fiction and nonfiction for children involved in religious education. The editors seek stories written by students, and "short fiction with a spiritual or moral lesson involved"; 1,500 words maximum. Acceptable nonfiction: profiles of historical figures, inspirational prose, and contemporary and social issues; 1,000 to 1,500 words. No occult material, vulgar language, unacceptable alternative lifestyles, or material that doesn't present Christian or doctrinal viewpoint.

☐Pays on publication: $.015 per word for articles and stories. Buys first serial rights (not negotiable). Prefers to receive entire manuscript. Interested in reprints. Simultaneous submissions and photocopies acceptable. Replies in 4 weeks. Author guidelines and sample issues available. Send SASE.

JUNIOR RIDERS, PO Box 63105, ST. LOUD, MO 63105. (314) 966-4330. Printed by Flegel Publishing Company. G. Alexander Smith, Publisher. National bimonthly magazine. Target audience: children, ages 12 to 14, who are knowledgeable about horses.

☐*Junior Riders* is especially interested in articles on horse care, training regimens, riding activities, profiles of riders or trainers, humor, and photo features; 1,200 to 2,500 words.

☐"The readers of *Junior Riders* are intelligent and knowledgeable, so don't make the mistake of talking down to them. Convey the information in a lively and entertaining fashion, and your chances of being published are greatly enhanced."

☐Pays on publication: $25 minimum for articles; will pay expenses of writers on assignment. No kill fee. Buys first North American serial rights. Prefers to receive query with detailed outline. Interested in reprints. Replies in 8 weeks. Author guidelines available; sample issues: $.80. Send SASE.

JUNIOR SCHOLASTIC, 730 Broadway, New York, NY 10003. (212) 505-3000. First published 1937. Printed by Scholastic, Inc. Lee Baier, Editor.

National biweekly magazine with 725,000 readers (ABC-audited). Target audience: students, ages 10 to 14. Average issue length: 16 pages.

☐Publishes articles of interest to children in grades 6 to 8. Acceptable topics: U.S. history, teens in other countries, national issues, and profiles of teens and young adults; 1,000 words. The editors especially seek manuscripts and photos about foreign teens that "tell about their country, its culture, history, and problems." Illustrations are done on commission only.

☐Pays on acceptance: $150 to $300 per article (1 to 3 pages). Buys first serial rights (negotiable). Prefers to receive query. Not interested in reprints. Simultaneous submissions and photocopies acceptable. Replies in 16 weeks; send SASE. Author guidelines an sample issues available for 9″ × 12″ SASE.

JUNIOR TRAILS, 1445 Boonville Ave., Springfield, MO 65802. (417) 862-2781. Printed by Gospel Publishing House. Charles Ford, Editor-in-Chief. National weekly journal with 65,000 readers. Target audience: "boys and girls, ages 9 to 12." Average issue length: 4 pages.

☐A Sunday school tabloid publishing articles and stories that have a spiritual emphasis for older elementary-age children. The editors look for a limited number of nonfiction articles on nature, science, history, and biography themes; 500 to 1,200 words. Fiction is heavily used. Stories should be relevant to the 9-to-12 age level. Involve character-building with a moral/spiritual emphasis; 1,000 to 1,800 words. Poetry relevant to the needs and feeling of children is also considered; length varies. Photos are purchased infrequently and illustrations are done either in-house or by commission; contact the art director for possible assignments.

☐"We are looking specifically for stories that present believable characters working through realistic situations via application of moral principles. Don't be afraid to address trends and issues affecting children (e.g., drugs, sex, alcohol, broken homes, suicide, fear of war, electronic media, occult)."

☐Pays on acceptance: $.03 per word for first right articles and stories; $.02 per word for reprints; $.03 per word for fillers; up to $5 for poetry. Buys first rights (not negotiable). Prefers to receive entire manuscript. Seldom interested in reprints. Simultaneous submissions acceptable. Replies in 6 to 8 weeks. Author guidelines and sample issue available. Send SASE.

LIGHTED PATHWAY, 922 Montgomery Ave., Cleveland, TN 37311. (615) 476-4512. First published 1929. Printed by Pathway Press (Church of God Publishing House). Marcus V. Hand, Editor. National monthly magazine with 30,000 readers. Target audience: "youth and young adults from 15 to 25 years old." Average issue length: 28 pages.

☐*Lighted Pathway* is a magazine dedicated to instilling youth with good Christian values. Interested in publishing nonfiction: exposés, how-to, interview, profile, devotional, travel, recreation, contemporary issues, and photo features; 1,000 to 1,500 words. Fiction should be youth-oriented (e.g., historical, romance, adventure) with believable characters, and should follow Christian beliefs; 800 to 1,200 words. Puzzles (crosswords, word finds) and games also are welcome. Youth-oriented photos are considered when submitted with manuscript.

☐Pays on acceptance: $.02 to $.04 per word for articles and stories; up to $25 for B&W photos. Buys first rights (negotiable). Prefers to receive either query or entire manuscript. Not interested in reprints. Simultaneous submissions and photocopies accepted. Replies in 4 weeks. Author guidelines and sample issues available. Send SASE.

LIGUORIAN, 1 Liguorian Dr., Liguori, MO 63057. (314) 464–2500. First published 1913. Printed by Redemptorist Fathers. Francine M. O'Connor, Managing Editor. National monthly magazine with circulation of 500,000. Readers: 1 million. Target audience: Catholic families, singles, teens, young adults, and elderly. Average issue length: 64 pages.

☐Publishes articles "that help young adults live fuller Christian lives in a predominantly non-Christian society." The editors are open to all nonfiction topics that fit this purpose, but are especially receptive to spiritual growth articles; 1,800 words. *The Liguorian* publishes one staff-written column each month for juveniles; good market for young adult material. Well-received article topics: Christian rock music, and Catholic Church history.

☐Pays on acceptance: $.07 per word for first-time purchases ("will go as high as $.10 or $.15 per word for quality writers in this field"). Buys all rights ("will return rights after publication upon written request"). Prefers to receive entire manuscript. Not interested in reprints. No simultaneous submissions or photocopies. Replies in 6 weeks. Author guidelines and sample issues available. Send SASE.

LISTEN, 6830 Laurel St., N.W., Washington, D.C. 20012. (202) 722–6725. First published 1948. Printed by Narcotics Education, Inc. Gary B. Swanson, Editor. National monthly magazine with 100,000 readers. Target audience: "American high-school teenagers." Average issue length: 32 pages.

☐Seeks a wide range of articles on dangers of drug abuse for teens and young adults, ages 13 to 19. The editors look for self-help and factual drug articles (1,200 words), and profiles/interviews of positive role models for teens regarding substance abuse (1,500 words). Puzzles of all types are welcome.

☐Pays on acceptance: $.04 to $.07 per word for articles. Buys first serial rights. Prefers to receive entire manuscript. Not interested in reprints. No simultaneous submissions; photocopies acceptable. Replies in 6 weeks. Author guidelines and sample issues available. Send SASE.

MAD MAGAZINE, 485 Madison Ave., New York, NY 10022. (212) 752–7685. First published 1952. Printed by E.C. Publications, Inc. Nick Meglin, Editor. John Ficarra, Editor. Charlie Kadau, Editorial Assistant. National magazine published 8 times annually; 1 million readers. Target audience: "a very wise readership: men and women ages 8 to 80." Average issue length: 48 pages.

☐Primarily a visual magazine, *Mad* publishes humor, parody, and satire. Cover ideas should incorporate famed Alfred E. Neuman ("What? Me Worry?") in the gag, but the editors will consider anything that is funny. The magazine is not interested in movie and TV satires, rewritten *Mad*-type articles, poetry, or topical material ("Remember, it takes six months from typewriter to newsstand! Very topical material could be dead and forgotten!").

☐ "Send us a paragraph or two explaining the premise of your humorous article with 3 or 4 examples of how you intend to carry it through, describing the action and visual content of each example. Rough sketches are welcomed but not necessary.

☐ "Don't be afraid to be stupid and don't edit yourself because it's what *you* think we're looking for," stress the editors. "Sometimes *we* don't know what we're looking for until we see it! Make us earn our money as editors!"

☐Pays on acceptance: $300 minimum per published page. Buys all rights (not negotiable). Prefers to receive either an outline or entire manuscript. Not interested in reprints. Simultaneous submissions acceptable if editor is so informed. Replies in 4 weeks. Author guidelines available; sample issue: $1.50. Send SASE.

MARVEL COMICS, 387 Park Ave. South, New York, NY 10016. (212) 696-0808. First published 1961. Tom DeFalco, Executive Editor. Jim Shooter, Editor-in-Chief. Howard Mackie, submissions editor. Lynn E. Cohen, Administrative Manager. National monthly magazines with 5 million readers. Target audience: "all ages." Average issue length: 32 pages.

☐Publishes 60 individual comic magazines each month for juveniles. Primary interest: fiction stories that can be readily illustrated, including adventure, science fiction, western, suspense, romance, horror and humor. Suggestion: a new author's best bet is to write stories using existing *Marvel* characters rather than trying to create and market new ones.

☐"Marvel wants new talent," report the editors. "We want to maintain our leadership of the graphic storytelling medium, and grow. There are no specific qualifications or training for being a *Marvel* writer, but since the comic industry is one where a good imagination is a necessity, you should read as much as possible, including many different types of literature—from the classics to mythology to modern literature—anything to lend inspiration to your imagination." New writers may want to examine *The Official Marvel Comics Try-Out Book*, which describes comic creation and production step-by-step. (You can buy this book at a bookstore or from Dept. F at the above address.)

☐Pays on acceptance: $20 to $60 per printed page plus royalties on magazine sales. Occasionally pays expenses of author on assignment. Regular contributors are offered company benefits. Buys all rights of company-owned cartoons; negotiates rights with creators of other cartoon characters. Prefers to receive query and *brief* plot synopsis (2 typed pages or less). No scripts, short stories, or long outlines. Not usually interested in reprints. Simultaneous submissions acceptable. Prefers to receive photocopy rather than original manuscript. Replies in 6 months. Author guidelines and sample issues available. SASE preferred.

MUPPET MAGAZINE, 300 Madison Ave., New York, NY 10017. (212) 687-0680. Printed by Telepictures Publications, Inc. Jim Lewis, Editor. National quarterly magazine. Target audience: "young children and their parents."

☐A long shot: "We are mostly a staff-written magazine and use very, very little freelance writing."

MUSCLE MAG INTERNATIONAL, 52 Bramsteele Road, Unit Two, Brampton, Ontario L6W 3M5, Canada. (416) 457-3030. First published 1974. Robert Kennedy, Editor. National monthly magazine with 250,000 subscribers and 1 million readers. Target audience: "high-school males and females who are physically active, and young adults up to 25 years of age." Average issue length: 100 pages.

☐Publishes articles about physical fitness and overall body improvement. The editors seek how-to articles, humor, testimonials, and factual and historical articles on nutrition, training tips, dieting, and competition; 1,500–2,000 words. Acceptable fillers include gossip about top bodybuilders, puzzles, and news items; variable length. Photos and line drawings are purchased with or without accompanying manuscript. Well-received articles: "How Tom Platz Trains Legs," and "Why Steroids Are Bad."

□Pays on acceptance: $125 to $250 for articles; $.10 per word for columns; $10 for B&W photos; $15 for color photos; up to $200 for color cover shots; $5 minimum for fillers. Buys first serial rights (not negotiable). Prefers to receive entire manuscript. Not interested in reprints. No simultaneous submissions or photocopied manuscripts. Replies in 3 weeks. Sample issue: $3. Send SASE.

NATIONAL GEOGRAPHIC WORLD, 17th and M Sts. N.W., Washington, D.C. 20036. (202) 857–7000. First published 1975. Printed by the National Geographic Society. Pat Robbins, Managing Editor. Eleanor Shannahan, submissions editor. Nancy White, Editorial Assistant. International monthly magazine with 1.3 million readers. Target audience: children, ages 8 to 13, who enjoy factual articles. Average issue length: 34 pages.

□Primarily publishes nonfiction articles of interest to young children: adventure, outdoors, science, natural history, technology, sports, geography, history, and archaeology; 250 to 1,500 words. Humor, puzzles, games, mazes, and recipes are also considered; 1 page. Illustrations and photos are welcome. Well-received articles: "Florida Panther," "Koko's New Kitten," "Herculaneum," and "Canine Companion."

□"Freelance writers are required to take a writer's test before an assignment is made," says White. "Write the editor and include sample copies of previously published work along with a current resume; no fee is paid."

□Pays on acceptance: fee varies with length of the story (e.g., $100 for 1 page; $400 for 6 pages). ("Text and legends are written after pictures have been selected and the layout has been designed.") Buys all rights (not negotiable). Prefers to receive query. Not interested in reprints. No simultaneous submissions or photocopies. Replies in 2 weeks. Author guidelines and sample issues available. SASE not required.

ODYSSEY, 1027 N. 7th St., Milwaukee, WI 53233. (414) 276–2689. First published 1979. Printed by Kalmbach Publishing Company. Nancy Mack, Editor. National monthly magazine with 80,000 readers. Target audience: "young people, ages 8 to 14, who have an interest in astronomy and space science." Average issue length: 40 pages.

□Mainly publishes short nonfiction articles on interesting aspects of astronomy and space science for juveniles and teens. The editors look for articles and photo features on stars, outer space, planets, spacecraft, and comets; 600 to 1,500 words. Interesting astronomy projects and experiments are also welcome; up to 1,000 words. No poetry, profiles, interviews, humor, puzzles, or fillers. Photos reviewed with or without accompanying manuscript. some "space art" is considered. Well-received articles: "Project Daedalus," "Miss Baker: Monkeynaut," and "Shuttle Food."

□"Information must be up-to-date, and accurate. For this reason, most of our writers are scientists."

□Pays on publication: $50 to $350 for articles, depending upon length and topic; variable rate for photographs. Occasionally pays expenses of authors on assignment. Buys first serial rights and limited reprint rights (negotiable). Prefers to receive query letter with writing clips. Not interested in reprints. Simultaneous submissions acceptable. Replies in 8 weeks. Author guidelines and sample issues available. Send SASE.

ON THE LINE, 616 Walnut Ave., Scottdale, PA 15683. (412) 887-8500. Printed by Mennonite Publishing House and Faith and Life Press. Virginia A. Hostetler, Editor. International monthly magazine published in weekly parts; 11,000 readers. Target audience: "children, ages 10 to 14, who attend Mennonite Sunday schools." Average issue length: 8 pages per weekly segment.
□*On The Line* publishes fiction and nonfiction which introduces children to the wonders of God's world—nature, art, music, poetry, human relationships—helps them appreciate their Christian heritage, Mennonite traditions, themselves, and other people. Nonfiction subjects include: science, nature, biography, craft ideas, safety, profiles, international themes, and seasonal events; 500 to 1,000 words. Fiction can explore these same areas, providing the story is realistic and the main characters are in the same age group as the reader; 750 to 1,200 words. Poetry (up to 24 lines), puzzles, and quizzes (with answer sheet) are also welcome. Quality B&W photos reviewed with manuscript.
□"Give children help in understanding and handling problem areas of life, as well as encourage them to live up to their potential, developing their unique skills and gifts," says Hostetler.
□Pays on acceptance: $.03 to $.04 per word for articles and stories; $.02 per word for simultaneous submissions; $.02 per word for second rights; $4 to $8 for puzzles, quizzes and poetry; $10 to $35 for B&W photographs. Buys one-time rights (not negotiable). Prefers to receive entire manuscript. Interested in reprints. Simultaneous submissions acceptable. Replies in 4 weeks. Author guidelines and sample issues available. Send SASE.

OWL MAGAZINE, 56 The Esplanade, Suite 306, Toronto, Ontario M5E 1A7, Canada. (416) 868-6001. Printed by The Young Naturalist Foundation. Sylvia Funston, Editor. International monthly magazine published 10 times a year. Target audience: children, ages 8 and up, who enjoy factual articles.
□Primarily publishes feature articles on environmental themes for children. Acceptable topics: animals, science, technology, natural phenomena, and people; 500 to 1,000 words. Stimulate children with a lively writing style, clear and logical presentation of ideas, and scientific accuracy. Bibliography and reference list for scientific data is required for all submissions. No sexist or ethnic stereotypes; do not give animals human characteristics. The editors also seek innovative puzzles, imaginative activities, and games; length varies.
□"*Owl* is informative and intellectually challenging in a lively, fun way," stress the editors. "And although it is a magazine with an environmental conscience, it is never preachy."
□Pays $200 to $600 (Canadian dollars) for feature articles, depending on the scope and research involved; $50 to $200 for photographs; varying fee for puzzles, games, and activities. Buys all rights (negotiable). Prefers to receive query and brief outline with paragraph or two to give an indication of the style; author credentials and clippings should accompany first-time queries. State availability of photos and/or illustrations to accompany manuscript. Submit seasonal material 6 to 8 months in advance. Replies in 6 to 8 weeks. Author

guidelines available; sample issue: $1.95. Send SASE with IRC or Canadian postage.

PLAYS, The Drama Magazine for Young People, 120 Boylston St., Boston, MA 02116. (617) 423-3157. First published 1941. Printed by Plays, Inc. Sylvia K. Burack, Editor and Publisher. National magazine published monthly from October through May (combined January/February issue) with 18,000 subscribers. Target audience: elementary and junior-high-school students and their teachers. Average issue length: 64 pages.

□Publishes 1-act plays for performance by public-school students from elementary- through junior-high-school level. Areas of interest: comedy, drama, mystery, melodrama, seasonal and holiday, history, environment, cultural, classical adaptations, fairy tales, and folk tales. The editors also consider monologues, puppet plays, skits, and creative dramatic programs. No music. Plays should be simple to produce, costume, light and stage (one setting is preferred). Desired manuscript lengths: lower grade audience, 6 to 10 pages (equates to 8 to 15 minutes playing time); middle grade audience, 12 to 15 pages (equates to 15 to 20 minutes playing time); and junior-high and high-school audiences, 15 to 20 pages (equates to 22 to 30 minutes playing time).

□Pays on acceptance: "rates vary depending on length of play and age level for which it is appropriate." Buys all rights (not negotiable). Prefers to receive entire manuscript (written to guideline specifications) with production notes (i.e., number of characters, costumes, playing time, settings, and special lighting and sound effects). Not interested in reprints. No simultaneous submissions. Photocopies acceptable. Replies in 3 weeks. Author guidelines available; sample issue: $2. Send SASE.

POCKETS, 1908 Grand Ave., PO Box 189, Nashville, TN 37202. (615) 327-2700. First published 1981. Printed by The Upper Room. Willie S. Teague, Managing Editor. Shirley Paris, Assistant Editor. National magazine published monthly (except January); 70,000 readers. Target audience: "Though some children share *Pockets* with their families, it is designed primarily for children, ages 6 to 12." Average issue length: 32 pages.

□A religious periodical for children, each issue of *Pockets* includes articles about the Bible and church history, role-model profiles, biographical sketches of famous or unknown-but-interesting persons, and articles about other cultures and various holidays; 400 to 600 words. Nonfiction should be related to a particular issue's theme. Fiction (realism or fantasy) should help children deal with real-life situations, and can be communicated via adventure, history, or legend, 600 to 1,500 words. Elaborations of Biblical stories are acceptable as long as the writer remains true to the story. *Pockets* will consider poetry (1 page), graphics, art, prayers, puzzles of all types, and activities. Material submitted by children, and seasonal material (secular and liturgical) also are desired.

□"Submissions do not need to be overtly religious," says Paris. "They should help children experience a Christian lifestyle that is not always a neatly-wrapped moral package, but is open to the continuing revelation of God's will."

□Pays on acceptance: $.07 minimum per word for stories and articles; $25 to $50 for poetry; $10 to $25 for activities. Buys magazine and newspaper rights (not negotiable). Prefers to receive entire manuscript. Interested in reprints.

No simultaneous submissions; photocopies acceptable. Replies in 8 weeks. Author guidelines available. Send SASE.

PURPLE COW, Suite 107, 1447 Peachtree St., Atlanta, GA 30309. (404) 872–1927. First published 1976. Printed by Purple Cow, Inc. Meg Thornton, Editor. Geri R. Forehand, Publisher. Regional monthly tabloid with 40,000 circulation and 120,000 readers. Target audience: "public- and private- school children, ages 13 to 18." Average issue length: 12 to 16 pages.
☐ A regional newspaper for teens in the Tampa/St. Petersburg area; 97% is nonfiction written by and for area teens.
☐ "Don't talk down or preach to teens!" stresses Thornton. "Challenge their abilities!"
☐ Pays on publication: $10 for articles and stories; $10 for B&W photos; $5 for filler material. Buys first and syndication rights (negotiable). Prefers to receive either a query letter with detailed outline and writing clips, or entire manuscript. Interested in reprints, but "only with prior approval!" Simultaneous submissions acceptable. Replies in 8 weeks. Author guidelines available; sample issue: $1. Send SASE.

R-A-D-A-R, 8121 Hamilton Ave., Cincinnati, OH 45231. (513) 931–4050. First published 1978. Printed by Standard Publishing. Margaret Williams, Editor. National weekly magazine. Target audience: children in grades 3 to 6. Average issue length: 12 pages.
☐ A religious magazine, *R-A-D-A-R*'s goal is to reach children with "the truth of God's Word, and to help them make it the guide of their lives." Acceptable topics: animals, nature, sports, science, hobbies, culture, and seasonal subjects; 400 to 500 words. "Articles should have religious emphasis." Fiction should feature a hero, age 11 or 12, in a situation involving one or more of the following: travel, adventure, sports, school, mystery, animals, friends, and parental relationships; 900 to 1,000 words (2,000 words for 2-part series). Stories should be wholesome, with plots, and involve Christian character-building. The editors also seek poetry (Biblical, nature), Bible puzzles, and cartoons that are appropriate for young children.
☐ "Many of our features, including our stories, now correlate with the Sunday school lesson themes," says Williams. "Send for quarterly theme list."
☐ Pays on acceptance: $.03 per word for articles and fiction; up to $.40 per line for poetry and verse; $10 to $15 for cartoons; variable payment for puzzles. Buys first serial rights (not negotiable). Must receive entire manuscript. Interested in reprints. No simultaneous submissions; photocopies acceptable. Submit seasonal material 1 year in advance. Replies in 6 to 8 weeks. Author guidelines and sample issues available. Send SASE.

RANGER RICK, 1412 16th St. N.W., Washington, D.C. 20036. (202) 797–6800. First published 1967. Printed by the National Wildlife Federation. Gerald Bishop, Managing Editor. National monthly magazine with 1.4 million readers. Target audience: "children, ages 6 to 12, of all interests; most reading material is aimed at 9-year-olds, or 4th graders." Average issue length: 48 pages.
☐ Publishes both fiction and nonfiction articles on nature, outdoor adventure and discovery, pets, science, conservation, and related subjects. Current nonfiction needs include wildlife, children's adventure, outdoor activities, and

profiles of either scientists or "heroes" of the environment; 900 to 1,000 words. For fiction, the editors seek science fiction, fantasy, adventure, and traditional stories; 1,000 words maximum. Poetry, puzzles, riddles, jokes, crafts, simple recipes, and humor of any length also are welcome.

□ "The only way you can write successfully for *Ranger Rick* is to know the kinds of subjects and approaches we like. And the only way you can do that is to read the magazine." Professional-quality transparencies are eagerly sought; B&W prints also used occasionally. Acceptable photo subjects: wild animals (wild shots preferred to zoo shots), pets (no wild creatures turned into house residents), humorous nature subjects, natural history, children (ages 6 to 14) involved with wildlife or outdoor activities, and adults participating in science. Submit no more than 40 captioned slides; accompanying manuscript required. Artwork and illustrations are assigned by the art director.

□ "We're especially looking for pieces on more obscure classes of animals such as reptiles and insects rather than birds and mammals." In fiction, the editors advise, "Avoid stereotyping any group, and keep your writing style light, breezy, spirited, not condescending or didactic. We need unique, creative approaches to subjects."

□ Pays on acceptance: up to $350 for feature articles; $250 to $350 for other articles, depending on extent of editing; $3 per line for poetry; $60 to $180 for B&W photos; $240 to $300 for color cover photos; $180 to $210 for inside color photos. If you submit artwork or photos with your manuscript, you will be paid separately if any are used. Buys all world rights (negotiable). Prefers to receive query letter (no phone queries) outlining intended subject, along with a lead or sample paragraph and professional writing credits, if any. Not interested in reprints. No simultaneous submissions; photocopied manuscripts acceptable, but "not recommended." Replies in 8 weeks. Author guidelines and sample issue available. SASE required.

READ MAGAZINE, 245 Long Hill Rd., Middletown, CT 06457. (203) 638-2400. Published by Field Publications. Edwin A. Hoey, Senior Editor. Louise C. Augeri, Senior Editorial Coordinator. National bimonthly digest. Target audience: "junior-high and middle-school students." Average issue length: 32 pages.

□ Plays and unusual fiction suitable for junior-high school readers are the specialties of *Read*. The editors look for general fiction and 10- to 12-part plays written to be read aloud in classrooms. Acceptable topics: fantasy, science fiction (stressing the human element rather than technical gadgetry), personal crisis, horror, supernatural, nature, adventure, and science; 1,000 to 4,000 words. Plays should possess action and drama and present thought-provoking ideas for classroom discussion. No animal, religious, or historical fiction.

□ "We avoid formula plots and stilted language, and prefer plot twists with surprise endings and perky language, word-play, and quick styles for easy reading," reports Augeri. "We prefer plays and stories that contain unusual elements that set them apart from the ordinary. We especially like to see writers take an unusual approach to an idea or use unusual language to portray an idea. In other words, we want to see first-rate writing that will spark young readers to read."

□ Pays on publication: $150 to $250 for article and stories. Buys first serial and/or all rights (negotiable). Prefers to receive entire manuscript ("we make decisions on final manuscripts only, not plot outlines or abstracts"). Interested in reprints. Simultaneous submissions and photocopies accepted. Replies in 8 weeks. Author guidelines and sample issues available. Send SASE.

SEEK, 8121 Hamilton Ave., Cincinnati, OH 45231. (513) 931-4050. Printed by the Standard Publishing Company. Eileen Wilmoth, Editor. National weekly magazine with 5,000 readers. Target audience: "young adults and Christians who attend Sunday school." Average issue length: 8 pages.
□Publishes fiction and nonfiction for young Christians. Current nonfiction needs include testimonial, devotional, and human-interest articles that concern social issues, ethics, contemporary matters controversial situations or decisions, family life, relationships, and parenting; 800 to 1,200 words. In fiction, the editors seek similar themes, as well as historical and humorous slants; 800 words maximum. Puzzles and interviews are also considered. Illustrations and photos are reviewed with or without an accompanying manuscript.
□ "We really want articles and stories that show Christian faith and ethics at their best in real-world applications."
□Pays on acceptance: $.03 per word for articles and stories; $10 minimum for B&W photos; plus complimentary issue upon publication. Buys first rights; negotiable. Prefers to receive entire manuscript. Interested in reprints. No simultaneous submissions. Replies in 4 to 6 weeks. Author guidelines and sample issue available. Send SASE.

SESAME STREET MAGAZINE, 1 Lincoln Plaza, New York, NY 10023. (212) 595-3456. Printed by Children's Television Workshop. National monthly magazine. Target audience: "young children, ages 2 to 6."
□A long shot: "We have a stable group of writers with whom we work. It is very difficult for freelancers to break into this market. For those who really want to try, though, approach the *Sesame Street Parents' Guide.*"

SESAME STREET PARENTS' GUIDE, 1 Lincoln Plaza, New York, NY 10023. (212) 595-3456. First published in 1985 as an inclusion within *Sesame Street Magazine.* Printed by Children's Television Workshop. Circulation: 1.3 million. Target audience: "the parents of children who read *Sesame Street Magazine* or watch the TV program."
□This publication-within-a-publication covers items of interest to parents of 2- to 6-year-olds. Although articles are assigned, the editors seek queries on reports (up to 1,500 words, plus sidebar and additional information) that explore common parental questions; these articles typically include interviews with educators, psychologists and child-care experts. First-person articles about how the parent solved a typical childrearing dilemma are also invited; 800 to 1,000 words.
□ "We like to work with our writers and shape the articles to the unique needs of the *Parents' Guide.* The adult reader wants practical information, including news of developmental research, tips on how to handle a child's tantrum, and useful medical information."
□Pays on acceptance: $300 to $800 for feature articles. Note: you must bill the magazine after acceptance of the article. Buys all rights (negotiable). Prefers to receive query letter with samples of previously published articles. Not interested in reprints. Simultaneous submissions acceptable if editors are so informed. Replies in 4 to 6 weeks. Author guidelines available; sample issue: $2. Send SASE.

SEVENTEEN, 850 3rd Avenue, New York, NY 10022. (212) 759–8100. Sarah Crichton, Senior Editor. National monthly magazine with 1.8 million readers. Target audience: young teenage women interested in their personal development: emotionally, physically and mentally.
☐*Seventeen* is becoming "more issue-oriented and down-to-earth." The editors are looking for articles and stories about contemporary issues affecting teenage women: the pros and cons of abortion; student-teacher relationships; and self-help features; 1,800 to 2,500 words. Acceptable fiction topics: (2,500 words average) common teen problems and concerns, family/social issues, relationships, and ethics. The magazine publishes a novelette annually in its July issue; 7,500 words maximum.
☐"Articles should be topical, entertaining, and helpful. When approaching us with a query, make certain that you've narrowed your subject enough. Too often we've been contacted by writers who propose grandiose and generic articles on such topics as 'Drugs' or 'Sex.'
☐"Avoid teenager stories that are too cliche and that are too sophisticated and detailed for a 16-year old—much less the editor—to comprehend."
☐Pays on acceptance: $350 to $1,500 for articles; $700 to $1,200 for stories; $15 per poem (teenagers only). Offers 25% kill fee to professional writers. Buys first North American serial rights. Prefers to receive query letter with lead paragraph and outline for articles; articles are commissioned after outlines are approved. Rarely interested in reprints. Simultaneous submissions acceptable. Responds in 6 weeks. Author guidelines available. SASE required.

SHARING THE VICTORY (formerly *The Christian Athlete*), 8701 Leeds Rd., Kansas City, MO 64129. (816) 921–0909. First published 1959. Printed by the Fellowship of Christian Athletes. Randy St. Clair, Managing Editor. Skip Stogsdill, Editor. National bimonthly magazine with 50,000 readers. Target audience: "athletes; coaches at the junior-high, high-school, and college level; plus parents, clergy, and business persons." Average issue length: 24 pages.
☐Publishes articles which "encourage/enable athletes and coaches to take their faith seriously on and off the field." The editors seek profiles and interviews of known and unknown athletes and coaches (1,000 words); articles for the magazine's "Sports Conscience" series (1,200 words); and humor. Photos (B&W and color) also are considered. Well-received topics: anorexia, suicide, alcohol abuse, and profiles/interviews of name athletes and coaches.
☐Pays on publication: $35 and up. Buys first serial rights (negotiable). Prefers to receive query. Occasionally interested in reprints. Simultaneous submissions acceptable; no photocopies. Replies in 1 to 2 weeks. Author guidelines available; sample issues: $1 plus postage. Send SASE.
☐Simultaneous submissions OK. Interested in reprints. Replies in 4 weeks. Author guidelines and sample issue both available for 10 ″ × 12 ″ manila SASE and $1.00. Send SASE with all submissions.

SPACE AND TIME, 138 W. 70th St., New York, NY 10023–4432. First published 1966. Printed by Space and Time, Inc. Gordon Linzner, Editor/Publisher. National, biannual magazine with 500 readers. Target audience: "science fiction and fantasy fans of all ages." Average issue length: 120 pages.
☐Seeks science fiction and fantasy stories with an unusual slant: supernatural, humor, horror, fantasy; 10,000 to 15,000 words (7,000 words average). Poetry,

especially narrative poetry, is welcome; no restrictions. Illustrations are done for specific stories by assignment only.

☐Pays on acceptance: $.01 per every 4 words for stories plus 2 contributor copies upon publication. Buys first North American serial rights (not negotiable). Prefers to receive entire manuscript. Not interested in reprints. No simultaneous submissions. Replies in 6 to 8 weeks. Author guidelines available; sample issue: $4. Send SASE.

STARWIND, PO Box 98, Ripley, OH 45167. (513) 392–4549. First published 1974. Printed by The Starwind Press. David F. Powell, Editor. Susannah C. West, Editor. National quarterly magazine with 2,000 readers. Target audience: "young adults, in either high school or college, who are interested in science, technology, and science fiction." Average issue length: 64 pages.

☐Publishes science fiction (both hard and soft) and fantasy stories that have positive storylines, well-created characters, and that show hope for the future; 2,000 to 10,000 words. The editors also are looking for interviews, profiles, how-to and factual articles that are not too technical for their readership, "but not too simplistic, either"; 2,000 to 7,000 words. Reviews of books, movies museums, and interesting scientific sites are also considered. Camera-ready ink illustrations and photos of people involved in science and technology are reviewed when accompanied by manuscript (model release form required).

☐Pays on acceptance and publication: $.01 to $.04 per word for articles and stories (25% on acceptance, remainder on publication). Buys either first or all rights (negotiable). For fiction, send entire manuscript; for nonfiction, query with outline and author credentials. ("We encourage disposable submissions. It's easier for us and the author.") Interested in reprints "mainly for nonfiction." No simultaneous submissions. Replies in 8 weeks. Author guidelines available; sample issue: $2.50. Send SASE.

STORY FRIENDS, 616 Walnut Ave., Scottdale, PA 15683. (412) 887–8500. Printed by the Mennonite Publishing House. Marjorie Waybill, Editor. National monthly magazine published in weekly issues. Target audience: children ages 4 to 9.

☐Publishes stories for children that reinforce Christian values; 300 to 800 words. Stories should achieve one or more of the following: provide ways for children to express love and caring; introduce children to other cultures; reinforce values taught by the church; introduce children to a wide range of people; reflect the emotions of a child in the story's characters; demonstrate that everyone is unique and important; and show that Jesus is the child's friend and helper. Poetry and activities that focus on children's needs are also considered.

☐Pays on acceptance: up to $.05 per word for stories and articles; $50 maximum per 1,000 words. Buys first serial rights (not negotiable). Prefers to recieve entire manuscript. Interested in reprints. Simultaneous submissions and photocopies acceptable. Submit seasonal material 6 months in advance. Reply requires several weeks. Author guidelines and sample issues available. Send SASE.

STRAIGHT, 8121 Hamilton Ave., Cincinnati, OH 45231. (513) 931–4050. Printed by Standard Publishing Company. Dawn Korth, Editor. Carla Crane, Assistant Editor. National magazine produced quarterly and distributed weekly; 80,000 readers. Target audience: "Christian junior-high and senior-high school students, ages 12 to 19, who receive the magazine through their churches.'' Average issue length: 12 pages.

☐Publishes religious/inspirational fiction and nonfiction that promotes Christian values. The editors seek articles dealing with church, school, service projects, family, part-time jobs, sports, entertainment and recreation; up to 1,100 words. Profiles of outstanding Christian teens are sought, especially when accompanied by B&W photos; 500 to 1,000 words. How-to articles also are of great interest (e.g., how to start a Bible club).

☐Humor written from a teen's point of view (500 to 1,000 words) and poetry written by teens (no restrictions) are welcome. Well-received articles: "Rock Music: Yes or No?,'' "Read No Evil,'' and "Careers for Christian Teens.''

☐Puzzles and illustrations are done by assignment only. Contact the editorial staff for consideration. Submit B&W photos that feature conservative-looking teens in wholesome activities.

☐"Fiction (1,000 to 1,500 words) must have an interesting, well-constructed plot. The main characters should be contemporary teens who cope with modern-day problems using Christian principles. Stories should be character-building, but not preachy. Conflicts must be resolved realistically, with thought-provoking and honest endings.''

☐Pays on acceptance: $.03 per word for articles and stories; $.01 to $.02 per word for reprints; $20 for B&W photos. Buys first and reprint rights (negotiable). Prefers to receive entire manuscript. Interested in reprints. Simultaneous submissions acceptable. Responds in 4 to 6 weeks. Author guidelines and sample issue available. SASE required.

THE STUDENT, 127 9th Ave., N., Nashville, TN 37234. (615) 251–2783. First published 1922. Printed by the Baptist Sunday School Board. Milt Hughes, Editor. Day Hardin, Assistant Editor. National monthly magazine with 25,000 readers. Target audience: high-school seniors and college students, ages 17 to 24. Average issue length: 50 pages.

☐Publishes fiction (700 to 900 words) and nonfiction (700 to 800 words) pertaining to Christian life and growth experiences for young adults. Areas of interest: religious, moral, self-help, and devotional. The editors also seek poetry (up to 20 lines), interviews (700 to 1,000 words), and humor (700 to 800 words). Photos and illustrations welcome.

☐Pays on acceptance: $.05 per word for articles and stories. Buys first serial rights (negotiable). Prefers to receive query or entire manuscript. Interested in reprints. No simultaneous submissions; photocopies acceptable. Replies in 4 to 6 weeks. Author guidelines and sample issues available. Send SASE.

SUPER TIMES (formerly *Happy Times*), 5600 N. University Ave., Provo, UT 84604. (801) 225–9000. First published 1983. Printed by Eagle Systems International. Steven R. Shallenberger, Publisher. Mark C. Avery, Managing Director. Colleen Hinckley, Managing Editor. National magazine published 10 times each year (combined March/April and August/September issues); 70,000 readers. Target audience: children ages 3 to 8. Average issue length: 32 pages.

☐A nondenominational periodical, *Super Times* publishes articles and stories that teach traditional values without being overly religious or preachy (e.g., don't litter; eat your vegetables). The editors seek fiction from which a puzzle can be made (300 words); biographies of interesting people (800 words); dot-to-dot and word-find puzzles; riddles; jokes; light, fanciful poetry; historical facts; and amazing animal facts (100 to 400 words). Animal and science articles are of special interest ("take a simple topic and make it exciting"). No blatantly religious material or material that shows kids/adults in a negative light. Articles should be wholesome, fun to read, informative, and stress strong character traits. Slides and transparencies also are considered. Well-received article: biography of Laura E. Wilder.

☐ "Biographies should focus on one part or aspect of a person's life, giving it sparkle, rather than provide an overview," suggests Hinckley. "Contact us for a list of biographies already published."

☐ Pays on publication: $20 to $80 for articles and stories. Buys first North American serial rights (negotiable). Prefers that authors send for guidelines and list of themes before submitting material for publication. Interested in reprints. Simultaneous submissions accepted if editor is so informed; photocopies acceptable. Replies in 1 to 3 weeks; final decision can take up to 1 year. Author guidelines and sample issues available. Send SASE.

TEACHER UPDATE, PO Box 429, Belmont, MA 02178. (617) 484-7327. First published 1977. Printed by Teacher Update. Donna Papalia, Editor. National newsletter published monthly (except July and August) with 12,000 readers. Target audience: "elementary and preschool teachers who want to learn more about early childhood education."

☐ Primarily publishes nonfiction articles to help preschool teachers teach and entertain children, including articles that describe classroom activities, teaching tactics, and innovative learning aids; length varies. Children's poetry, fingerplays, puzzles, and games also are welcome; no restrictions. Artwork is considered when accompanying manuscript.

☐ "Feel free to submit an entire issue. We are always open to ideas for special sections, even if it's not related to a specific month's theme."

☐ Pays on acceptance: $20 per printed page for articles. Buys all rights (negotiable). Interested in reprints. Simultaneous submissions acceptable. Responds in 4 to 6 weeks. Author guidelines and sample issue available. SASE required.

TEEN MAGAZINE, 8490 Sunset Blvd., Hollywood, CA 90069. (213) 854-2222. Roxanne Camron, Managing Editor. National monthly magazine with 1.2 million readers. Target audience: girls, ages 13 to 17. Average issue length: 100 pages.

☐ *Teen Magazine* is heavily staff written, limiting freelance publication. Publishes only fiction about contemporary/social issues of interest to teenage girls. The editors look for romance, mystery, suspense, and humor; 2,000 to 4,000 words. "No graphic sex, language, or violence, or cliche stories involving cheerleaders or prom queens."

☐ Pays on publication: $100 minimum for stories. No kill fee. Buys all rights (negotiable). Prefers to receive entire manuscript. Not interested in reprints. Simultaneous submissions accepted if editor is so informed. Replies in 8 to 12 weeks. Author guidelines available. Send SASE.

TEENAGE MAGAZINE, 928 Broadway, New York, NY 10010. (212) 505-5350. First published 1981. Printed by Highwire Associates. Ellen Lander, Managing Editor. Jeannie Ralston, Editor. National magazine published 6 times annually; 1.5 million readers. Target audience: "young, college-bound women, 15 to 19 years old, who are interested in fashion,news, entertainment, and services." Average issue length: 76 pages.

□Publishes fiction and non-fiction for—and from—young people. The editors are interested in how-to, interviews, general interest, humor, profile and factual articles dealing with entertainment, services, social and family issues, contemporary concerns, careers, education, health, technology and relationships; 1,500 to 2,200 words. Profiles and interviews should be of interesting people or entertainers; 1,500 words maximum. Acceptable fiction themes include adventure, mystery, romance, humor and suspense. No poetry, puzzles, illustrations, or photographs. Well-received articles: "Rock and Politics," "Fears and Phobias," "The Truth About College Life," "Heroes," and "The TeenAge 100—100 Exceptional Young People."

□Pays on acceptance: $50 to $750 for articles; up to $350 for stories; $20 to $25 for fillers. Buys first North American rights (negotiable). For nonfiction, prefers to receive query letter with outline and credentials; for fiction, send entire manuscript. Not interested in reprints. No simultaneous submissions. Replies in 12 weeks. Author guidelines available. No sample issues. Send SASE.

TEENS TODAY, 6401 The Paseo, Kansas City, MO 64131. (816) 333-7000. Printed by the Nazarene Publishing House (PO Box 527, Kansas City, MO 64141). Karen DeSollar, Editor. National weekly magazine with 65,000 readers. Target audience: "junior and high-school children affiliated with the Church of the Nazarene." Average issue length: 8 pages.

□Published for teenagers attending Sunday School, *Teens Today* seeks Christian-based fiction and nonfiction that deals with today's teen issues. Nonfiction should be first-person or how-to articles about family life, relationships, Christian living, careers, and contemporary concerns of teens; 1,200-1,500 words. For fiction, the editors are looking for stories (1,500 words maximum) about "teens involved in situations and struggles where they must put their Christian principles into practice, such as situations involving relationships with family and friends, moral and ethical decisions, and adventure stories." No poetry, fillers, interviews, profiles, humor or puzzles. Illustrations are done by assignment only. Contact the editorial staff for consideration. B&W photos of teens in groups ("especially close-ups of individual kids in a variety of mood poses") are considered with or without an accompanying manuscript; make certain that dress and styles are current.

□Pays on acceptance: $.035 per word for word for articles and stories. Buys first rights (negotiable). Prefers to receive entire manuscript. Interested in reprints. Simultaneous submissions acceptable. Replies in 6 to 8 weeks. Author guidelines and sample issues available. Send SASE.

3-2-1 CONTACT, 1 Lincoln Plaza, New York, NY 10023. (212) 595-3456. First published 1979. Printed by the Children's Television Workshop. Richard Chevat, Senior Editor. National monthly magazine with 400,000 readers. Target audience: children ages 8 to 12. Average issue length: 32 pages.

□A science magazine for young children, *3-2-1 Contact* publishes articles about current trends and discoveries in all areas of science and technology: computers, artificial intelligence, robotics, space exploration, physiology, zoology, and oceanography; 1,000 words. Profiles of scientists and/or children also are welcome; 1,000 words. Well-received articles: "How Do You Go to the Bathroom in Space?," and "What Makes Babies Cute?"

☐ "Focus on what things interest today's intelligent child," suggests Chevat. "If you find yourself doing a lot of library research, chances are good that the article won't be what we or the readers want."

☐ Pays on acceptance: $300 to $400 for 1,000-word features; occasionally pays expenses of authors on assignment. Buys all rights (negotiable). Prefers to receive query ("please read the magazine before querying."). Not interested in reprints. Simultaneous submissions and photocopies accepted. Replies in 3 weeks. Author guidelines available; sample issue: $1.25. Send SASE.

TIGER BEAT, 1086 Teaneck Rd., Teaneck, NJ 07666. (201) 833-1800. First published 1965. Printed by D.S. Magazines. Diane Umansky, Editor. National monthly magazine with 500,000 readers (ABC-audited). Target audience: "teenage girls, 14 to 18, who are interested in entertainment." Average issue length: 72 pages.

☐ A celebrity-oriented magazine for teenage girls, *Tiger Beat* is particularly interested in articles with new angles and exclusive interviews with persons to whom the staff doesn't have access. Profiles and interviews should be celebrity- and entertainment-oriented; varying length. Also will consider quizzes, puzzles, and humor. All types of fiction are considered, including romance, mystery, adventure and suspense; 1,500 words minimum. Ideally, the main characters should be in the same age group as the reader. No fillers or poetry. Photos are considered with or without an accompanying manuscript.

☐ Pays on publication: $50 to $125 for articles and stories; $25 for B&W photos; $50 for color photos; $75 minimum for color cover photos. Buys first North American rights (negotiable). Prefers to receive entire manuscript. Interested in reprints. Simultaneous submissions acceptable. Replies in 6 weeks. No author guidelines; sample issue available. SASE preferred.

TIGER BEAT STAR, 1086 Teaneck Rd., Teaneck, NJ 07666. (201) 387-0880. First published 1976. Printed by Edrei Communications. Lisa Arcella, Editor. International monthly magazine with 350,000 readers (ABC-audited). Target audience: "teenage girls interested in celebrities." Average issue length: 68 pages.

☐ Publishes interviews/profiles of pop and television celebrities for teenage girls; acceptable length varies. The editors will also consider humor and puzzles that fit the editorial slant. Photos (B&W and some color) and illustrations welcome.

☐ Pays on publication: $50 for 1 page; $100 for 2 pages. Buys entertainment-related rights (negotiable). Prefers to receive query. Interested in reprints. Simultaneous submissions and photocopies acceptable. Replies in 3 weeks. Sample issues available. SASE preferred.

TURTLE MAGAZINE FOR PRESCHOOL KIDS, 1100 Waterway Blvd., PO Box 567, Indianapolis, IN 46206. (317) 636-8881. Printed by Children's Better Health Institute, Benjamin Franklin Literary & Medical Society, Inc. Beth Wood Thomas, Editor. National magazine published monthly (bimonthly February/March, April/May, June/July, and August/September). Target audience: children ages 2 to 5. Average issue length: 48 pages.

☐ Interested in publishing bedtime or naptime fiction stories that can be read to a child. Animal, fantasy, and humorous rhyming stories are sought, especially if they effectively teach morals and ideals in a subliminal, non-lecturing fashion; 200 to 600 words. Not interested in nonfiction due to the age of the target audience. Well-received articles: "Buddy Bear's Tooth Discovery" by Mary Beth Stevens and "Animals' Safety Rhymes" by Marge O'Harra.

☐ "Seasonal stories, as well as humorous stories and poems, are especially needed. There is always a need for material that emphasizes good health, safety, nutrition, and exercise."

☐ Pays on publication: $.06 per word for stories and articles; $10 minimum per poem; variable rate for puzzles and games; plus 2 contributor copies upon publication. Buys all rights. Prefers to receive entire manuscript. Interested in reprints. No simultaneous submissions. Replies in 8 to 10 weeks. Note: submissions are considered for publication in all 6 of this publisher's magazines, so do not resubmit material to another publication at this address (see listing for *Children's Better Health Institute*). Author guidelines available for SASE; sample issue: $.75. Send SASE.

VENTURE, PO Box 150 Wheaton, IL 60189. (312) 665–0630. Printed by the Christian Service Brigade. Stephen P. Neideck, Editor. National magazine published 6 times annually; 25,000 readers. Target audience: "boys to 15, who are involved in their church's Service Brigade." Average issue length: 32 pages.

☐ Material is intended to promote Christian ideals and to present a positive image of what it means to be a Christian man in today's society. The editors are looking for factual and true-adventure articles about social issues, contemporary concerns affecting today's youth, family life, and relationships; 1,200 to 1,500 words. Articles should reveal or demonstrate good Christian qualities in some fashion. All types of fiction are reviewed, including adventure and suspense; 1,000 to 1,200 words. Stories should have a Christian theme or teaching. Puzzles and quizzes are occasionally considered.

☐ Pays on publication: $50 minimum for articles and fiction; $35 for assigned B&W photos; up to $100 for B&W cover photos. Buys first rights (negotiable). Prefers to receive query and outline for nonfiction, entire manuscript for fiction. Not interested in reprints. Simultaneous submissions acceptable. Replies in 3 to 4 weeks. author guidelines available; sample issue: $1.50. Send SASE.

WEE LITTLE PEOPLE, PO Box 411, Keansburg, NJ   07734. (201) 787–1437. Printed by Mattmar Press. Maryann Vandre, Editor. National newsletter published 10 times each hear. Target audience: preschoolers and their parents.

☐ Publishes general interest articles of interest to parents regarding common family issues: child psychology, recreation, crafts, and communication; 2,500 words. Short stories (1,500 words), poems (100 line limit), and fillers (riddles, anecdotes; 50 words) also are considered.

☐ "We're looking for short articles that give our adult readers ideas on how to help their children, and become emotionally closer to them," says Vandre.

☐ No payment; offers contributor copies with author bio upon publication. Prefers to receive entire manuscript. Interested in reprints. Simultaneous submissions acceptable. Replies in 4 to 6 weeks. Author guidelines available; sample issue $1. Send SASE.

WEE WISDOM MAGAZINE, Unity Village, MD 64065. (816) 524–3550. First published 1893. Printed by the Unity School of Christianity. Verle Bell, Editor. International magazine published 10 times each year (2 bimonthly issues); 175,000 subscribers. Target audience: "children, ages 3 to early teens, teachers, and librarians." Average issue length: 48 pages.

☐Publishes stories and articles that are "uplifting and of good moral content" for young children and their educators; 500 to 800 words. The editors also seek appropriate poetry and puzzles; length varies. Seldom purchases photos; illustrations are commissioned to local artists.

☐Pays on acceptance: about $.04 per word for articles and stories (averages $20 to $35). Buys first serial rights (not negotiable). Prefers to receive entire manuscript. Not interested in reprints. No simultaneous submissions or photocopies. Replies in 6 weeks. Author guidelines and sample issue available. Send SASE.

WITH, PO Box 347, Newton, KS 67114. (316) 283–5100. Published by the Faith & Life Press and the Mennonite Publishing House. Susan E. Janzen, Editor. National monthly magazine. Target audience: senior-high students.

☐ *With* tries to help high-school students make a commitment to Christ amidst the complex and conflicting values they encounter in the world. Acceptable topics: profiles and personal experiences about real people in real-life situations, relationships with the opposite sex, discipleship, lifestyle ethics, education, peers, Christianity in action, and social issues; 1,200 to 1,500 words. Fiction should show how a problem can be solved without the characters breaking Christian principles or being disobedient to Christ; 2,000 words. *With* also seeks short poetry about youth inn relation to the world (up to 25 lines). Photos and illustrations are accepted.

☐"Do not try to be 'in' with youth by using their jargon," warns Janzen. "It dates quickly. Use adult language. Anecdotes and fast-paced articles are most appealing to youth."

☐Pays on acceptance: up to $.04 per word for stories and articles. Buys first serial rights (not negotiable). Prefers to receive entire manuscript. Interested in reprints. Simultaneous submissions and photocopies accepted. Reply requires several weeks. Author guidelines and sample issue: $1.25. Send SASE.

WONDER TIME, 6401 The Paseo, Kansas City, MO 64131. (816) 333–7000. Printed by the Nazarene Publishing House (PO Box 527, Kansas City, MO 64141). Evelyn J. Beals, Editor. National weekly journal with 45,000 readers. Target audience: "first- and second-grade children, ages 6 to 8." Average issue length: 4 pages.

☐Publishes character-building fiction for young children. Considers stories dealing with family life, divorce, drugs, death, unemployment, latch-key children, and social issues; 450 to 550 words. If the story concerns church doctrine, remember to keep it in line with the Church of the Nazarene's beliefs. Puzzles (½ page) and seasonal or religious poetry (8 lines) are welcome. Illustrations (⅔ page, B&W and color photos) are considered with or without an accompanying manuscript. Well-received articles: "Baby Sister," "Nobody Home," and "Chad's Prayer is Answered."

☐"Avoid being preachy or talking down to the reader," cautions the editor.

☐Pays on acceptance: $.035 per word for stories; $.25 per line for poetry. Buys first and, occasionally, second rights (negotiable). Prefers to receive en-

tire manuscript. Not interested in reprints. Simualtaneous submissions acceptable. Replies in 6 weeks. Author guidelines and sample issues available. Send
SASE.

YABA WORLD, 5301 S. 76th St., Greendale WI 53129. (414) 421–4700. First
published 1982. Printed by the Young American Bowling Alliance. Paul R.
Bertling, Editor. National magazine published monthly, November through
April; 700,000 readers. Target audience: "bowlers, ages 8 to 21." Average
length: 24 pages.
☐Publishes articles on tenpin bowling and activities connected with the Young
American Bowling Alliance. Most articles are staff-written.
☐Pays on publication: $30 to $100 for articles; $5 minimum for B&W photos.
Buys all rights (not negotiable). Prefers to receive entire manuscript; queries
for any special nonfiction article. Interested in reprints. Simultaneous submis-
sions acceptable. Replies in 3 to 4 weeks. Author guidelines and sample issues
available. Send SASE.

YM (formerly *Young Miss* and *Calling All Girls),* 685 3rd Ave., New York,
NY 10017. (212) 878–8700. First published 1941. Printed by Gruner & Jahr
Publishing. Nancy Comer, Executive Editor. Mary Kaye Schilling, Articles
and Fiction Editor. National monthly magazine with 800,000 readers. Target
audience: "young women, between the ages of 14 and 18, who are interested in
fashion, entertainment, beauty, and human interest stories." Average issue
length: 100 pages.
☐ *YM* publishes well-researched, sophisticated, and provocative stories and
articles for teenage women: romance, human interest, advice, and health; 650
to 2,000 words. Profiles/interviews of entertainers or people of distinction are
also considered; up to 1,200 words. Fiction should be of interest to mature
teens; 2,500 to 3,000 words. *YM* also publishes poetry written by teens, as well
as fillers (romance, anecdotal) and some humor (romance, family oriented);
length varies. The editors are especially interested in "good ideas for teen market that are not too juvenile." Well-received articles: "18, Married and a
Mother"; and "Hooked on Cocaine: A True Story."
☐"Writers often toss off stories for this age group;" says Schilling, "they
underestimate the readers' intelligence".
☐Pays on acceptance: $.50 to $1 per word for articles and stories, depending
upon complexity. Buys first North American serial rights (negotiable). Prefers
to receive query for nonfiction; entire manuscript for fiction. Not interested in
reprints. Simultaneous submissions and photocopies acceptable. Replies in 6
weeks. Author guidelines available. Send SASE.

YOUNG AMERICAN, America's Newsmagazine for Kids, PO Box 12409,
Portland, OR 97212. (503) 230–1895. First published 1983. Printed by Young
American Publishing Co., Inc. Kristina T. Linden, Editor. Regional biweekly
newspaper with 437,000 readers (Pulse Research-audited). Target audience:
"kids, ages 4 to 15, and their families. As a supplement to suburban and small
newspapers, we reach a highly-educated audience." Average issue length: 24
pages.
☐Publishes articles and stories for and about children: humor, mystery, fantasy, true-to-life, and science; up to 1,000 words (300 word limit for nonfiction). Interested in profiles/interviews of newsworthy kids and their projects;

350 words. The editors also consider all types of humor, light verse, short fillers, and puzzles; length varies. Photos and illustrations are welcome; send for artist guidelines. No drugs, sex, violence, religious, or condescending material. Well-received topics: an interview with a child movie-star and a science fiction story about a boy learning how to fly a spaceship.

☐Pays on publication: $.07 per word for articles and stories; $5 for photos. Buys first North American serial rights (not negotiable). Prefers to receive entire manuscript (''queries discouraged''). Not interested in reprints. No simultaneous submissions; photocopies acceptable. Replies in 16 weeks. Author guidelines available; sample issue: $1.50. Send SASE.

YOUNG AUTHOR'S MAGAZINE, 3015 Woodsdale Blvd., Lincoln, NE 68502. (402) 421-3172. First published 1985. Printed by Theraplan, Inc. Traci Austin, Managing Editor. National bimonthly magazine. Target audience: writers, ages 19 and younger.

☐Here is a paying market for young adults who enjoy writing articles and/or stories. The editors seek works that will interest high-school students. Nonfiction articles of interest include how-to, profiles, photo features, and general interest articles; 1,000 to 2,500 words. Acceptable fiction includes adventure, science fiction, mystery, suspense, humor and fantasy; 2,500 words maximum. The editors also will consider poetry (any style), short stories (no word limit), and fillers (including humor), but will not consider stories with excessive violence or explicit sex. Submit seasonal material at least 6 months in advance.

☐Pays on publication: $.03 per word for articles and stories; $5 for poems and fillers. No kill fee. Buys all rights (negotiable). Prefers to receive query letter for articles; entire manuscript for stories. Not interested in reprints. Simultaneous submissions acceptable if editor is so informed. Responds in 6 weeks. Author guidelines available; sample issue: $2. SASE required.

YOUR BIG BACKYARD, 1412 Sixteenth St., N.W., Washington, D.C. 20036. (202) 797-6800. Printed by the National Wildlife Foundation. Dr. Jay D. Hair, Executive Vice-President. Trudy D. Farrand, Editorial Director. Sallie A. Luther, Editor. National monthly magazine. Target audience: preschool children, ages 3 to 5; widely read in preschool and day-care centers. Average issue length: 20 pages.

☐Developed to help teach children about nature and to appreciate the responsibility everyone shares in conserving it. The editors seek articles and stories with a nature/wildlife slant that encourage children to learn preschool tasks. Areas of interest: nature crafts; activities to teach word, color, and number identification; science; math; games (e.g., dot-to-dot); outdoor activities; instructive questions; and nature facts; 50 to 300 words. Acceptable fiction must have a nature focus; length varies. Rebus stories and illustrative poetry (rhyming preferred) also are considered. Articles should be well-written, accurate, entertaining, challenging, and creative.

☐''We have designed each issue to help children start on that magic path of discovery toward beginning reading.''

☐Pays on acceptance: variable fee. Buys all rights. Prefers to receive query with outline and list of credentials. Will consider appropriate reprints. No simultaneous submissions. Replies in 6 to 8 weeks. Author guidelines and sample issues available. Send SASE.

YOUTH! PO Box 801, Nashville, TN 37202. (615) 749–6463. First published 1985. Printed by the United Methodist Publishing House. Sidney D. Fowler, Editor. Carol Atkins, Editorial Secretary. National monthly magazine with 50,000 readers. Target audience: "teenagers of all Christian denominations in junior- and senior-high school." Average issue length: 48 pages.

☐ "The purpose of *Youth!* is to help teenagers live out the Christian faith in contemporary culture." The editors are seeking fiction and nonfiction. They look for how-to and factual articles about social issues and interaction, youth interests and decisions, relationships, and family living; 700 to 2,000 words. All articles should strengthen the reader's Christian identity. For fiction, the editors are interested in adventure, romance, science fiction, fantasy, relationship stories, and humor; 700 to 2,000 words. Avoid heavy slang, sex-roles, racial discrimination, and teenage stereotypes of the so-called "pretty people" (athletes and homecoming queens).

☐ "We want stories that involve the reader's mind and feelings. Simplistic situations and sentimental resolutions do not help Christian youth deal with their world." "We are delighted when we discover a surprise twist, a lovable and laughable character, a simple, clever use of words, or a real faith experience. We treasure creativity in use of words, storyline and format." Illustrations and photos (color and B&W) are considered with or without an accompanying manuscript; writers are encouraged to submit both with their articles. "The approach of this magazine is to provide help for individual youth—not a youth group. Although an article may focus on a group, it should illustrate the effects on individual youth or ways an individual youth might make a difference."

☐ Pays on acceptance: $.04 per word for articles and stories (higher payments must be negotiated with the editor). Buys first North American serial rights (not negotiable). Prefers to receive entire manuscript. Not interested in reprints. Simultaneous submissions acceptable. Replies in 6 to 8 weeks. Author guidelines and sample issues available. Send SASE.

THE YOUTH REPORT, 226 W. Pensacola St., Suite 301, Tallahassee, FL 32301. (904) 681–0019. First published 1985. Printed by Loiry Publishing House. William S. Loiry, Editor. Regional/national monthly news magazine. Target audience: anyone involved in or interested in child/youth adovcacy.

☐ *The Youth Report* concentrates on the efforts of those attempting to improve conditions for children. The editors accept articles on how to improve conditions, reviews of related books, editorials from children about their perceptions of social issues, and essays on controversial matters affecting today's youth; length varies. Profiles and interviews with prominent child advocates and policy-makers also are welcome. This magazine plans to gradually broaden its initial focus in Florida to include national issues. Fiction, humor, and poetry are not considered.

☐ Pays on publication: $200 average for articles. No kill fee. Buys all rights. Prefers to receive query letter with detailed outline. Not interested in reprints. Simultaneous submissions acceptable. Responds in 4 to 6 weeks. Author guidelines and sample issue available for large envelope (10″ × 12″) and $.30 postage. SASE required.

YOUTH UPDATE, 1615 Republic St., Cincinnati, OH 45210. (513) 241–5615. First published 1982. Printed by St. Anthony Messenger Press.

Carol Ann Morrow, Editor. National monthly newsletter with 53,000 readers. Target audience: "Catholic teenagers of high-school age, interested in religious topics." Average issue length: 4 pages.

□Publishes Catholic-oriented nonfiction of interest to teens; 2,500 words. Interviews should be of experts in areas of personal growth; 2,500 words. The editors are specifically looking for sensitive treatments of homosexuality; the church's role in a young person's life; self-image of teens, including specific attitudes toward one's body; and an exploration of the reasons for being Catholic. Well-received topics: dating, suicide, drinking, loneliness, feelings, lifetime decisions, rock music, popularity, peer pressure, stress, alcoholism, tension at home, and getting along with parents.

□"I look for practical, down-to-earth treatment of a clearly defined dilemma or concern of young people, addressed from a moral perspective," says Morrow. "Concrete examples, anecdotes, and references to the current scene are expected."

□Pays after revisions suggested by youth advisors are made; $300 per article (negotiable according to condition of the piece). Buys first North American serial rights. Prefers to receive outline. Interested in reprints. No simultaneous submissions; photocopies acceptable. Replies in 6 to 8 weeks. Author guidelines and sample issues available. SASE preferred.

FOUR

BOOK PUBLISHERS

You know you finally have made it as a writer when an editor believes in your talent enough to accept a book-length manuscript for publication or to ask you to write a book about a specific topic. According to the Authors Guild, the organization that represents some 6,000 book authors, more than 50,000 books—both fiction and nonfiction—are published each year in the United States. This figure might sound impressive (and it is), but when you consider that it represents only 1% to 5% of manuscripts *submitted* to the publishing industry, you begin to appreciate the selective nature of book publishing.

As you use this section, be alert to the specific information in each entry. If, for example, a publisher states that she is looking for picture books of 32 pages, don't submit a 128-page manuscript; it won't work.

To improve the chances of your manuscript being accepted, learn as much as possible about your prospective publisher. If author guidelines and book catalogs are available, send for them. Then study them from cover to cover to see what the editors consider acceptable manuscripts. A book catalog can provide you with a wealth of what professional writers call "unspoken knowledge." Such invaluable data includes the number of new titles published annually by the house, who the intended readership is, the average book lengths and the trends and topics that are in demand.

After examining these materials—in addition to researching *Literary Market Place (LMP)* and *Publishers Weekly* for detailed, current information—you can objectively critique your proposed book to determine whether it really is what the publisher wants. If it isn't, you must either change your proposal or search for another publisher.

If your manuscript *is* what the publisher desires, follow the publisher's guidelines for submitting queries or manuscripts. Most editors prefer that a typed, book-length manuscript be mailed to them in a ream box (you can use the same one you emptied in writing the story), unbound. Your name should appear at the top right of every numbered page. Include a cover letter summarizing the storyline and your credentials.

Make certain that the front page of your manuscript contains a copyright notice. You can use the copyright symbol, the word "Copyright," or the abbreviation "Copr." For example: "Copyright © 1987 by S.F. Tomajczyk."

Finally, include enough postage for the return of manuscript should it be rejected. If you don't want your manuscript returned and just want the editor's decision, do what many professional authors do: mail a self-addressed postcard (SAPC) instead of an SASE. Pre-stamped SAPCs can be purchased from any U.S. Post Office. To use, simply type on the back of the postcard:

CWMP-RP

_____ Accepted, we love it!
_____ Sorry, but we can't use it. Thanks anyway.
_____ We need more information. Please send us:

You can even code the card so that you know what manuscript/query and publisher it refers to (e.g., "CWMP-RP" to represent Running Press' decision on *Children's Writer's Marketplace)*. This procedure saves you money and provides you with quick information about your book's status with the editor. (Most book acceptances are typewritten on company letterhead by an editor, so if you receive a letter instead of your postcard, you know it must be good news!)

Never, under any circumstances, send an unsolicited book manuscript to an editor. Most unsolicited material ends up in a "slush pile," where it sits for weeks or months before being mailed back to you *unread*. Publishing houses that do not accept unsolicited material, such as Doubleday, must be queried first with a letter describing your book's plot, characters, and your qualifications.

Optional information to include in your query package are clips of your published works, a detailed table of contents, character profiles, and a sample chapter. You will have to decide which of these will best support your book. However, most editors tend to want detailed, specific information about your credentials for nonfiction titles and a synopsis and character profiles for fiction titles.

When a publishing house accepts your book and sends you a contract, be prepared to pull out a magnifying glass. The fact is, there is no standard book contract that is used by each and every publishing house; book contracts all differ from one another to some extent. Second, contrary to popular belief, nearly all terms of a contract are negotiable, unless the contract is a work for hire agreement—in which case the publisher asks you to surrender all rights to the work in exchange for a flat fee.

When you receive your contract, it's a good idea to sit down with either an attorney or an agent and go over the contract point by point until you fully comprehend it. Don't be afraid to pencil in queries or suggest changes. Take your time. The more time you spend on your contract, the more likely you are to spot unfair conditions that need to be modified or replaced.

Although each contract is unique, these are some of the standard provisions:

Advance. An advance is prepayment of a portion of the royalties you are expected to earn on the sale of your book. It is often paid half upon the signing of the contract, with the remainder paid on acceptance of the completed manuscript; or it may be payable in thirds, with the final third payable upon publication. If you do not deliver the manuscript, you will be asked to return the advance.

The size of the advance usually reflects the publisher's commitment to the book. A low advance means you can expect very little marketing of the book; a large advance may mean a book tour. Advances start at around $1,000 and as high as six figures, but the majority are less than $10,000.

Co-authors and author-illustrator teams usually divide the advance evenly. When a writer is assigned to work with a so-called "expert" in writing a book, it is customary for the author to receive the entire advance; the expert receives a share of the royalty.

Guarantee. This advance payment to a writer is guaranteed and is not returnable, unlike an advance.

Royalty. Payment based upon a percentage of the book's sales is made to the author every six or 12 months. The standard payment structure for hardcover books is 10% of sales for the first 5,000 or 10,000 books, escalating to 12½% for the next 5,000; and 15% for all sales thereafter. Most publishers base the rate on the retail price of the book; if your contract is based upon the wholesale price, start negotiating.

Take note: An increase of 2.5% in the royalty rate means an additional $250 in royalty for every 1,000 copies of a $10 list-price book. If your $10 book sold 10,000 copies at 10% royalty, your payment would be $10,000. However, if you had negotiated the royalty to 12.5% after 5,000 copies, this same book would earn $11,250. So negotiate for higher royalty and a faster escalation whenever possible.

Here are some common royalty structures you can expect:

- *Picture books:* Royalties are divided by author and illustrator. However, only one member of the team can negotiate so-called "step-ups" in the royalty clause (e.g., the author receives 5%, increasing to 7% at a predetermined point; the illustrator receives a straight 5% on all copies sold). In this genre, it's not uncommon for illustrators to receive more favorable royalty rates than the writers of the text (e.g., illustrator, 6%; author, 4%). Typical royalty rates for writers of children's picture books are 2.5%, 3%, 3.75%, and 4%.
- *Books for ages 8 to 12:* Here the royalty payments favor the writer rather than the illustrator, since most books for this age group are not dependent upon illustration. Illustrators of these books receive a smaller royalty or sell their work outright to the publisher.
- *Books for teens:* This is where the money is for writers; the full royalty is awarded to the author of the text. Illustrators usually receive a flat fee for decorative artwork, or a separate, small royalty of 2% to 4% for extensive artwork in nonfiction titles.
- *Trade paperback titles (all genres):* Royalties range from 5% to 15% of the retail price, depending upon the type of book. A 1986

Authors Guild study lists some of the more common royalty terms:

    5% of all copies sold
    5% on the first 15,000 copies; 6% thereafter
    6% on the first 25,000 to 50,000 copies; 8% thereafter
    7% on all copies sold
    7.5% on all copies sold
    7.5% on first 40,000 copies; 10% thereafter
    8.5% on first 25,000 copies; 10% thereafter
    10% on all copies
    10% on first 15,000 copies; 12.5% thereafter
    10% (15,000 copies); 12.5% (next 15,000); 15% thereafter
    10% (5,000 copies); 12.5% (next 5,000); 15% thereafter

Satisfactory manuscript. Most contracts require the author to submit a manuscript satisfactory to the publisher in "form and content" by a certain date. This appears to be reasonable; all professional writers are willing to update, revise, and rewrite a manuscript until is sparkles. However, an unethical publisher who is in financial difficulty might claim that a manuscript is unacceptable and demand that the advance by returned. If this happens to you, contact your attorney. If nothing can be worked out with your publisher, find another publisher who will purchase the manuscript.

Indemnity clause. In this clause, you agree to indemnify your publisher against any claims of libel, plagiarism, or invasion of privacy resulting from the publication of your book. Try to change this clause so that you are held responsible only for suits that result in actual judgment against you and the publisher. Try also to limit your liability to the amount of your advance.

Some large publishers now have a libel "umbrella" for their contracted authors which extends the publisher's own insurance to writers. Protection can range up to $10 million, with deductibles ranging from $15,000 to $100,000; authors are sometimes expected to pay 50% of the deductible.

Manuscript delivery. Make certain that this date is realistic: that it includes adequate time both to research and to write the book. Try to reword this clause so that you can obtain an extension if necessary.

Out-of print clause. Be sure that within a specific period of time after your book goes out of print all rights of the publisher terminate and revert to you. This gives you an opportunity to sell your book to another publishing house, one that might be able to find a new niche for it in the marketplace.

Free copies. Negotiate for 15 to 25 free copies. You'll want to give them to friends and relatives, and you'll also need them for promotional purposes. You may be surprised by the number of people who will ask you for a free, autographed copy of your book, so try to add a clause that allows you to buy copies of your own book from the publisher at a discount.

Option clauses. You might be flattered that your publisher wants your next book, but you should look over the option clause very carefully. If it binds you to the same terms of the current book, negotiate to improve the terms.

Foreign and subsidiary rights. If you have a good literary agent, try to retain as many of these rights as possible. An agent can turn these rights into income though sales to book clubs, magazines and even movie companies and some publishers will assign to the author upwards of 80% royalty for non-profit and subsidiary rights. If you do not use an agent, you should ask your publishers' subsidiary rights department to pursue these sales.

Most U.S. publishers acquire only the right to sell books in the United States and Canada. It's not uncommon for agents to request up to 50% of your foreign subsidiary sales and 10% of the domestic sales that they negotiate for you. Such statistics might sound gluttonish, but agents can give you access to the international market.

Author keystrokes. This area is so new that you'll probably be the one to initiate this clause.

Through computerization, a publisher now can cut production costs dramatically, especially if one of its authors uses a computer and modem. With a touch of a key the writer can send an entire book to the publisher's typesetter via telephone, eliminating the need for on operator to keystroke the text. This savings, typically around $5 per page for nontechnical books, can save a publisher $1,500 on a 300-page text.

But who gets this savings? Many writers feel that they should be compensated for reducing the publisher's costs. Try to add an amendable clause to your contract to cover this situation. Since this is relatively new territory, be prepared to negotiate this clause. Your publisher may agree to share the savings with you!

The market for children's books is large. It's also volatile. Many publishing houses have recently merged with competing firms, and other mergers and shifts in editorial direction will surely follow.

Current editorial trends in the children's writers marketplace, as reflected in questionnaires completed by publishers for this book, include:

- Biographies
- Manuscripts that can be turned into computer games
- "Select your own ending" books
- Suspense romance for young adults
- Audiocassettes
- Bears (both in fiction and nonfiction)
- Science/high-tech fiction

The following section lists more than 100 publishers of books for juveniles (ages 2 to 12), teens (13 to 16), and young adults (17 and up). These publishing houses range in size from such giants as E.P. Dutton, publisher of *Winnie-The-Pooh,* to smaller, newer publishers such as Elephant Walk, founded in 1985. Most book publishers are located in New York City, but you'll also find high-quality publishers in other cities across the country.

An index of book publishers is located at the end of this book; use it to quickly locate potential markets for your manuscript. If you are a published writer who would like to consider asking a literary agent to represent your book proposals and manuscripts, turn to Chapter 10.

ABBEY PRESS, St. Meinrad, IN 47577. (812) 357–8011. Keith McClellan, O.S.B., Publisher. A Catholic publishing house that publishes up to 15 nonfiction paperbacks each year.
□ "While Abbey Press does not publish children's books or programs per se," reports McClellan, "it does publish books for parents that have an effect on

their children." Recent titles: *When Your Child Needs a Hug* by Larry Loson-cy and *When God Is At Home With Your Family* by David M. Thomas.
☐Pays royalty on net sales. Prefers query with outline and one or two sample chapters. Replies in one month. SASE required.

ABINGDON PRESS, 201 8th Ave. South, PO Box 801, Nashville, TN 37202. (615) 749-6404. Etta Wilson, Children's Editor; Jim Deming, Children's Pro-duct Manager. Publishes about 20 children's books each year, 65% hardcover.
☐The publishing house of the United Methodist Church, Abingdon Press issues books for children ages 2 to 4 with emphasis on picture books, read-alouds and some Bible-related titles. The editors also seek juvenile fiction with religious values (i.e., no explicit sex or graphic violence); length varies. Recent picture book title: *Amelia's Nine Lives* by Lorna Balian.
☐ "Short, pointed books have a better chance with us right now."
☐Pays standard royalty and occasional advance. Buys all rights. Prefers to receive complete manuscript. Not interested in reprints. Simultaneous submis-sions acceptable if editor is so informed. Replies in 4 to 6 weeks. Author guide-lines and catalog available. Send SASE.

ADDISON-WESLEY PUBLISHING CO., Route 128, Reading, MA 01867. (617) 944-3700.
☐Since the purchase by Harper and Row Junior Books of the Addison-Wesley Juvenile list, Addison-Wesley no longer accepts manuscripts or proposals for children's books.

ALBA HOUSE, a division of the Society of St. Paul, 2187 Victory Blvd., Staten Island, NY 10314. (212) 761-0047. Anthony L. Chenevey, Editor-in-Chief.
☐Specializes in religious books, 80,000-120,000 words. Publishes 15 books a year. Interested in young-adult books about family issues, and sociology, as well as textbooks and general nonfiction. Does not want any books for chil-dren under 16 years old.
☐Pays 10% royalty on retail price. Advance varies. Query with outline and synopsis. Replies in one month. Catalog available. SASE required.

ALYSON PUBLICATIONS, INC., 40 Plympton St., Boston, MA 02118. (617) 542-5679. Founded 1977. Sasha Alyson, President. Publishes 3 paper-back books each year for young adults.
☐Alyson specializes in homosexual fiction for young adults: romance and other stories with strong, positive, gay or lesbian characters; 50,000 to 70,000 words. Recent titles: *One Teenager in Ten, All-American Boys,* and *Reflec-tions of a Rock Lobster.*
☐Pays 10% to 13% royalty of net sales; offers variable advance upon signing. Buys all rights. Prefers to receive query. Interested in reprints. Simultaneous submissions and photocopies acceptable. Replies in 3 to 8 weeks. Author guidelines and catalog available. Send SASE.

ARCO PUBLISHING INC., 215 Park Ave. South, New York, NY 10003, (212) 777-6300. Phil Friedman, Managing Editor. Debra Jeffer, Editorial Assistant. Submissions editors: Linda Bernback, Educational Books, and Ellen Lichtenstein, Career Guidance and Study Guide.

☐Specializes in test-preparation, and educational books (150 to 600 pages in length; also publishes science and how-to titles for young adults.

☐"It's best to contact us first with a query letter before writing a book," says Ms. Jeffer. "You'd be surprised at the duplication of projects we have already in-house."

☐Advance and royalty varies with the book project. Buys all rights. Not interested in reprints. Simultaneous submissions acceptable. Replies in 2 weeks. Guidelines and catalog available. SASE required.

ATHENEUM PUBLISHERS, INC., 115 5th Ave., New York, NY 10003. (212) 614-1300; (212) 486-2700. Jonathan J. Lanman, Editorial Director. Publishes up to 75 books each year for children ages 3 to 16; 80% hardcover. (See also entry for Margaret K. McElderry Books.)

☐Atheneum publishes quality nonfiction books and young-adult novels and picture-books; length varies with intended readership and topic.

☐"We publish whatever comes into our offices that interests us. The more literary manuscripts stand a better chance with us for publication."

☐Pays variable royalty and occasional advance. Buys all rights. Prefers to receive query letter with outline and sample chapter; send entire manuscript for picture books. Interested in reprints. Simultaneous submissions acceptable if editor is so informed. Replies in 6 to 8 weeks. Catalog and guidelines available. Send SASE.

AUGSBURG PUBLISHING HOUSE, 426 S. 5th Street, PO Box 1209, Minneapolis, MN 55440. (612) 330-3432. Founded in 1890. Roland Seboldt, Director of Book Development. Publishes 12 juvenile, 2 to 4 teen, and 2 young-adult paperbacks each year.

☐A Christian publisher, interested in publishing textbooks, contemporary stories with a Christian theme, health, and self-help. Recent titles: *Jesus Lives* by Ron and Lyn Klug, *Growing Up Isn't Easy, Lord* by Stephen Sorenson and the *Dear God* series (12 books) illustrated by Annie Fitzgerald.

☐"We publish books with a Christian message," reports Seboldt. "to apply to feelings, needs, and aspirations of children and youth, and books parents and other adults can use to teach values."

☐Pays 5% royalty on children's picture books (10% royalty on other books); advance varies. Buys all rights. Prefers to receive an outline with either synopsis or sample chapters. Interested in reprints. Simultaneous submissions acceptable. Replies in 6 weeks. SASE required.

AVON BOOKS (imprints include Camelot and Flare), 1790 Broadway, New York, NY 10019. (212) 399-4500. Founded 1925. Ellen Krieger, Senior Editor, Books for Young Readers. Gwen Montgomery, Editorial Assistant. Publishes 1 to 5 books for 6- to 8-year-olds, 24 books for 9- to 12-year olds, and 24 books for teens each year, all paperback.

☐Interested exclusively in all areas of fiction: romance, adventure, fantasy, historical, mystery, science fiction, suspense, and mainstream; 30,000 to 50,000 words. Recent titles: *Bunnicula* by James Howe, *The President's Daughter* by Ellen White, and *Behind The Attic Wall* by Sylvia Cassedy.

☐Pays $1,000 to $2,500 for first novel; half on signature and half on acceptance of final manuscript. Buys world rights. Prefers to see entire manuscript. Interested in reprints. Simultaneous submissions acceptable. Replies in 6 to 8 weeks. Author guidelines available. SASE required.

BAKER STREET PRODUCTIONS, LTD., 502 Range St. PO Box 3610, Mankato, MN 56001. (507) 625-2482. Founded 1981. Karyne Jacobsen, Managing Editor. Publishes 12 hardcover titles each year for 6- to 8-year-olds.
☐Publishes fiction and nonfiction for children from kindergarten to grade 3. Acceptable topics: educational materials (32 pages), biographies, and fiction "with a message or moral"; 500 to 1,000 words. Recent titles: *Beast Has Too Much To Do, Ugly Beast,* and *Homesick.*
☐Pays either royalty or flat fee, up to $1,500 (depending upon length of manuscript); offers variable advance upon signature and acceptance. Buys North American or all rights. Prefers to receive sample chapter. Not interested in reprints. Simultaneous submissions and photocopies acceptable. Replies in 8 to 12 weeks. Author guidelines available. Send SASE.

BANTAM BOOKS, INC., 666 5th Ave., New York, NY 10103. (212) 765-6500. Linda Grey, Publisher. Judy Litenstein, Editor, Young Readers; Carolyn Nichols, Editor, "Loveswept"; Alicia Condon, Senior Editor, "Loveswept." Publishes a varying number of childrens and young-adult titles each year.
☐Publishes mass market, trade paperback, and hardcover titles for children, ages 8 to 12, and young adults, ages 12 to 17; length varies.
☐Pays royalty and advance; amount determined by author's experience, quality of the manuscript, and the market. Does not accept unsolicited queries or manuscripts: query through an agent. Interested in reprints.

BARNES & NOBLE (A division of Harper & Row), 10 E. 53rd Street, New York, NY 10022. (212) 207-7000. Jeanne Flagg, Editor. Publishes 25 to 40 young-adult and adult titles each year, mostly paperback.
☐Specializes in publishing educational handbooks and study guides. The editors are interested in titles for their existing College Outline series (summations of college-level courses), as well as nonfiction self-help, craft, hobby, and skills manuscripts. Most authors are teachers or experienced in the subject they are writing about.
☐Pays standard royalty; advance varies. Buys all rights. Prefers to receive query letter with outline, synopsis and sample chapters. Interested in reprints. Simultaneous submissions acceptable if editor is so informed. Replies in 4 to 6 weeks. Catalog available. Send SASE.

BC STUDIO PUBLICATIONS, PO Box 5908, Huntington Beach, CA 92615. Founded 1983. B.H. Camp, Owner/Manager. S. Kaye, Managing Editor. Publishes a varying number of booklets and reports for juveniles and adults each year, all paperback.
☐Publishes nonfiction how-to booklets and pamphlets for recreation, projects, solving a problem, and self-improvement; 2 to 28 pages. Considers B&W photos by assignment or with manuscript. Fillers that can be expanded to report size are welcome.
☐Pays 8% to 10% royalty on net sales, and occasionally buys manuscript outright; no advance. Buys either first North American or all rights; occasionally second rights. Prefers to receive entire manuscript. Interested in reprints. Simultaneous submissions acceptable. Replies to queries in 2 to 3 weeks; to manuscripts in 4 to 6 weeks. Author guidelines, catalog, and sample reports: $2. Send SASE.

BENNETT & McKNIGHT PUBLISHING CO., 809 W. Detweiller Dr., Peoria, IL 61615. (309) 691-4454. Founded 1899; acquired by Macmillan in 1983. Submissions editors: Pattyann Des Marais, Home Economics; Robert Cassel, Career Education, Art, and Health; Michael Kenny, Industrial Education. Publishes 10 teen and 10 young-adult books each year, 60% hardcover.
□Interested in publishing textbooks for junior and senior high-school students. Acceptable topics: economics, industrial education, art, career education, and health occupations; length varies according to subject. Recent titles: *Food for Today,* and *Succeeding in the World of Work.*
□"Books must be carefully planned to fit into the curriculum for the areas mentioned," says Kenny. "We want to hear only from writers who are qualified to write textbooks in our fields; nearly always this means teachers."
□Pays 6% to 10% royalty; no advance. Buys all rights. Prefers to receive query with outline and sample chapters. No simultaneous submissions. Not interested in reprints. Responds in 4 to 6 weeks. Author guidelines sent after receipt of outline. SASE preferred.

THE BERKLEY PUBLISHING GROUP, 200 Madison Ave., New York, NY 10016. (212) 686-9820. Nancy Coffey, Editor-in-Chief. Publishes a varying number of paperbacks each year for young adults.
□Of Berkley's 8 imprints, 3 are for juvenile and teen readers: Second Chance at Love, To Have and To Hold, and Tempo Young Adult. Primary interest for these imprints is fiction: adventure, suspense, historical, romance, and science fiction; length varies. Not poetry or textbooks.
□Pays up to 10% royalty on the retail price; advance varies. Buys all rights. Prefers to receive query with outline and synopsis. Interested in reprints. Simultaneous submissions acceptable if editor is so informed. Replies in 6 to 8 weeks. Catalog available. Send SASE.

THE BESS PRESS, PO Box 22388, Honolulu, HI 96822. (808) 734-7159. Founded 1979. Benjamin E. Bess, Managing Editor. Publishes 1 title for 6- to 8-year-olds, 2 titles for 9- to 12-year-olds, and 2 teen titles each year, 80% paperback.
□Specializes in regional history, text and trade titles that focus on Hawaiian, Pacific and Asian cultures; acceptable length varies. The editors also are interested in history textbooks about Hawaii and other regions. No poetry. Recent titles: *Fax to da Max* (humor), *Ethnic Foods of Hawaii* (cookbook), *The Hawaiian Baby Book* (scrapbook), and *Hawaiians Of Old* (textbook).
□Pays either 10% royalty on net sales, or negotiable flat fee; no advance. Usually buys all rights (negotiable). Prefers to receive query. Interested in reprints. Simultaneous submissions and photocopies acceptable. Replies in 6 weeks. Catalog available. Send SASE.

BETHANY HOUSE PUBLISHERS, 6820 Auto Club Rd., Minneapolis, MN 55428. (612) 944-2121. Carol Johnson, Editor. Publishes a varying number of books each year for children and young adults, mostly paperback.
□An evangelical publisher, Bethany House seeks well-written Christian stories, especially historical and contemporary romance novels for its existing Heartsong Books and Springflower Books imprints. Acceptable nonfiction for children and teens includes contemporary, family, and social issues; length varies. The editors also are looking for manuscripts for their young-adult cur-

riculum series, "Building Blocks" (34-lesson student workbooks). Recent titles include: *The Wedding Dress* and *Love's Fragile Flame.*
☐Pays 6% royalty on mass market books; 10% on other titles. Offers negotiable contract and advance. Buys all rights. Prefers to receive query with outline and simple chapter. Not interested in reprints. Simultaneous submissions acceptable if editor is so informed. Replies in 6 to 8 weeks. Author guidelines and catalog available; specific guidelines for Heartsong and Springflower imprints are available. Send SASE with all submissions.

BRADBURY PRESS (An affiliate of Macmillan, Inc.), 866 3rd Ave., New York, NY 10022. (212) 702-1409. Barbara Lalicki, Editor-in-Chief. Publishes about 30 hardcover titles each year for children and young adults.
☐Publishes original picture books and novels of adventure, fantasy, and suspense. The editors are willing to take chances on first novels! Successful titles: *The All-New Jonah Twist* by Natalie Honeycutt, and *The Pain and the Great One* by Judy Blume.
☐ "Use real dialogue and real situations," suggest the editors.
☐Pays up to 10% royalty; advances average $3,000. Buys all rights. From established writers, prefers to receive query with outline and sample chapters; Unpublished writers should send entire manuscript. Not interested in reprints. Simultaneous submissions acceptable if editor is so informed. Replies in 8 to 10 weeks. Catalog available. Send SASE.

BRANDEN PUBLISHING CO., 17 Station St., PO Box 843, Brookline Village, MA 02147. (617) 734-2045. Founded 1963. Adolph Caso, Editor. Publishes an average of 2 juvenile titles for ages 6 to 12, and 3 young-adult books each year.
☐Publishes general trade texts, especially "well-written books with positive, even polemical messages." Interested in biographies, historical events, and textbooks. No religion or philosophy. For fiction, Branden looks for adventure, historical biographies, romance and juvenile-level books about computers. Poets should submit at lest 5 poems with manuscript outline; no religious or autobiographical poetry. Successful titles: *Young Rocky* by Kinney, Erebus; *Child Of Chaos* by Sam Saladino, and *Story Pilgrims and Indian Friends* by Cauper.
☐Pays 10% royalty on sales; 50% on other rights. Typically purchases all rights. No advances for children's literature. Prefers to receive query letter with SASE. Interested in reprints Simultaneous submissions acceptable. Replies to queries in 1 week; to manuscripts in 8 to 10 weeks. Catalog available. SASE required.

BYLS PRESS, 6247 North Francisco Ave., Chicago, IL 60659. (312) 262-8959. Daniel Stuhlman, Editor. Publishes 3 paperback or computer software titles each year.
☐A part-time publisher, BYLS publishes books and computer software for Jewish children, parents, teachers, and librarians. Subjects of interest include how-to, historical, education, and cooking. Acceptable children's fiction includes religious stories (especially those that center around Jewish holidays. No expository fiction.
☐Pays up to 15% royalty on wholesale price; no advance. Prefers query with vitae. Editors deal directly with authors (no agents). Replies in 2 weeks. Catalog available.

CALEDONIA PRESS, PO Box 245, Racine, WI 53401. (414) 637-6200. Caledonia no longer accepts juvenile material.

CAMELOT BOOKS. *See* Avon.

CAREER PUBLISHING, INC., 910 N. Main St., PO Box 5486, Orange, CA 92667. (714) 771-5155; (800) 821-0543 (CA); (800) 854-4014 (outside CA). Sherry Robson, Editor. Publishes up to 25 guidance texts, educational software titles, and health books each year. However, Career Publishing has suspended its review of new book ideas until the end of 1987.

CAROLRHODA BOOKS, INC., 241 First Ave. North, Minneapolis, MN 55401. (612) 332-3344. Founded 1969. Emily Kelley, Editorial Director. Submissions editor: Inga Thelander. Typically publishes 28 titles each year for ages 3 to 13.
□Specializes in fiction and nonfiction picture books with an emphasis on quality rather than mass-market appeal. For fiction, the editors look for folktales from other countries and from specific ethnic groups (1,000 words); mysteries, and novelettes (for ages 8 to 13). For nonfiction: nature- and conservation-oriented manuscripts (2,500 to 3,000 words), photo essays (1,500 to 2,000 words), easy-to-read history, biographies of creative personalities (past and present) such as musicians and artists (4,000 words). Successful titles: *Harriet And The Rollercoaster* by Nancy Carlson and *Saving The Peregrine Falcon* by Caroline Arnold.
□Payment depends upon length, retail price and the nature of the book. Buys all rights. Prefers to receive entire manuscript. Simultaneous submissions acceptable if editor is so informed. Replies in 3 to 4 months. Author guidelines and catalog available. Send SASE.

CLIFF'S NOTES, INC., PO Box 80728, Lincoln, NE 68501. (402) 477-6971. Founded 1958. Michele Spence, Editor. Submissions editors: Gary Carey (Cliff's Notes series) and Michele Spence (all other publications). Publishes 10 to 15 paperbacks each year for teens and young adults.
□Cliff's Notes issues student self-help material, literary study aids, test preparation guides, and textbooks for junior- and senior-high school audiences; length varies. Most authors hold advanced degrees and are experienced teachers. Recent titles: *Cliff's SAT Preparation Guide, Cliff's Notes on the Scarlet Letter* and *Cliff's Notes on Hamlet.*
□"Most of our books are purchased directly by the student and fill a specific academic need," reports Michele Spence.
□Royalty and advance payments vary. Buys all rights. Prefers to receive query letter with outline and sample chapters. Not interested in reprints. No simultaneous submissions. Replies in 5 weeks. Author guidelines available after interest is shown in manuscript or query. SASE preferred.

COACH HOUSE PRESS, INC., PO Box 458, Morton Grove, IL 60053. (312) 967-1777. Founded 1954. David Jewell, President. Hetty Mayer-MacDowell, submissions editor. Publishes 1 title for ages 6 to 8, 3 titles for ages 9 to 12, and 1 teen title each year, all paperback.
□Specializes in plays for young audiences; 60 to 75 minutes running time. The editors look for scripts that emphasize children's intelligence, zest for life, car-

ing, and cooperative nature. Successful titles: *Wiley & The Hairy Man, Blue Horses,* and *Wind in the Willows.*

☐"Plays should receive at least two high-caliber productions before being published," suggests Jewell.

☐Pays 10% royalty on book sales; 50% royalty on production. No advance. Buys all rights. Prefers to receive query with outline/synopsis. Not interested in reprints. No simultaneous submissions; photocopies acceptable. Replies in 8 weeks. Author guidelines and catalog available. Send SASE.

COMPUTER SCIENCE PRESS, INC., 1803 Research Blvd., Rockville, MD 20850. (301) 251-9050. Founded 1974. Arthur D. Friedman, Editor-in-Chief. Publishes introductory technical books for teens and young adults, 75% paperback.

☐Interested in publishing high-school textbooks about computers, telecommunications, computer education, and mathematics. No fiction. Successful titles: *Computing without Mathematics* by Marcus, *Bits 'n Bytes about Computing* by Heller and Martin, and *Learning PASCAL Step-By-Step* by McDermott and Fischer.

☐Royalty varies; no advance. Buys all rights. Prefers to receive manuscript, author bio, and a written comparison of the proposed book with other books already on the market. Not interested in reprints. No simultaneous submissions. Replies in 8 to 12 weeks. Catalog available; no author guidelines. SASE preferred.

CONCORDIA PUBLISHING HOUSE, 3558 S. Jefferson Ave., St. Louis, MO 63118. (314) 664-7000. Founded 1869. Mervin A. Marquardt, Family Book Developer. Typically publishes 12 titles for ages 2 to 5; 18 titles for ages 6 to 8; 8 titles for ages 9 to 12; 2 titles for teens and 6 titles for young adult each hear; 65% paperback.

☐Interested in explicitly Christian (i.e., Christ-centered, gospel motivation) nonfiction books harmonious with Lutheran teachings. Contemporary fiction also accepted; editors are looking for juvenile picture books that deal with Bible stories and Bible history. Successful titles: *Numbers in God's World, Time in God's World* and *My Bible Story Book.*

☐Says editor Marquardt, "We look for texts that show how readers can apply Christian principles to everyday life. However, few freelance manuscripts are currently accepted."

☐Variable royalty; children's picture books typically secure a 5% royalty. Buys all rights. Prefers to receive entire manuscript for short children's books; query letter with outline and sample chapter for all other manuscript ideas. Not interested in reprints. Simultaneous submissions acceptable. Responds in 12 weeks. Author guidelines available. Send SASE.

DAVID C. COOK PUBLISHING (Chariot Books), 850 N. Grove Ave., Elgin, IL 60120. (312) 741-2400. Founded 1875. Catherine L. Davis, Managing Editor. Marcia Fay, Editorial Coordinator. Issues an average of 60 titles per year, for ages 1 to 14; 90% paperback.

☐Looks for fiction and nonfiction books with a moral and spiritual foundation. Nonfiction subjects: animals, sports, science, and biographical adventures (all of which must help a child grow emotionally or spiritually). Length depends upon readers' age level: for example, 20,000 words for ages 8 to 10.

Acceptable fiction usually is both entertaining and compelling. The editors look for material that illuminates biblical truth without being didactic; plots typically concern external and spiritual conflict which the characters resolve through faith. Average length is 30,000 words. Picture books should be no longer than 60 printed pages. Successful titles: *In Grandma's Attic* by Arleta Richardson and *Potter* by Walter Wanguin Jr.

☐Pays standard royalty: half of advance is paid upon signature; half upon acceptance of final manuscript. Buys all rights. Prefers to receive query letter with outline and sample chapter. Not usually interested in reprints. Simultaneous submissions acceptable. Replies in 12 weeks. Author guidelines and catalog available. Send SASE.

COWARD McCANN INC. (An imprint of G.P. Putnam's Sons), 51 Madison Ave., New York, NY 10016. (212) 576-8900. Margaret Frith, Publisher. For details, see entry for Putnam Young Readers Group.

CROSSWAY BOOKS, 9825 W. Roosevelt Rd., Westchester, IL 60153. (312) 345-7474. Founded 1938. Ted Griffin, Managing Editor. Typically publishes 2 titles for ages 6 to 8; 2 titles for ages 9 to 12; and 1 title for teens each year; all paperback.

☐Books that communicate Christian issues and lifestyles, written from an evangelical perspective, are the focus of Crossway. Editors are interested in buying fictional adventure, science fiction, and fantasy novels with Christian themes; up to 50,000 words. Nonfiction topics: home and family, Christian living, the Bible, and contemporary issues. No poetry, picture books, short stories, or formula romance. Successful juvenile fiction: *The Dragon King Trilogy* by Steve Lawhead, *The Blooming Of The Flame Tree* by Roberta Kehle, and *The Door in the Dragon's Throat* by Frank Peretti.

☐Negotiable royalty and advance. Buys first rights. Prefers to receive a query letter with sample chapters. Not interested in reprints. Simultaneous submissions acceptable. Replies in 12 weeks. Author's guidelines available. Send SASE.

MAY DAVENPORT, PUBLISHERS, 26313 Purissima Road, Los Altos Hills, CA 94022. (415) 948-6499. Founded 1976. May Davenport, Editor-Publisher. Publishes 3 to 5 books for ages 6 to 8; 3 books for ages 9 to 12; and 3 young-adult books each year, 95% paperback.

☐Although currently overstocked with manuscripts, Davenport is interested in humorous fiction narratives of 1,500 to 40,000 words. Prefers animal narrators for grades K to 5, human narrators for older children. Davenport will also consider working with teachers on special textbooks about art education, music education and drama written for children. Successful titles: *The Zebra Who Learned to Dance* by Pamela Neubacher, and *Child of the Field* by Ron Bliss.

☐"Remember," says Davenport, "children will remember the message if they laugh while reading."

☐Pays 15% royalty on retail price; no advance. Buys all rights. Prefers to receive query letter. Not interested in reprints. Send SASE.

DELMAR PUBLISHERS INC., 2 Computer Dr., West, PO Box 15015, Albany, NY 12212. (518) 459-1150. G.C. Spatz, Vice-President. Publishes a varying number of young adult titles each year; most are paperback.

□Primarily a publisher of educational textbooks for secondary and post-secondary students, Delmar is interested in manuscripts in these areas: vocational, mathematics, child care, agriculture, and health; length varies. Editors will consider photos and illustrations that accompany proposals. Suggestion: your best bet is to submit vocational and career manuscripts.

□Pays royalty and small advance. Buys all rights. Prefers to receive query letter with outline and sample chapters. Not interested in reprints. Simultaneous submissions acceptable if editor is so informed. Replies in 6 to 8 weeks. Catalog available. Send SASE.

DIAL BOOKS FOR YOUNG READERS (A division of E.P. Dutton, A division of NAL Penguin Inc.), 2 Park Ave., New York, NY 10016. (212) 725–1818. Skip Skwarek, Managing Editor. Paula Wiseman, Editor. Publishes, on the average, 8 titles for ages 2 to 4; 20 titles for ages 4 to 8; 4 titles for ages 8 to 12; and 8 titles for ages 12 and over each year. Also publishes 12 paperback picture books per year that are reprints of Dial's own hardcover titles.

□Dial is particularly interested in fiction (e.g., adventure, romance, historical, mystery, humor, fantasy) and nonfiction for the middle grades, plus innovative picture book manuscripts (e.g., animals, history and nature). Also seeks easy-to-read texts for first- and second-grade readers. No games, riddles, plays, or alphabet books. Successful fiction titles: *Best Friends* by Steven Kellogg, *The Revenge of the Wizard's Ghost* by John Bellairs, and *The Mare on the Hill* by Thomas Locker.

□"Due to the small size and high quality of our book list, we are most selective in choosing manuscripts for publication," says editor Paula Wiseman. "Acceptable texts should be well-written, with an involving, convincing plot and believable characters. Subjects or themes should be unusual, not overworked in previously published books."

□Pays variable royalty and advance. Negotiates the purchase of publishing rights. For fiction, prefers to receive complete manuscript; for nonfiction, a query letter with outline and several sample chapters. No simultaneous submissions. Replies to queries in 2 weeks; to manuscripts in up to 3 months. Author guidelines and catalog available. Send SASE.

DILLON PRESS INC., 242 Portland Ave. South, Minneapolis, MN 55415. (612) 333–2691. Founded 1964. Ms. Uva Dillon, Editorial Director. Thomas Schneider, Senior Editor. Publishes 5 titles for ages 6 to 8; 15 titles for ages 9 to 12; 10 teen and 2 young-adult titles each year, 95% hardcover.

□"Dillon Press primarily publishes nonfiction supplemental educational books for K to 12 readers," reports Schneider. The publisher seeks nonfiction biographies, both contemporary and historical, for mid-to-upper-elementary and junior-high students: material about U.S. cities and states and foreign countries; unusual approaches to science and nature topics for elementary pupils; nonfiction humorous subjects; and photoessay coverage of a wide variety of educational topics.

□Acceptable manuscript length: 10 to 120 pages, depending upon age level; biographies should be 20 to 25 pages for *Taking Part* books, 90 to 100 for *People in Focus* books, and all should focus on well-known subjects. Successful titles: *Bill Cosby: Making America Laugh and Learn,* and *Incredible Facts about the Ocean.*

☐Negotiable royalty and flat fee; advances not usually offered. Buys all rights. Prefers to receive entire manuscript, but will review outline and synopsis if accompanied by sample chapter. Not interested in reprints. Simultaneous submissions acceptable, but not preferred. Replies in 6 to 8 weeks. Catalog available for SASE with $1 postage; author guidelines on request.

DODD, MEAD & COMPANY, 71 Fifth Ave., New York, NY 10011. (212) 627-8444. Jo Ann Daly, Children's Editor. Publishes a varying number of juvenile and young-adult titles each year.
☐Dodd, Mead publishes book-length (2,000 to 75,000 words) fiction and nonfiction in these areas: picture books, biographies, sports, science, romance, suspense, mysteries, music, adventure and travel. Dodd, Mead does not publish textbooks. Suggestion: Carefully scrutinize the book catalog to see what is being published before considering a submission.
☐Negotiable advance and royalty. Buys all rights. Prefers to receive query letter with outline and a sample chapter; send manuscripts only if requested. Simultaneous submissions acceptable if editor is so informed. Replies in 6 to 8 weeks. Catalog available. Send SASE.

DOUBLEDAY & COMPANY INC., 245 Park Ave., New York, NY 10167. (212) 953-4561. William Barry, Managing Editor.
☐"We do not consider unsolicited queries, proposals, or manuscripts," warns Barry. "Any such submission is returned unopened." Doubleday does, however, consider proposals submitted by literary agents.
☐Offers standard royalty scale; negotiable advance. Prefers to receive query with outline and sample chapters for fiction and nonfiction titles. Typically buys all rights. Replies in 8 to 10 weeks. Author guidelines and catalog available. Send SASE.

DOWN EAST BOOKS, PO Box 679, Camden, ME 04843. (207) 594-9544. Karin Womer, Editor. Publishes 1 or 2 juvenile books each year.
☐This regional publisher rarely issues juvenile fiction, but does look for nonfiction with a strong Maine or New England focus for the juvenile level. Topics include history, nature and recreation.
☐Pays 10% to 15% royalty; offers small advance. Typically buys all rights. Prefers to receive query with outline and a sample chapter. Simultaneous submissions acceptable if editor is so informed. Replies to queries in 2 weeks; to manuscripts in 8 weeks. Author guidelines and catalog available. Send SASE.

E.P. DUTTON, 2 Park Ave., New York, NY 10016. (212) 725-1818. Ann Durell, Editor-in-Chief. Publishes from 40 to 50 juvenile titles each year, hardcover except for Unicorn Paperback Picture Books.
☐Fiction for children, ages 3 to 12, is Dutton's specialty. Editors are looking for manuscripts to add a new series for beginning readers, as well as picture books, short "chapter books" for ages 7 and 8; and novels for ages 9 up to 14. Illustrations and photos are considered with proposals. (See Dial Books for Young Readers for additional information.) Successful titles include: *Watch the Stars Come Out* by Riki Levinson, and *The Illyrian Adventure* by Lloyd Alexander.
☐Pays standard royalty on list price; negotiable advance. Buys all rights. Prefers to receive entire manuscript for picture books; send query letter with

synopsis for other manuscripts. Not interested in reprints. Simultaneous submission acceptable if editor is so informed. Replies in 8 to 10 weeks. Catalog available. Send SASE.

EAKIN PRESS, 8800 Tara Lane, PO Box 23066, Austin, TX 78735. (512) 288-1771. Founded 1978. Edwin M. Eakin, Publisher and Acquisitions Editor. Buys 4 titles for ages 6 to 8; 8 titles for ages 9 to 12; 4 teen titles; and 1 young adult title each year, 95% hardcover.
☐ Juvenile fiction, primarily with a Texan theme, is Eakin's primary product: biographies of well-known people associated with Texas, and easy-to-read, illustrated books for grades 2 and 3. Eakin also is broadening its publishing interests to include contemporary subjects with a wider interest range; query first. Successful titles: *Glory Girl, A Queen Named King, The Dark Ships,* and *Where the Pirates Are.*
☐ "Manuscripts must have a Texas flavor with an emphasis on history, culture, and ethnic groups," comments Eakin.
☐ Pays minimum 10% royalty on net sales; usually offers advance variable upon signing. Buys all rights. Prefers to receive query with 500-word synopsis. Not interested in reprints. Simultaneous submissions and photocopies acceptable. Replies in 6 weeks. Author guidelines and catalog available. Send SASE.

ELEPHANT WALK (A division of Little House Group), 2544 N. Monticello Ave., Chicago, IL 60647. (312) 342-3338. Founded 1985. Gene Lovitz, Senior Editor. Publishes a variable number of children's paperbacks each year.
☐ Seeks fiction for juveniles, ages 4 to 15: mystery, nature, adventure, and fantasy (in the manner of J.R.R. Tolkien), as well as romance novels (with nonexplicit sex) for young adults; length varies.
☐ "Don't contact us unless you have a completed manuscript or one near to completion," advises Lovitz.
☐ Pays 10% royalty on the retail price; negotiable advance. Buys all rights. Prefers to receive entire manuscript. Not interested in reprints. Simultaneous submissions acceptable. Replies in 2 to 4 weeks. Send SASE.

ENSLOW PUBLISHERS, Bloy St. and Ramsey Ave., PO Box 777, Hillside, NJ 07205. (201) 964-4116. Founded 1976. Patricia Culleton, Vice President and Managing Editor. Publishes 3 books for ages 6 to 8, and up to 30 books for teens each year, 95% hardcover.
☐ Primarily publishes nonfiction for juveniles: science, social issues, and biographies that are either 64-, 96- or 128-pages long. Will review nonfiction translations. Successful nonfiction titles: *Cloning and the New Genetics* by Margaret Hyde, *Leaders of the Middle East* by James Haskins, and *Mr. President* by Mary Fox.
☐ Pays 10% to 15% royalty; up to $5,000 advance. Buys all rights. Prefers to receive query letter with outline and sample chapter. Not interested in reprints. Simultaneous submissions acceptable. Replies in 2 to 4 weeks. Book checklist available. Send SASE.

ENTELEK, PO Box 1303, Portsmouth, NH 03801. (603) 436-0439. Founded 1961. A.E. Hickey, Editor. Publishes 4 teen and young-adult paperbacks each year.
☐ Specializes in computer books for teens and young adults; length varies.

Successful titles: *Fun and Games with the Computer, 3-D Computer Graphics,* and *Physics with the Computer.*

□Pays variable royalty or flat fee; no advance. Buys all rights. Prefers to receive either query or complete manuscript. Simultaneous submissions and photocopies acceptable. Interested in reprints. Replies in 4 weeks. Catalog available. Send SASE.

ESPRESS, INC., PO Box 55482, Washington, D.C. 20011. (202) 723–4578. Founded 1969. Rev. Henry J. Nagorka, President. Steven Matias, Editor. Publishes 1 title for ages 6 to 8; 1 title for ages 9 to 12; 1 teen and 2 young-adult titles each year, all paperback.

□Primarily interested in nonfiction that deals with parapsychology, spirituality, new-age subjects, and psychotronics; 80 to 200 pages. Biographies should be related to metaphysics and parapsychology; 120 to 250 pages. No textbooks, poetry, or illustrated books. Successful titles: *Who's the Matter with Me?* by Steadman, and *The Blue Island* by W.T. Stead.

□Pays up to 35% royalty (no advance). Negotiates publishing rights. ("We merchandise the books we publish," says Nagorka.) Prefers to receive query with outline and sample chapter. Not interested in reprints. No simultaneous submissions. Replies to queries in 2 to 4 weeks; to manuscripts in 8 weeks. Author guidelines and catalog available. Send SASE.

EXPOSITION PRESS OF FLORIDA, 1701 Blount Rd., Pompano, FL 33069. (305) 979–3200. Steve Berner, Editor. Cheryl Guessford, Editor. Publishes 4 titles for ages 2 to 5; 12 titles for ages 6 to 8; 8 titles for ages 9 to 12; 6 teen, and 5 young-adult titles each year, 60% hardcover.

□Interested in nonfiction topics that include animals, art, health, hobbies, music, nature, recreation, and sports; length varies. For fiction, the editors seek adventure, fantasy, humor, mystery, romance, science fiction and westerns. Poets of all genres are welcomed. No pornographic or racist material.

□Pays 40% royalty first edition; 20% royalty on second and subsequent editions. No advance. Negotiates publishing rights. Prefers to receive entire manuscript. Interested in publishing reprints. Simultaneous submissions acceptable. Replies in 3 weeks. Author guidelines and catalog available. SASE preferred.

FARRAR, STRAUS & GIROUX, 19 Union Square West, New York, NY 10003. (212) 741–6900. Founded 1946. Stephen Roxburgh, Editor-in-Chief. Margaret Ferguson, Senior Editor. Typically publishes 25 to 30 hardcover titles, and about 10 paperback titles for children and young adults each year, selected for backlist books.

□Primarily seeking fiction: picture books ("Send complete manuscript," suggests Ferguson, "and, when appropriate, dummies and photocopies or slides of sample art work."), and juvenile novels (length averages 192 pages). Editors also review illustrator's portfolios. Artists should call for an appointment. Publishes very little nonfiction, so query first. Successful titles: *A Wrinkle in Time* by Madeleine L'Engle, *The Cricket In Times Square* by George Selden, and *Duffy and the Devil* by Margot Zemach.

□Pays variable royalty and advance against earnings. Publishing rights purchased "depend on whether or not an agent is involved." Prefers to receive query letter with outline and sample chapters. No simultaneous submissions. Replies in 6 to 8 weeks. Author's guidelines and catalog available. Send SASE.

FLARE BOOKS (An imprint of Avon Books).

FLEET PRESS, 160 Fifth Ave., New York, NY 10010. (212) 243-6100. Founded 1953. Susan Nueckel, Editor. P. Scott, submissions editor. Publishes 2 to 4 teen titles each year, 50% hardcover.
☐Interested in nonfiction books about history, social science, and biography; up to 50,000 words. No fiction. Successful titles: *Customs & Holidays,* and the Heroes series.
☐Pays variable royalty; variable advance paid upon signing, upon acceptance, and upon publication. Buys all rights. Prefers to receive query letter with outline. Not interested in reprints. Simultaneous submissions acceptable. Replies in 12 weeks. Catalog available. SASE not required.

FRIENDSHIP PRESS (A division of the National Council of Churches). 475 Riverside Dr., New York, NY 10115. (212) 870-2495. Nadine Hundertmark, submissions editor. Audrey Miller, Editor. Publishes 1 title for ages 6 to 8; 1 title for ages 9 to 12; and 1 young-adult title each year, all paperback.
☐An ecumenical publisher, Friendship Press is interested is social issues (hunger, poverty), ecumenical inter-faith, and international themes. The editors also look for religion-oriented, general resource books for children's use in churches. Publishes very little fiction, usually stories of children from other countries and cultures; length varies. Successful titles: *The Whole World Singing* (children's songs from around the world), *Clue to Creativity* (craft projects for children), *Children's Festivals from Many Lands,* and *Children's Games from Many Lands*.
☐"We have two themes each year on which we publish at least one juvenile title, but most of these are assigned (to established writers)."
☐Pays variable royalty; advance paid upon acceptance and upon publication. Buys North American and first rights. Prefers to receive query with outline/synopsis and sample chapter; entire manuscript if very small. Interested in reprints. Simultaneous submissions acceptable if editor is so informed; photocopies acceptable. Replies in 4 weeks. Catalog available. Send SASE.

GIFTED EDUCATION PRESS (The Reading Tutorium), 10201 Yuma Court, PO Box 1586, Manassas, VA 22110. (703) 369-5017. Founded 1981. Maurice D. Fisher, Publisher. Publishes 6 paperbacks each year for ages 4 to 18.
☐Publishes fiction and nonfiction for gifted children and their educators. Current interests: how-to books on educating and counseling gifted children (primarily for parents); biographies of creative heroes whom the gifted can admire; psychology; and practical books on how to teach reading/comprehension skills. Average length for texts is 13,000 words. Successful titles: *Humanities Education for Gifted Children* by Michael E. Walters, *How to Use Computers with Gifted Students* by Patricia J. Terry, and *How to Improve Gifted Student's Creative Thinking and Imagination* by Win Wenger.
☐"Criteria for acceptance include an innovative idea, good imagination, and inventive style," says Fisher.
☐Pays $1 royalty per book; no advance. Buys all rights. Prefers to receive query letter with outline. Interested in reprints. Simultaneous submissions acceptable. Replies in 6 to 8 weeks. Author guidelines and book ads available. Send SASE.

GINN. *See* Silver Burdett & Ginn.

GOLDEN BOOKS (An imprint of Western Publishing Co., Inc.), 850 Third Ave., New York, NY 10022. (212) 753–8500. Founded 1942. Rosanna Hansen, Editor-in-Chief. Doris Duenewald, Publisher. Natalie Provenzano, Art Director. Publishes about 100 titles for ages 2 to 5; 20 titles for ages 6 to 8; and 2 titles for ages 9 to 12 each year. Of these, 75% are hardcover.
☐Publishes children's picture books (e.g., *Pat the Bunny*) for the mass market. Although the editors accept very few unsolicited fiction manuscripts, they typically look for full-color picture books and humor; 600 words. Golden Books publishes very few nonfiction titles (mostly concept books) and very little poetry (collections are selected and edited in-house). Successful titles: *Poky Little Puppy,* and *Richard Scarry's Best Word Book Ever.*
☐Payment agreements range from work-for-hire to standard royalty with full contracts. Pays variable advance: upon signing, upon acceptance, and upon publication. Buys all rights. Prefers to receive entire manuscript; artists should send a query letter with samples. Interested in reprints. Simultaneous submissions acceptable. Time period for a reply varies. Author guidelines and catalog available. SASE preferred.

GREENWILLOW BOOKS (A division of William Morrow & Co.), 105 Madison Ave., New York, NY 10016. (212) 889–3050. Founded 1974. Susan Hirschman, Editor-in-Chief. Judith Fried, Assistant Managing Editor. Publishes 35 titles for ages 2 to 5; 30 titles for ages 6 to 8; 5 titles for ages 9 to 12; and 5 teen titles each year, all hardcover.
☐Interested in picture books, easy readers, fantasy, poetry, humor, biographies, and young-adult fiction, as well as illustrations to accompany juvenile material. Successful titles: *Whiskers and Rhymes* by Arnold Lobel, *Have You Seen My Duckling?* by Nancy Tafuri, and *The Hero and the Crown* by Robin McKinley.
☐Pays variable royalty and advance. Buys all rights. Prefers to receive entire manuscript and sample illustration for picture books; sample chapter and synopsis for other titles. Not interested in reprints. No simultaneous submissions. Replies in 6 weeks. Author guidelines available; catalog can be ordered from William Morrow & Co., Children's Marketing Department. Send SASE.

GRYPHON HOUSE, INC., 3706 Otis St., PO Box 275, Mt. Rainier, MD 20712. (301) 779–6200. Larry Rood, Editor. Publishes 3 children's paperbacks each year.
☐Concentrating exclusively on how-to and educational material for teachers of preschool, nursery school, day care, and kindergarten, Gryphon House looks for activity workbooks, supplements, and textbooks; length varies.
☐"Remember," says editor Larry Rood, "you're dealing with young children, write clearly and interestingly. Know your subject well."
☐Pays 10% to 12.5% royalty on retail price; offers small advance up to $500. Buys all rights. Prefers to receive query with outline and sample chapter. Not interested in reprints. Simultaneous submissions acceptable if editor is so informed. Replies in 3 to 4 weeks. Author guidelines and catalog available. Send SASE.

HARCOURT BRACE JOVANOVICH, 1250 Sixth Ave., San Diego, CA 92101. (619) 699–6598. Laura Lance, Editorial Assistant. Submissions editors:

Maria Modugno, Bonnie Ingber, and Susan Tehrani. Publishes 10 to 15 titles for ages 2 to 5; 10 to 12 titles for ages 6 to 8; 10 to 12 titles for ages 9 to 12; and 5 to 10 teen titles each year, 85% hardcover. Publishes simultaneous hardcover and paperback editions, and reprints of backlist; no original paperbacks.

□Picture books are a current interest of Harcourt, as well as middle-grade and young-adult fiction, mysteries, and fantasy/science fiction. The editors are also looking for nonfiction for all ages, particularly the very young; biographies (64 pages) of well-known contemporary figures, such as athletes; and board books are also desired. Artists should submit all kinds of work, since Harcourt maintains a file of art and photo samples (no original artwork is kept on file). HBJ publishes a limited amount of poetry, mainly picture-book length poems and anthologies. Successful titles: *A Visit to William Blake's Inn* by Nancy Willard, *The Napping House* by Audrey Wood, and *Friends Like That* by Patricia Hermes. (If you are interested in proposing a juvenile textbook, contact Harcourt Brace Jovanovich, School Department, Orlando, FL 03887.)

□"HBJ Children's Books publishes books suitable for bookstores, schools, and libraries," reports Lance. "We are looking for honestly-approached and thoughtfully-written manuscripts with special appeal for children and young adults."

□Pays advance against royalty (upon signature, upon acceptance and upon publication); payment varies. Rights purchased varies. Prefers to receive entire manuscript for picture books; outline and sample chapters for other titles. Not interested in reprints. No simultaneous submissions. "No dot-matrix submissions unless very heavily inked and readable." Replies in 6 to 8 weeks. Author guidelines and catalog available. SASE preferred.

HERALD PRESS, 616 Walnut Ave., Scottdale, PA 15683. (412) 887-8500. Founded 1908. Paul M. Schrock, General Book Editor. Publishes about 1 title for ages 2 to 5; 1 title for ages 6 to 8; 4 titles for ages 9 to 12; 2 teen, and 2 young-adult titles each year. Of these, 90% are paperback.

□Specializes in fiction and nonfiction for the Christian market. The editors seek historical fiction and juvenile novels for grades 4 to 9, which focus on social concerns; length varies. The editors also seek nonfiction biographies, devotionals and manuscripts concerned with social issues; 25,000 to 50,000 words. Photos and illustrations are assigned by the editorial staff. No humor, poetry or textbooks. Successful titles: *Remember the Eagle Day* by Guenn Martin, *And I'm Stuck with Joseph* by Susan Sommer, and *Danger in the Pines* by Ruth Nulton Moore.

□Pays 10% royalty on the retail price; no advance. Buys all rights. Prefers to receive outline with sample chapters. Not interested in reprints. No simultaneous submissions. Replies in 4 weeks. Catalog: $.50. Send SASE.

HOLIDAY HOUSE, 18 East 53rd St., New York, NY 10022. (212) 688-8085. Founded 1935. Barbara Walsh, Editor. Linwood Harrison, submissions editor. Publishes 35 juvenile and young-adult hardcovers each year.

□Publishes trade fiction and nonfiction for young readers, from preschool to high school; length varies. Holiday themes are strongly recommended. Successful titles: *The Twisted Witch and Other Spooky Riddles* by Adler.

□Pays variable royalty; advance against royalty paid upon signature, upon acceptance, and upon publication. Buys North American or all rights. Prefers to receive query letter with outline. Not interested in reprints. Would rather not receive simultaneous submissions. Replies in 6 to 8 weeks. No author guidelines or catalog. Send SASE.

HOUGHTON MIFFLIN COMPANY, 2 Park St., Boston, MA 02108. (617) 725-5000. Publishes 50 to 60 hardcover originals for children each year.
□Publishes both nonfiction and fiction, including history, mystery, suspense, biographies, and books about animals, nature and health; length varies. Will consider any proposal. Illustrations and photos reviewed with manuscript.
□Pays 10% to 15% royalty; offers negotiable advance. Buys all rights. For nonfiction, send query with outline and sample chapters; for fiction, send complete manuscript. Interested in reprints. Simultaneous submissions acceptable if editor is so informed. Replies in 6 to 8 weeks. Catalog available. Send SASE.

HUMANICS LIMITED, 1389 Peachtree St., N.E., Atlanta, GA 30309. (404) 874-2176. Gary Wilson, Publisher; Sarah Gregory, Editorial Director. Publishes 10 to 15 juvenile paperbacks each year.
□Humanics Limited, which primarily publishes nonfiction textbooks and resource books for juveniles and instructors, is looking for manuscripts about infant development, health, parenting, early childhood, social issues, and self-help. Length varies with intended audience.
□Pays up to 12% royalty on net sales; occasionally buys manuscript outright; no advance. Buys all rights. Gregory prefers to receive query with outline and several sample chapters. Not interested in reprints. Simultaneous submissions acceptable if editor is so informed. Replies in 10 to 12 weeks. Author guidelines and catalog available. Send SASE.

HUNTER HOUSE, INC., PO Box 1302, Claremont, CA 91711. (714) 624-2277. Founded 1978. Kiran S. Rana, Publisher. Wendee Streeter, submissions editor. Publishes 2 to 4 teen and young-adult paperbacks each year.
□Primarily prints nonfiction books of 96 to 124 pages. The editors look for non-preachy books that take young adults seriously. Hunter's new Infobook series is designed to be informational and useful; the idea is not to manipulate, but to inform young adults and leave them free to draw their own conclusions.
□"Our books are reviewed by 11- to 17-year-olds for style and content, and above all, tone," says Rana.
□Pays royalty ranging from 5% to 7½% to 10%; offers small advance, half payable upon signing and half upon publication. Buys all rights. Prefers to receive outline/synopsis with sample chapters. Interested in reprints. Simultaneous submissions acceptable. Replies to queries in 6 weeks; to manuscripts in up to 16 weeks. Send SASE.

INCENTIVE PUBLICATIONS, INC., 3835 Cleghorn Ave., Nashville, TN 37215. (615) 385-2934. Founded 1970. Sally D. Sharpe, Editor. Publishes 4 titles for ages 2 to 5; 4 titles for ages 6 to 8; and 4 titles for ages 9 to 12 each year, all paperback.
□A publisher of supplementary educational materials for teachers and parents. Incentive Publications is interested in activity textbooks that include reproducible patterns, and nonfiction educational materials; 64 to 200 pages. Successful titles: *I Can Make a Rainbow*, the Tabletop Learning series, and *If*

You're Trying to Teach Kids How to Write.
☐Pays either royalty or flat fee; no advance. Buys all rights. Prefers to receive outline/synopsis and sample chapters. Sumultaneous submissions and photocopies acceptable. Replies in 3 to 4 weeks. Catalog available. Send SASE.

INTERSTATE PRINTERS & PUBLISHERS, INC., 19 N. Jackson St., PO Box 50, Danville, IL   61834. (217) 446–0500. Founded 1908. Ronald L. McDaniel, Vice President/Editorial. Publishes 5 titles for ages 2 to 5; 5 titles for ages 6 to 8; 5 titles for ages 9 to 12; 15 teen, and 10 young-adult titles each year. Of these, 50% are hardcover.
☐This educational publisher sells primarily to schools and is currently interested in textbooks for vocational education (agriculture, agribusiness, home economics, business education, trade) and special education (speech-language pathology, audiology, learning disabilities, aphasia); length varies. Successful titles: *The Meat We Eat* (12th ed.) by Romans, Jones, Costello, Carlson and Ziegler, *Speech and Language Rehabilitation* (vols. 1 & 2) by Robert L. Keith, and *Agriculture in Our Lives* (5th ed.) by Alfred H. Krebs.
☐"We publish special-education materials at all levels, and agricultural texts and related materials for upper elementary, high-school and college students," reports McDaniel. "We favor items that are designed to sell on a class-quantity basis rather than on a single-copy basis."
☐Pays standard 10% royalty; no advance. Buys all rights. Prefers to receive query with outline and synopsis. Interested in reprints. Simultaneous submissions acceptable if editor is so informed. Replies in 6 to 8 weeks. Author guidelines and catalog available. SASE preferred.

JALMAR PRESS (B.L. Winch & Associates), 45 Hitching Post Dr., Bldg. 2, Rolling Hills Estates, CA   90274. (213) 547–1240. Founded 1971. Bradley L. Winch, President. Suzanne Mikesell, Editor. Publishes 1 title for ages 6 to 8; 1 title for ages 9 to 12; and 1 teen and 2 young-adult titles each year, all paperback.
☐Issues nonfiction elementary and secondary textbooks and how-to books about positive self-esteem (100 to 300 pages); and illustrated books that focus on expressing feelings (64 to 100 pages). Jalmar also publishes crossover books on self-esteem that can be used by teachers and parents. First-time authors welcomed. Successful titles: *Reading, Writing and Rage* by Dorothy Ungerleider, *Feelings Alphabet* by Judy Lalli, and *TA for Tots* by Alvyn M. Freed.
☐"Books must match our editorial philosophy," emphasizes president Bradley Winch.
☐Pays royalty of between 7.5% and 10% of net sales; variable advance, paid upon signature, upon acceptance and upon publication. Buys all rights. Prefers to receive query with both outline/synopsis and sample chapters. Interested in reprints. Simultaneous submissions acceptable. Replies in 6 to 10 weeks. Author guidelines and catalog available. Send SASE.

JAMESTOWN PUBLISHERS, 544 Douglas Ave., PO Box 9168, Providence, PI 02940. (401) 351–1915 or (800) USA-READ. Founded 1969. Theodore Knight, Senior Editor. M. Fontaine and D. Laurila, submissions editors. Averages 6 to 8 paperback titles each year for ages 6 to 12, teens, and young adults.
☐An educational publisher, Jamestown is interested in reading-improvement

textbooks and workbooks for K to 12, college, and adult education; length varies. Fiction is considered only if it supplements comprehension exercises and drills. Published authors are usually—but not always—recognized leaders in the fields of reading improvement and study skills development. Successful titles: *Monsters* by Dan Dramer, *The Man Who Stopped Time* by Judith Andrews Green, and *Best Short Stories* by Raymond Harris.

☐ "Typically the reading passage (for workbooks), short or long, is followed by exercises and questions that help develop specific reading skills," explains Knight.

☐ Pays either 10% royalty or a variable flat fee. Buys all rights. Prefers to receive query with outline and sample chapters. Not interested in reprints. Simultaneous submissions acceptable. Replies in 3 weeks. Catalog available. SASE preferred.

JOY STREET BOOKS. *See* Little, Brown & Company

KAR-BEN COPIES, 6800 Tildenwood La., Rockville, MD 20852. (301) 984-8733. Founded in 1975. Madeline Wikler, Executive Editor. Usually publishes 6 to 8 hardcover titles each year for children 2 to 8 years of age, and simultaneously releases each title in paperback.

☐ Jewish themes, developed through fiction and nonfiction, are Kar-Ben's specialty. The editors seek nonfiction subjects that relate to Jewish holidays and customs, and that are appropriate for juveniles. Fiction storybooks and picture books for preschool and primary readers are welcome. Juvenile fiction can also include adventure, fantasy, and history-related themes. Average book length: 32 to 48 pages. Successful titles: *The Odd Potato* by Eileen Sherman (A Chanukah Story), and two series of toddler board books.

☐ Pays royalty of 10% to 15% of the net sales (divided between author and illustrator); variable advance paid upon signature. Buys all rights. Prefers to receive entire manuscript. Interested in reprints. Simultaneous submissions acceptable. Replies in 4 to 6 weeks. Catalog available. Send SASE.

ALFRED A. KNOPF, INC., Books for Young Readers, 201 E. 50th St., New York, NY 10022. (212) 572-2341. Janet Shulman, Editor-in-Chief; Frances Foster, Anne Schwartz, Senior Editors. Publishes 10 titles for ages 2 to 5; 14 titles for ages 6 to 8; 8 titles for ages 9 to 12; 7 titles for ages 10 to 13; and 6 young adult titles each year. Of these, 90% are hardcover.

☐ Knopf will consider all fiction submitted (length and level of difficulty depends upon the intended audience); unique, solid, and readily-accessible nonfiction for any age group; and humorous fiction (especially for middle-grade readers). The editors also welcome science fiction and fantasy for young readers. No poetry, biographies, or textbooks. Successful titles: *Frederick's Fables* by Leo Lionni, *Like Jake and Me* by Mavis Jukes, and *Beyond the Chocolate War* by Robert Cormier.

☐ Our markets are the trade and library/institutional ones. We do no mass-market-quality books.

☐ Pays royalty of up to 10%; variable advance, paid half upon signature, half upon acceptance. Buys North American and first rights. Prefers to receive entire manuscript. Simultaneous submissions acceptable if editor is so informed. Replies in 4 to 8 weeks. Author guidelines and catalog available. Send SASE.

DAVID S. LAKE PUBLISHERS (formerly Pitman Learning), 19 Davis Dr., Belmont, CA 94002. Mel Cebulash, Publisher. Publishes about 30 juvenile titles each year.

☐Publishes easy-to-read fiction with juvenile characters for middle-grade readers; 25,000 words. The editors look for believable characters and situations, and will consider any theme except pornography. Successful title: *Dangerous Waters* by Ken Girard.

☐Pays up to 10% royalty; occasionally buys manuscript outright; rarely offers advance. Buys all rights. Prefers to receive query with outline for nonfiction; entire manuscript for fiction. Not interested in reprints. Simultaneous submissions acceptable if editor is so informed. Replies in 4 to 6 weeks. Catalog available. Send SASE.

LEE'S BOOKS FOR YOUNG READERS, 813 West Ave., PO Box 111, Wellington, TX 79095. (806) 447-5445. Lee Templeton, Publisher. Publishes up to 10 hardcover juvenile and young adult titles each year.

☐Biographies of young American heroes of both sexes for juveniles ages 10 to 15 are the specialty of Lee's; length varies. This publisher seeks manuscripts that are technically correct, interesting, and well-written. Suggestion: do some thorough research and find a little-known young hero to write about.

☐Pays 10% to 12% royalty on wholesale price; no advance. Buys all rights. Prefers to receive query with outline, synopsis, and sample chapter. Not interested in reprints. Simultaneous submissions acceptable if editor is so informed. Replies in 4 to 6 weeks. Catalog available. Send SASE.

LITTLE, BROWN & COMPANY, 34 Beacon St., Boston, MA 02106. (617) 227-0730. John G. Keller, Publisher. Karen Klockner and Stephanie O. Lurie, submissions editors. Publishes 30 titles for ages 2 to 5; 20 titles for ages 6 to 8; 10 titles for ages 9 to 12; and 6 teen titles each year, all hardcover. Also publishes juvenile books under its new Joy Street Books imprint (Melanie Kroupa, Editor-in-Chief).

☐Little, Brown seeks fiction for early- and middle-grade children (25,000 to 30,000 words), as well as young-adult novels, nonfiction that deals with activities, crafts, and hands-on experiences. The editors also accept humor ("always welcome!"), some children's poetry, juvenile biographies, and photos/illustrations for preschool picture books. Successful titles include: *No More Secrets for Me* by Wachter, *St. George and the Dragon* by Hodges and Hyman, and *You Never Can Tell* by Conford.

☐Pays from 5% to 12.5% royalty on hardcover sales; variable advance, paid upon signature and upon delivery of acceptable manuscript. Buys all rights. Prefers to receive entire manuscript. Not interested in reprints. Simultaneous submissions acceptable if editor is so informed. Replies in 8 to 10 weeks. Author guidelines available. Send SASE.

LODESTAR BOOKS (A Division of E.P. Dutton), 2 Park Ave., New York, NY 10016. (212) 725-1818. Founded 1981 (formerly called Elsevier/Nelson). Virginia Buckley, Editorial Director. Rosemary Brosnan, submissions editor. Usually publishes 8 hardcover titles for ages 9 to 12 each year.

☐Publishes quality fiction and nonfiction for young adult and middle-grade readers, and occasionally for younger readers. Favored nonfiction themes include space, science, technology, contemporary issues, social issues, and wildlife; 30,000 to 40,000 words. Fiction is published for juveniles and young adults only. Themes include adventure, contemporary, humor, family, science fiction and westerns; up to 40,000 words. The editors also are interested in receiving biographies of Jews written for young adults; 35,000 to 40,000 words. Successful titles: *Come Sing, Jimmy Jo* by Katherine Paterson, *Encyclopedia Brown* series by Donald Sobol, and *Halley: Comet 1986* by Franklyn Branley.

□ "Juvenile novels should be fast-paced and well-written," advises Buckley.
□ Pays 10% royalty; advances of $2,000 to $10,000 are paid upon signature and upon acceptance. Buys all rights. Prefers to receive outline/synopsis and sample chapter for nonfiction; entire manuscript for fiction. Not interested in reprints. Simultaneous submissions acceptable. Replies in 2 to 4 months. Author guidelines and catalog available. Send SASE.

LOIRY PUBLISHING HOUSE, 226 W. Pensacola St., Suite 301, Tallahassee, FL 32301. (904) 681–0019. William Loiry, Executive Editor. Publishes a variable number of hardcover and paperback children's books each year.
□ Will consider any nonfiction topic, but is especially interested in how-to, self-help, and textbook proposals.
□ Pays up to 12% royalty; no advance. Buys all rights. Prefers to receive query with outline. Not interested in reprints. Simultaneous submissions acceptable. Replies in 4 to 6 weeks. Catalog available. Send SASE.

LOTHROP, LEE & SHEPARD BOOKS (A Division of William Morrow Co.), 105 Madison Ave., New York, NY 10016. (212) 889–3050. Laura Woodworth, Managing Editor. Dorothy Briley, Editor-in-Chief. Dinah Stevenson, Executive Editor. Publishes 35 titles for ages 2 to 5; 14 titles for ages 6 to 8; 10 titles for ages 9 to 12; and 12 teen titles each year. Of these, 99% are hardcover.
□ This publisher, whose primary buying audience is libraries and bookstores, is interested in picture book manuscripts (2 pages), fiction for children 8 to 12, and juvenile novels for children 12 and older (100 to 200 pages). The editors also seek general nonfiction for ages 8 to 12 (30 to 96 pages), and some photo essays for ages 6 to 10 (20 to 40 pages). Successful titles include: *Pterosaurs, the Flying Reptiles* by Helen Roney Sattler and *Drawing from Nature* by Jim Arnosky.
□ "We look for new twists on old stories, originality, and good writing," reports Woodworth.
□ Pays 10% royalty to authors of novels; 5% to authors of picture books. Advance varies: half paid upon signature; half upon acceptance. Buys all rights. Prefers to receive query, but send entire manuscript if under 20 typewritten pages. Not interested in reprints. No simultaneous submissions. Replies in 5 to 8 weeks. Catalog available. Send SASE.

MACMILLAN PUBLISHING COMPANY, 866 Third Ave., New York, NY 10022. (212) 702–2000. Publishes about 140 juvenile titles each year, both hardcover and paperback.
□ One of the largest children's publishers, Macmillan publishes fiction and nonfiction books of varying length. This is a very difficult market to break into, since Macmillan receives so many manuscripts.

□Pays negotiable royalty and advance. Buys all rights. Prefers to receive query with outline and sample chapters for longer manuscript proposals; entire manuscript for shorter works. Interested in reprints. Simultaneous submissions acceptable if editor is so informed. Replies in 6 to 8 weeks. Catalog available. Send SASE.

MARGARET K. McELDERRY BOOKS (An imprint of Macmillan Children's Book Group), 115 5th Ave., New York, NY 10003. (212) 614-1355. Margaret K. McElderry, Publisher.
□Publishes fiction for children in grades 4 to 7 and for young adults. Contemporary fiction, fantasy, and science fiction are welcome (30,000 to 60,000 words), as well as non-rhyming picture books (with or without accompanying illustrations). Send photocopies, photographs or slides of illustrations rather than original artwork. McElderry publishes few nonfiction books; those that have been published in recent years feature such topics such as history, archaeology, and architecture (25,000 to 50,000 words). Successful titles: *The Silver Cow* by Susan Cooper, and *Friends* by H. Heine.
□"We publish books of high quality—in terms of content, design and production," says McElderry. "We look always for outstanding quality in the ideas within a manuscript."
□Pays 8% to 12.5% royalty on list price; variable advance, often paid partially upon signature, upon acceptance, and upon publication. Buys all rights. Prefers to receive query and/or entire manuscript. Not interested in reprints. Simultaneous submissions acceptable if editor is so informed; photocopied manuscripts not acceptable. Replies in 6 to 8 weeks. Author guidelines and catalog available. Send SASE.

MERIWETHER PUBLISHING LTD., 880 Elkton Dr., Colorado Springs, CO 80907. (303) 594-4422. Founded 1965. Arthur Zapel, Managing Editor. Publishes 3 teen and 5 young adult paperbacks each year. (See also Contemporary Drama Service in Chapter 6 and Meriwether Publishing in Chapter 7.)
□Primarily publishes juvenile nonfiction sold via mail order: how-to, speech, drama, theater, humor and youth ministry; 100 to 150 pages. Not interested in young adult fiction at this time, but will look at well-written religious plays and comic 1-act plays. Successful titles: *Theater Games for Young Performers, Fundraising for Youth,* and *The Youth in Action Book.*
□"We sell our books to students, teachers, the general public, and to religious youth ministries," says Zapel.
□Pays 10% royalty on wholesale or retail prices; no advance. Buys North American and United Kingdom rights. Prefers to receive query with outline and sample chapters. Interested in reprints. Simultaneous submissions acceptable. Replies in 4 to 6 weeks. Author guidelines: $1. Send SASE.

CHARLES E. MERRILL PUBLISHING CO., 1300 Alum Creek Dr., Columbus, OH 43216. (614) 890-1111. Ann G. Turpie, Editor-in-Chief, Elhi Division. Tim McEwen, Editor-in-Chief, College Division. Publishes up to 400 textbook and supplementary titles each year.
□A textbook publisher, Merrill publishes elementary, high school, and college texts. Length ranges from just a few pages for kindergarteners to about 600 pages for 12th-grade texts. At the elementary/high school level, the editors

seek texts for language arts, mathematics, social studies, literature (but no juvenile stories or novels!), science, and bilingual science and math (particularly Spanish). For college texts, all courses (including childhood education and childhood development) are welcome.

☐ Pays variable royalty and flat fee, depending upon the nature of the book and its market; no advance. Buys various publishing rights. Prefers to receive query with outline and sample chapters. Not interested in reprints. Simultaneous submissions acceptable if editor is so informed. Replies in 8 to 10 weeks. Catalog available. SASE preferred.

MINDBODY PRESS, 1427 Milvia St., Berkeley, CA 94709. (415) 527-4980. Founded 1980. Marianne Morgan, Managing Editor. Lewis Mehl, Editor Associate. Publishes 1 title for ages 6 to 8; 1 title for ages 9 to 12; and 1 teen title each year, all paperback.

☐ Publishes science fantasy, fables, and nonfiction with themes of peace, conflict, and resolution; length varies. No humor.

☐ A combination subsidy/standard press; author retains all rights. Prefers to receive query. Interested in reprints. Simultaneous submissions and photocopies acceptable. Replies in 8 weeks. Catalog available. Send SASE.

WILLIAM MORROW AND COMPANY, 105 Madison Ave., New York, NY 10016. Children's imprints: Greenwillow Books; Lothrop, Lee & Shepard. For details, see these entries.

MOTT MEDIA INC., PUBLISHERS, 1000 E. Huron St., Milford, MI 48042. (313) 685-8773. Founded 1974. George Mott, Executive Editor. Ruth Beechick, Curriculum Editor. Publishes 20 titles each year.

☐ Specializes in Christian curriculum materials. Mott is looking for writers who can produce narrative history. Acceptable nonfiction for teens is marketed to the Christian school and home school markets.

☐ Says Mott, "All manuscripts should reflect excellent writing, scholarship, depth of treatment, and a biblical worldview."

☐ Royalty schedule ranges from 7% to 10%. Prefers to receive query with author's qualifications, outline and sample chapters. Not interested in reprints. Simultaneous submissions acceptable. Replies in 6 weeks. Author guidelines and catalog available. Send SASE.

NATIONAL PRESS, INC., 7508 Wisconsin Ave., Bethesda, MD 20814. (301) 657-1616. Linda Lee Stringer, Editor. Jillian Stoneback, Submissions Editor. Publishes 2 to 4 hardcover titles each year for children ages 2 to 8.

☐ Publishes a limited amount of children's fiction; 30 pages average length. National also issues nonfiction for juveniles, travel, how-to, health, cookbooks, sports and Jewish material. The editors are not presently interested in humor or illustrated books, although they have published both in the past. Recent successful titles: *The Father/Son Book*, *Employee's Rights in Plain English* and *The Glove Compartment Book*.

☐ Pays a variable royalty of 5% to 15% on retail price; advance varies. Buys all rights, including foreign rights. Prefers to receive query with sample chapter. Interested in reprints. Simultaneous submissions acceptable. Replies in 4 weeks. Catalog available. Send SASE.

NATIONAL TEXTBOOK COMPANY, 4255 W. Touhy Ave., Lincolnwood, IL 60646. (312) 679–5500. Leonard Fiddle, Editor-in-Chief. Publishes about 30 to 40 juvenile and young adult paperbacks each year.
☐Specializes in foreign-language, ESL and language-arts textbooks for secondary-level teen and young-adult students; length varies with intended readership and topic. The editors look for material in all areas of language comprehension, including workbooks and supplements, but only experienced language authors and teachers should attempt this market. National Textbook demands very high standards of its writers. Successful title: *Building Real Life English Skills* by Penn & Storkey.
☐Pays varying royalty and an occasional flat fee; offers small advance. Buys all rights. Prefers to receive query with detailed outline and sample chapter. Not interested in reprints. Simultaneous submissions acceptable if editor is so informed. Replies in 10 to 12 weeks. Author guidelines and catalog available. Send SASE.

THOMAS NELSON PUBLISHERS, Nelson Place at Elm Hill Pike, Nashville, TN 37214. (615) 889–9000. Lawrence Stone, Editorial Director. Publishes a variable number of children's titles each year, hardcover and paperback.
☐A Christian publisher, Thomas Nelson seeks nonfiction manuscripts adhering to principles of orthodox Christian theology (e.g., *Abortion and the Conscience of the Nation* by Ronald Reagan); length determined by the book's goals. Query for guidelines and immediate needs. Will consider illustrations and photos.
☐Pays negotiable royalty; occasionally buys manuscript outright. Offers variable advance to established authors only. Buys all rights. Prefers to receive query with outline and a chapter-by-chapter summary. Interested in reprints. Simultaneous submissions acceptable if editor is so informed. Replies in 6 to 8 weeks. Author guidelines and catalog available. Send SASE.

OAK TREE PUBLICATIONS, 9601 Aero Dr., Suite 202, San Diego, CA 92123. (619) 560–5163. Paul Lapolla, Acquisitions Editor. Buys a variable number of titles for ages 2 to 5; publishes 15 hardcover titles each year for ages 6 to 8.
☐Primarily publishes picture books; averaging 32 pages. The editors also seek educational read-aloud books that are entertaining and well-illustrated. Successful titles: *Value Tales* (an ongoing series of 30 titles created by Dr. Spencer Johnson), *Candy Clause* by Joan Chase Bowden; and *I Wish I had a Computer That Made Waffles,* by Dr. Fitzhugh Dodson.
☐Pays standard royalty; pays variable advance upon signature. Buys North American rights. Prefers to receive outline/synopsis and full-color sample illustrations. Interested in reprints. Simultaneous submissions and photocopies acceptable. Replies in 4 to 6 weeks. Author guidelines and catalog available. Send SASE.

ODDO PUBLISHING, INC., PO Box 68, Fayetteville, GA 30214. (404) 461–7627. Paul C. Oddo, Publisher.
☐Oddo publishes children's textbooks and supplemental texts for language arts, reading, science, social studies, writing, and mathematics.
☐Purchases manuscripts outright for negotiable flat fee; royalty offered only

in special cases. Buys all rights. Prefers to receive entire manuscript. Replies in 12 weeks. Catalog available. Send SASE.

PACIFIC BOOKS, PUBLISHERS, PO Box 558, Palo Alto, CA 94302. (415) 856–0550. Founded 1945. Henry Ponleithner, Publisher & Editor. Publishes 1 teen and 1 young-adult title each year, 50% hardcover.
☐Interested in general-interest trade books and textbooks at all levels, but primarily at high-school and college levels; length depends upon topic and intended reader. Pacific Books also publishes books for parents (e.g., *You and Your Retarded Child* by Kirk, Karnes & Kirk). Other nonfiction titles: *How to Study Successfully* by Bamman & Brammer, *How to Use the Library* by Santa & Hardy, and *How to Write a Research Paper* by Taylor.
☐Accepts nonfiction "only with educational value."
☐Pays a variable royalty; no advance. Buys all rights. Prefers to receive a query. Interested in reprints. Simultaneous submissions acceptable. Replies in 3 weeks. Catalog available. Send SASE.

PACIFIC PRESS PUBLISHING ASSOCIATION, PO Box 7000, Boise, ID 83707. (208) 467–7400. Herbert Douglass, Editor. Publishes a variable number of children's books each year, most paperback.
☐Sponsored by the General Council of the Seventh-Day Adventists, Pacific Press publishes nonfiction titles for children in these areas: biography, textbooks (for use in religious schools), self-help, health, nature, and contemporary issues written from a Christian perspective; up to 128-pages. Successful titles include: *What Jesus Said about* by Morris Venden, and *The Cry of a Lonely Planet* by G.E. Vandeman.
☐Pays 7% royalty; offers advance of $100. Buys all rights. Prefers to receive query with outline and sample chapter. Not interested in reprints. Simultaneous submissions acceptable if editor is so informed. Replies in 8 to 10 weeks. Author guidelines and catalog available. Send SASE.

PANTHEON BOOKS, 201 E. 50th St., New York, NY 10022. (212) 572–2341. Address all queries and manuscripts to Juvenile Editorial Department, 6th Floor.
☐Publishes a limited number of juvenile fiction and nonfiction each year. A first-time writer's best bet is a how-to book. Illustrations and photos are considered when accompanying the manuscript. Successful titles: *The Animal Family* by Randall Jarrell, *Frederick's Fables* by Leo Lionni, and *Bike Factory* by Harold Roth.
☐Although Pantheon prefers to work only with experienced authors, it promises, "All submissions sent to the Juvenile Editorial Department will be read."
☐Pays variable royalty on the invoice price; negotiable advance. Typically buys all rights. Prefers to receive entire manuscript along with a marketing brief. Not interested in reprints. Simultaneous submissions acceptable if editor is so informed. Replies in 4 to 8 weeks. Catalog available. Send SASE.

PARENTS MAGAZINE PRESS, 685 Third Ave., New York, NY 10017. (212) 878–8700. Christopher Medina, Editor. Typically publishes 10 titles each year.
☐The editors note: "We are not reviewing any manuscripts at this time, but hope to resume reviews late 1987. In the past, Parents Magazine Press has pub-

lished easy-to-read picture books for 2- to 7-year-old children (450 to 600 words)."

□Pays both royalty and flat fee; advance varies. Prefers to receive entire manuscript. Replies in 6 to 8 weeks. Send SASE.

PELICAN PUBLISHING COMPANY, 1101 Monroe St., PO Box 189, Gretna, LA 70053. (504) 368-1175. Founded 1926. Dean Shapiro, Assistant Editor. Publishes 3 titles for ages 6 to 8; 1 title for ages 9 to 12; and 1 teen title each year, 80% hardcover.

□Publishes fiction for ages 5 to 16 on any theme except romance, as well as regional fiction (southern and Louisiana); no set length. The editors are not actively looking for general nonfiction, but will consider inspirational, motivational and religious works; no set length. They also would like to see more biographical submissions (especially collections of biographical sketches) and juvenile textbooks. No poetry. Successful titles: *Cajun Night before Christmas* illustrated by James Rice, *Henry Hamilton, Graduate Ghost* by Marilyn Redmond, *Clovis Crawfish and Petit Papillon* by Mary Alice Fontenot, and *Famous Firsts of Black Americans* by Sibyl Hancock.

□Pays variable royalty; advances not normally offered to first-time authors. Buys all rights. Prefers to receive query with outline and synopsis. Interested in reprints. No simultaneous submissions. Replies to queries in 2 weeks; to manuscripts in 12 weeks. Catalog available. Send 8½″ × 11″ SASE with .50 postage.

PERFECTION FORM COMPANY, 8350 Hickman, Suite 15, Des Moines, IA 50322. (515) 278-0133. Perfection has discontinued its young-adult novel program.

PHILOMEL BOOKS (an imprint of Putnam Young Readers Group), 51 Madison Ave., New York, NY 10010. (212) 689-9200. Patricia Lee Gauch, Editor-in-Chief; Victoria Rock, Editor. Publishes about 30 juvenile books each year, some of which are hardcover imports. (See also entry for Putnam Young Readers Group.)

□Philomel Books publishes a wide range of high-quality children's picture books, and middle- and young-adult fiction; length varies. The editors will consider any topic as long as it is well-written, interesting and readily marketable. Successful title: *The Very Hungry Caterpillar* by Eric Carle.

□Pays standard royalty; offers negotiable advance. Buys all rights. Prefers query. Replies in 4 to 6 weeks. Catalog available. Send SASE.

P.P.I. PUBLISHING, 835 E. Congress Park, PO Box 335, Dayton, OH 45459. (513) 433-2709. Founded 1973. Kim Brooks, Vice-President. Publishes 20 to 30 teen titles and 20 to 30 young-adult titles each year, all paperback.

□Controversial issues and current events of interest to junior- and senior-high students are P.P.I.'s specialty. The editors seek appropriate "hot topic" nonfiction themes: terrorism, arms race, suicide, abused children, classroom discipline, drugs, teenage pregnancy, adoption, sexual assault, family stress, birth control, gay rights, domestic violence, children in pornography, runaway children, and one-parent families: 15,000 to 20,000 words. Manuscripts should include a complete bibliography. P.P.I. also considers photos and illustrations for their booklets. Successful titles: *Teenage Suicide in America, Anorexia and Bulimia,* and *AIDS: Myths and Realities.*

□"When writing on controversial issues, we request that equal time be presented for both sides of the issue," emphasizes Brooks. "We are also open to a manuscript dealing entirely with one viewpoint as well, (and) to more than one publication on a particular topic."

□Pays 10% royalty on gross profits (quarterly basis); no advance. Books are jointly copyrighted by P.P.I. and the author. Prefers to receive either outline/synopsis or entire manuscript. Interested in reprints. Simultaneous submissions acceptable; photocopies acceptable as long as they are readable and clear. Replies in 10 to 12 weeks. Author guidelines and book catalog available for 2 first-class stamps. Send SASE with all submissions.

PRENTICE-HALL INC., Children's Book Division, Englewood Cliffs, NJ 07632. (201) 592-2643; (201) 592-2618. Founded 1913. Barbara Francis, Editor-in-Chief. Rose Lopez, submissions editor. Publishes 30 hardcover books and about 15 paperback reprints from its backlist each year.

□Prentice-Hall publishes up-market picture books in full color. For fiction, the editors are interested in mystery, humorous novels, and autobiographical novels. Acceptable nonfiction includes juvenile picture books ("full-color with the accent on humor"), sports for ages 6 to 10, social sciences, history (with an unusual slant), and creative, often idiosyncratic nonfiction; length varies with topic. No poetry ("very difficult to market"), biographies, or textbooks. Will occasionally consider B&W and full-color photos and illustrations for picture books. ("All the illustrators we use are known and have successful track records," reports Francis. "I would, however, occasionally consider using an unknown artist with genuine talent and promise.") Successful titles: *Strega Nona* by Tomie de Paola, *Happy Birthday Moon* by Frank Asch, and *Life on a Fishing Boat* by Huck Scarry.

□"We do not wish to see manuscripts dealing with topical subjects, drugs, alcohol, teenage sex, abortion, or divorce!"

□Pays advance against royalty; partial payment upon signature, upon acceptance, and upon publication. Buys all rights. Prefers to receive query with outline and sample chapters from established authors; entire manuscript from unpublished authors. Simultaneous submissions acceptable. Replies in 6 weeks. Catalog available. Send SASE.

THE PRESS OF MacDONALD & REINECKE (a division of Padre Productions), PO Box 1275, San Luis Obispo, CA 93406. (805) 543-5404. Founded 1974. L.P. MacDonald, Publisher. Publishes 2 hardcover titles each year for ages 8 to 14.

□This publisher issues both fiction and nonfiction. Its fiction—primarily fantasy and adventure themes—is written for juveniles between 8 and 14; 140 to 160 pages. Nonfiction subjects for young readers include California history, hobbies, and how-to; length varies with topic. The editors will also consider biographies. No humor or poetry. Manuscripts stand a better chance of acceptance when accompanied by illustrative samples. Successful titles: *Pioneer California* by Margaret Roberts and *Joel In Tananar* by Robert M. Walton (a fantasy adventure in the J.R.R. Tolkien tradition).

□Pays royalty of 6% to 10%; small advance of $200 to $1,000 paid upon signature. Buys all rights. Prefers to receive query with sample chapters. Interested in reprints but only of books on California subjects. Simultaneous submissions acceptable. Replies in 10 weeks. Catalog available. Send SASE.

PRICE/STERN/SLOAN, INC., PUBLISHERS, 360 N. La Cienega Blvd., Los Angeles, CA 90048. Contact: Editorial Department. Publishes more than 100 juvenile titles each year. (*See also* Troubador Press.)

□Publishes these imprints: Storybook Specials™, Laugh and Learn™, Wee Sing™, Laughter Library, Troubador Press, and Enrich (educational). The editors look for juvenile fiction and nonfiction: humor, satire, and self-help; length varies with topic and intended audience. Suggestion: write to the imprints' publishers for specific information concerning immediate needs before submitting a proposal.

□Pays standard royalty; offers negotiable advance. Buys all rights. Prefers to receive query describing author's qualifications and the intended submission. Not interested in reprints. Simultaneous submissions acceptable. Replies in 10 weeks. Author guidelines and catalog available. Send SASE.

PRINTEMPS BOOKS, INC., PO Box 746, Wilmette, IL 60091. (312) 251-5418. Contact: Editor. Publishes 3 to 5 children's books each year, mostly paperback, as well as textbooks.

□This educational publisher specializes in fiction for secondary-level students. The editors are presently interested in adventure, humor, suspense, fantasy and short stories; length varies with topic.

□Buys manuscripts outright; no advance. Buys all rights. Prefers to receive complete manuscript. Not interested in reprints. Simultaneous submissions acceptable. Replies in 4 to 6 weeks. SASE required.

PUTNAM YOUNG READERS GROUP, 51 Madison Ave., New York, NY 10010. (212) 689-9200. Founded as a group of Putman in 1982. The Putnam Young Readers Group has 3 members: G.P. Putnam's Sons (including Coward-McCann); Philomel Books; and Grosset & Dunlap (including Platt & Munk). Managing Editors: Nora Cohen, Putman & Philomel; Michael Beacom, Grosset. Submissions editors: Margaret Frith and Refna Wilkin, Putnam; Ann Beneduce, Philomel; Bernette Ford, Grosset. Collectively, this group publishes 70 titles for ages 2 to 5; 50 titles for ages 6 to 8; 20 titles for ages 9 to 12; and 10 teen titles each year, 95% hardcover. Philomel Books publishes about 10 books each year, mostly imports. (*See also* Philomel Books.)

□This group publishes fiction and nonfiction titles spanning the range of juvenile genres, including board books, picture books, pop-up and novelty books but the editors do not read unsolicited manuscripts. The editors look for fiction of all types for readers ages 8 to 18 (160 pages), including humor, romance, fantasy, mystery, and adventure. Acceptable nonfiction includes: science; nature; photo essays written for an existing series; biographies by established authors on scientists, inventors, and Black Americans (160 pages); picture story books with full color or pre-separated art (24 to 32 pages); and B&W wildlife photo essays as a series or package deal. Successful titles: *Where's Spot?* by Eric Hill (Putnam), *The Very Hungry Caterpillar* by Eric Carle (Philomel), and *The Little Engine that Could* by Watty Piper (Grosset & Dunlap).

□Pays standard royalty; variable advance, paid upon acceptance and upon publication. Buys North American, first rights, or all rights. Prefers to receive query with outline/synopsis/description of idea. Unsolicited manuscripts are returned unopened. Not interested in reprints. No simultaneous submissions.

Replies in 2 to 4 weeks, but this "depends on complexity of the idea, how much discussion is required." Catalog available. SASE not required.

RAINTREE PUBLISHERS, INC., 330 E. Kilbourn Ave., Milwaukee, WI 53202. (414) 273-0873. Russell Bennet, Editor-in-Chief. Publishes 40 to 50 children's hardcovers each year.
☐Publishes juvenile fiction and nonfiction: nature, historical, science fiction, health, animals, and adventure; length varies with topic and intended readership. Considers illustrations and photos with manuscript. The editors also are seeking book series for sale to school and library systems.
☐Pays variable royalty, and occasionally buys a manuscript outright; no advance. Buys all rights. Prefers to receive query with outline and several sample chapters. Not interested in reprints. Simultaneous submissions acceptable if editor is so informed. Replies in 6 to 8 weeks. Catalog available. Send SASE.

REGAL BOOKS (a division of Gospel Light Publications), 2300 Knoll Dr., Ventura, CA 93003. (805) 644-9721. Keith Wintermute, Acquisitions Editor. Publishes a variable number of children's books each year, mostly paperback.
☐An independent Christian publisher, Regal focuses on quality nonfiction for children, teens, and young adults: self-help, biographies, inspirational, and devotional; 100 to 200 pages.
☐Pays 8% to 10% royalty for paperbacks; 10% royalty on net sales for hardcover curriculum titles. Typically offers a small advance. Buys all rights. Prefers to receive query with detailed outline and several sample chapters; no complete manuscripts. Not interested in reprints. Simultaneous submissions acceptable. Replies in 10 weeks. Author guidelines and catalog available. Send SASE.

REGENTS PUBLISHING COMPANY, INC., 2 Park Ave., New York, NY 10016. (212) 889-2780. Founded 1948. Mary Vaughn, Vice President. John Chapman, Acquisitions Editor. Publishes 1 title for ages 6 to 8; 1 title for ages 9 to 12; 10 teen titles; and 10 young-adult titles each year, all paperback.
☐Specializes in textbooks (averaging 96 pages) for students of all ages who are learning English as a second or a foreign language (ESL/EFL). The books are typically written by experienced teachers with at least a Masters degree in applied linguistics or ESL, and overseas experience. Successful titles: *Spectrum, Hopscotch,* and *I Love English.*
☐"We rarely accept a manuscript which is not the result of an in-house process of conception and review by editorial, marketing, sales and financial divisions," says Chapman. "After the project is clearly outlined, we begin to look for authors who are able to write to spec and add their own creativity to the materials."
☐Pays royalties of 1% to 10% depending upon degree of input; flat fees average $1,000 to $1,500 for a 96-page text. Pays partial advance upon signature; remainder upon publication. Buys all rights. Prefers to receive query with outline and marketing analysis (i.e., why textbook is unique, who would buy it). Not interested in reprints. Simultaneous submissions acceptable. Replies in 8 to 10 weeks. No author guidelines or book catalog available. SASE not required.

REVIEW AND HERALD PUBLISHING ASSOCIATION, 55 West Oak

Ridge Dr., Hagerstown, MD 21740. (301) 791–7000. Founded 1861. Penny Estes Wheeler, Acquisitions Editor. Publishes 1 title for ages 2 to 5; 2 titles for ages 6 to 8; 2 titles for ages 9 to 12; 2 teen titles; and 1 young-adult title each year, all paperback.

□Owned and operated by the Seventh-day Adventist Church, Review and Herald publishes nonfiction that reflects the philosophy of the church. Themes include Bible history, health, church doctrine, inspirational, and nature (32 to 96 pages). Biographies with a religious slant also are welcome (96 to 128 pages). No fiction. Illustrations and photos are considered with manuscript. Successful titles: *Bible Promises for Tiny Tots, No More Alphabet Soup,* and *Miss Dr. Lucy.*

□Pays royalty of 7% for the first 20,000 sold; 10% thereafter. Occasionally makes outright purchases of 32-page books for small children. Pays minimum advance of $100 upon acceptance. Buys all rights. Prefers to receive entire manuscript. Not interested in reprints. Simultaneous submissions acceptable. Replies in 12 weeks. Author guidelines available. Send SASE.

ROSEBRIER PUBLISHING CO., PO Box 1725, Blowing Rock, NC 28605. (704) 295–7614. Founded 1979. Beverly Donadio, Editor/Publisher. Publishes 1 title for ages 2 to 5; 1 title for ages 6 to 8; and 1 title for ages 9 to 12 every 3 to 4 years, all hardcover.

□Rosebrier exclusively publishes 4-color picture books for young children; 30 to 35 pages.

□Pays variable royalty. Buys all rights. Prefers to receive query with art work. Not interested in reprints. Simultaneous submissions and photocopies acceptable. Replies in 12 weeks. Send SASE.

THE ROSEN PUBLISHING GROUP, 29 E. 21st St., New York, NY 10010. (212) 777–3017. Founded 1950. Roger Rosen, President. Ruth C. Rosen, Editor. Publishes 35 young adult hardcover titles each year.

□Primarily publishes fiction and nonfiction for schools and libraries. Young-adult fiction is typically the "problem romance" type; 40,000 words. Nonfiction subjects include career guidance, personal guidance, theatre, art, health, music, social adjustment, and journalism; 40,000 to 50,000 words. Popular book series include "Exploring Careers In . . . ," "Aim For A Job In . . . ," and "Coping With . . . " Successful titles: *Coping With Academic Anxiety* by Allen Ottens, *High School Journalism* by Homer Hall, and *Exploring Careers In Robotics* by Mary Price Lee.

□Pays variable royalty; no advance. Buys all rights. Prefers to receive either query or outline with sample chapters. Not interested in reprints. Simultaneous submissions acceptable. Replies in 3 weeks. Catalog available. Send SASE.

RUNNING PRESS, 125 S. 22nd St., Philadelphia, PA 19103. (215) 567–5080. Founded 1971. Lawrence Teacher and Stuart Teacher, Publishers. Publishes more than 50 titles each year, mostly paperback, for adults and children.

□One of America's largest independent trade paperback publishers, Running Press issues nonfiction books, coloring books, and books based on classic children's stories. Accepts no new fiction for children. Successful titles: *The Gray's Anatomy Coloring Book, The Velveteen Rabbit,* and *The Classic Tale of Peter Rabbit.*

HAROLD SHAW PUBLISHERS, PO Box 567, 388 Gundersen Dr., Wheaton, IL 60189. (312) 665-6700. Founded 1967. Ramona Cramer Tucker, Director of Editorial Services. Publishes very few juvenile titles. 99% paperback.

☐Half of Harold Shaw's titles are Bible study guides for teens and young adults. The editors look for high-quality, nonfiction religious/Bible guides (32 to 96 pages), biographies of famous persons, some poetry (only 1 volume every other year), and general-interest titles. No fiction. Uses own freelance artists and designers. Successful titles: The Fisherman and Young Fisherman Bible Studyguide series and *Song for Sarah* by Paula D'Arcy.

☐Pays 5% to 10% royalty on retail, but prefers to pay a negotiable flat fee. Offers a small advance to established writers only. Buys all rights. Prefers to receive query; outline and sample chapters are requested later if the proposal interests the editors. Not interested in reprints. Simultaneous submissions acceptable. Replies within 4 weeks. Author guidelines and catalog available. Send SASE.

SILVER BURDETT & GINN, 191 Spring St., Lexington, MA 02173. (617) 861-1670. Sandra Brever, Publisher. Publishes up to 100 children's titles each year.

☐Publishes basal reading textbooks and other instructional materials (e.g., workbooks and supplements) for elementary-school students. Will consider any proposal; length varies with topic and with age of readers. The editors seek authors who know their subject; teachers have the best chance here.

☐Occasionally offers work-for-hire fee. Buys all rights. Prefers to receive either partial or complete manuscript. Not interested in reprints. Simultaneous submissions acceptable if editor is so informed. Replies in 4 weeks. Catalog available. Send SASE.

SIMON & SCHUSTER, 1230 Ave. of the Americas, New York, NY 10020. (212) 698-7000. Founded 1924. Michele LaMarca, Managing Editor. Rose Lopez, submissions editor. Grace Clarke, Vice-President/Editorial Director, Juvenile Division. Publishes 80 titles for ages 2 to 5; 90 titles for ages 6 to 8; 59 titles for ages 9 to 12; and 34 teen titles each year, 54% paperback.

☐Publishes a wide selection of books for children: classic poetry, poetry anthologies of previously published works, humor (Prentice-Hall imprint), biographies for ages 7 to 12 (Julian Messner and Prentice-Hall imprints), fiction of all types for ages up to 16, and nonfiction (history, science, current events) for ages 8 to 12 (Julian Messner imprint); length varies with age and topic. The editors also seek photos and illustrations from known artists. No coffee table books. Successful titles: *The Velveteen Rabbit,* by Margery Williams; *Mooncake,* by Frank Asch; and *Seventeenth Summer,* by Maureen Daly.

☐"We are looking for books with wide appeal, rather than highly specific topics," reports Clarke.

☐Pays either royalty or flat fee depending upon title, length, and experience and reputation of the author. Offers variable advance, paid in several segments beginning with the contract signing. Buys all rights; purchases paperback rights for books written for older children. Prefers to receive query for young adult books; outline/synopsis for ages 6 to 16; and entire manuscript for picture books for ages 2 to 6. Photocopies acceptable. Simultaneous submissions acceptable if editor is so informed. Replies in 6 to 8 weeks. Author guidelines and book catalog not available. SASE preferred.

SQUARE ONE PUBLISHERS, 501 Prospect Ave., Madison, WI 53711. (608) 255–8425. Lyn Miller-Lachmann, Editor/Publisher. Founded 1985. Publishes 2 to 4 books for juveniles and teens, ages 14 to 19, each year, all paperback.
☐ This new publishing house is interested in fiction for juveniles and teens on subjects not currently in the spotlight; will consider social issues, political themes, alternative lifestyles, minority situations, relationships; length varies. The editor asks teenagers to help select manuscripts for publication.
☐ "Manuscripts must focus on encouraging teens to pursue alternative solutions to problems confronting them today," says Miller-Lachmann.
☐ Pays 5 to 6% royalty; no advance. Buys all rights. Prefers to receive either completed manuscript or query letter with detailed outline and sample chapters. Not interested in reprints. Simultaneous submissions acceptable if editor is so informed. Replies to queries in 4 weeks; to manuscripts in 8 to 10 weeks. Author guidelines available. Send SASE.

STANDARD PUBLISHING, 8121 Hamilton Ave., Cincinnati, OH 45231. (513) 931–4050. Founded 1866. Eugene H. Wigginton, Publisher. Mark Plunkett, Editor. Marjorie Miller, Acquisitions Editor. Publishes 40 titles for ages 2 to 5; 12 titles for ages 6 to 8; 16 titles for ages 9 to 12; 12 teen titles; and 6 young-adult titles each year, all paperback.
☐ Publishes primarily for the religious market: churches, Christian schools, and homes. Juvenile nonfiction titles—activity books, puzzle books, workbooks, coloring books, novelty books, how-to, crafts—must pertain to Christian education, Bible studies, or devotional reading; length varies. Acceptable fiction includes picture books and adventure stories with strong Biblical principles and/or values; length varies with intended audience. Editors also welcome all types of photos and illustrations, particularly full color. Successful title: *It's Me, Jennifer* by Jane Sorenson.
☐ "When writing children's books, make the vocabulary level correct for the age you plan to reach," stresses Miller, "and keep your material true to the Bible."
☐ Pays 8% to 10% royalty on net sales for larger books; variable flat fee for small picture books. Occasionally offers advance up to $1,500, paid upon acceptance. Buys all rights. Prefers to receive query and outline for large books; entire manuscript for small books. Not interested in reprints. No simultaneous submissions; photocopied submissions acceptable, but only if readable. Replies in 12 weeks. Author guidelines and catalog available. Send SASE.

STEMMER HOUSE PUBLISHERS, INC., 2627 Caves Rd., Owings Mills, MD 21117. (301) 363–3690. Founded 1975. Barbara Holdridge, President/Editor. Usually publishes 2 titles for ages 5 to 8, and "an occasional" title for ages 9 to 12, all hardcover.
☐ Stemmer House is not reviewing new manuscripts until September, 1987. However its goal is to publish "books worth having on the bookshelves in 50 years." Successful titles: *The First Teddy Bear* by Helen Kay, *Dooley's Lion* by Gudrun Alcock, and *Why The Possum's Tail is Bare* by James E. Connolly.

☐Pays 5% to 10% royalty on wholesale price; variable advance paid upon publication. Buys all rights. Prefers to receive query with outline for most proposals; entire manuscript for picture books. Not interested in reprints. Simultaneous submissions acceptable. Replies to queries in 2 weeks; to manuscripts in 6 weeks. Catalog available. Send SASE.

STERLING PUBLISHING COMPANY, INC., 2 Park Ave., New York, NY 10016. (212) 532-7160. Anne Kallem, Managing Editor. Sheila Anne Barry, Juvenile Book Editor. Publishes 4 titles for ages 6 to 8; and 16 titles for ages 9 to 12 each year, 60% paperback.
☐Publishes only nonfiction: humor, easy-to-understand activity books, records, fun books, how-to, riddles and joke collections (e.g., knock-knocks); 128 pages. The editors will consider photos and drawings to illustrate how-to and humor books. Successful titles: *Biggest Riddle Book in the World, The Funny Songbook,* and *Tricks and Stunts to Fool Your Friends.*
☐ "Most of our books are how-to books that are suitable for teen and young-adult markets, as well as adult," says Barry.
☐Pays 10% royalty on retail price on trade editions; 10% royalty on net sales on paperbacks. Offers variable advance; half upon signature, half upon publication. Buys all rights. Prefers to receive query. Not interested in reprints. Simultaneous submissions and photocopies acceptable. Replies in 8 to 12 weeks. No author guidelines or catalogs. Send SASE.

SUCCESS PUBLISHING, 10258 Riverside Dr., Palm Beach Gardens, FL 33410. (305) 626-4643. Founded 1978. Allan Smith, Editor. Publishes a variable number of children's books each year.
☐Interested in nonfiction books for junior-high and high-school students: how-to, self-help and craft books on almost any subject; 100 to 300 pages long. No poetry, religious or technical titles. Successful titles: *Teenage Moneymaking Guide* by Allan Smith, and *Sewing For Profits* by Judy and Allan Smith.
☐NOTE: About one-fourth of Success' titles are subsidized.
☐Pays up to 10% royalty on wholesale price; occasionally offers $1,000 flat fee purchase of manuscript. No advance. Buys North American rights. Prefers to receive query with sample chapters. Not interested in reprints. Simultaneous submissions acceptable. Replies in 4 weeks. Author guidelines and catalog available. SASE preferred.

TEMPO BOOKS (A division of the Berkley Publishing Group), 200 Madison Ave., New York, NY 10016 is no longer an active line.

TEXAS CHRISTIAN UNIVERSITY PRESS, PO Box 30783, TCU, Fort Worth, TX 76129. (817) 921-7822. Founded 1966. Judy Alter, Editor. Publishes 2 teen hardcover titles each year.
☐This regional publisher seeks fiction and nonfiction with a Texas slant for young-adult readers. Regional historic novels up to 60,000 words, and biographies of famous Texans (50,000 words) are your best bet. However, the editors will consider any nonfiction manuscript as long as it is well-written, lively, accurate, and interesting (and, of course, somehow related to Texas). Successful titles: *Luke and the Van Zandt County War* by Alter, and *Tame the Wild Stallion* by Williams.

☐Pays 10% royalty on net sales; no advance. Buys all rights. Prefers to receive query with outline. Interested in reprints. Simultaneous submissions acceptable. Replies in 6 weeks. No author guidelines or book catalogs available. Send SASE.

T.F.H. PUBLICATIONS, INC., 211 W. Sylvania Ave., Neptune City, NJ 07753. (201) 988–8400. Founded 1952. Neal Pronek, Managing Editor. Cynthia J. Kalin, Editorial Assistant. Publishes 5 titles for ages 2 to 5; 5 titles for ages 6 to 8; 10 titles for ages 9 to 12; 10 teen titles; and 30 young-adult titles each year, 95% hardcover.
☐Specializes in nonfiction animal, nature, and pet books for all ages; 30 to 50 pages. (Its textbooks are typically scientific animal books; e.g., *Encyclopedia of Reptiles and Amphibians*.) No fiction, biographies or poetry. Suggestion: look through the catalog, see what has already been published, and then submit a proposal for a marketable, original book about a pet (dog, cat, fish, bird). The editors consider photos and illustrations; submit 35mm slides. Successful titles: *Your German Shephard Puppy* by Ernest Hart, and *Handbook of Discus* by Jack Wattley.
☐Usually pays variable flat fee for manuscripts (royalty arrangement is reserved for "special books"; basic payment is about $10 per page. Also pays variable advance upon signature, upon acceptance, and upon publication. Buys all rights. Prefers to receive query with outline and sample chapters. Interested in reprints. Simultaneous submissions acceptable. Replies in 2 to 3 weeks. Catalog available. Send SASE.

THREE TREES PRESS, 2 Silver Ave., Toronto, Ontario M6R 3A2. (416) 534–4456. Founded 1976. Wence Horak, Managing Editor. Publishes 4 to 5 paperbacks for ages 6 to 8 each year.
☐Publishes exclusively picture books for young children; 500 to 1,000 words. Successful titles: *There's an Alligator Under My Bed,* by Gail E. Gill; *Who's Going to Clean Up the Mess?* by Anita Krumins; and *Highwire Spider: Poems for Children,* by George Swede.
☐"For funding reasons, we can publish books by Canadian citizens only," says Horak.
☐Pays variable royalty; no advance. Buys all rights. Prefers to receive query with outline/synopsis. Not interested in reprints. No simultaneous submissions; photocopies acceptable. Replies in 10 to 12 weeks. Send SASE.

TRILLIUM PRESS, INC., PO Box 921, Madison Square Station, New York, NY 10159. (914) 783–2999. Founded 1978. T. Holland, Managing Editor. Myrna Kaye, Vice-President of Marketing (submissions editor). Publishes 25 titles for ages 2 to 17 each year, 99% paperback. Trillium has 270 current juvenile titles.
☐Specializes in materials for use by gifted students, ages 4 to 17, and their teachers, parents, and administrators: humor, poetry, biography, textbooks (emphasis on science topics), workbooks, and resource books; up to 600 pages. Successful titles: *Suppose the Wolf were an Octopus, A New Way to Use Your Bean,* and *Stories to Stretch Minds.*
☐Pays variable royalty; no advance. Buys all rights. Prefers to receive either outline/synopsis or entire manuscript. Interested in reprints. Simultaneous submissions and photocopies acceptable. Replies in 3 weeks. Author guidelines and catalog available. SASE preferred.

TROUBADOR PRESS (A subsidiary of Price/Stern/Sloan), 410 N. La Cienega Blvd., Los Angeles, CA 90048. (213) 657-6100. Suite 205, San Francisco, CA 94104. (415) 397-3716. Incorporated 1970. Malcolm K. Whyte, Founder and Editorial Director. Publishes 4 paperback books each year for ages 5 and up.

☐Publishes children's activity, coloring, cut-out, puzzle, joke, and paper doll books; 32 to 48 pages long. The editors are looking for manuscripts to expand existing nonfiction series. Successful titles: *Hot Air Ballooning Coloring Book* by Marilyn Senum, *Teddy Bear Paper Dolls* by Terra Muzick, and *Make Me Laugh* (a joke book series) by Sam Schultz.

☐Pays either royalty or buys manuscript outright, depending upon the interest of the author/artist. An advance up to $500 is paid partially upon signature, partially upon acceptance, and partially upon publication. Buys all rights. Prefers to receive query with synopsis and sample art. Simultaneous submissions acceptable. Replies in 4 to 6 weeks. Catalog available. Send SASE.

J. WESTON WALCH PUBLISHER, PO Box 658, Portland, ME 04104. (207) 772-2846. Jane Carter, Editor. Publishes a variable number of school-related young people's titles each year, in formats ranging from softcover books to filmstrips and software.

☐Specializes in supplementary educational material for secondary schools: art, English, history, mathematics, social studies, music, home economics, foreign languages, and science. Length varies with topic and intended readership. Illustrations and photos are considered with the proposal. Most of Walch's authors have teaching experience, and most titles are determined by the publisher; very few proposals are accepted, so query.

☐"Author/artist teams have a good chance with us," says Carter, "especially if the writer can write for young people 12 to 18 years old."

☐Pays 10% to 15% royalty on gross sales; occasionally buys a manuscript outright; rarely offers an advance. Buys all rights. Prefers to receive query with detailed outline and sample chapter. Not interested in reprints. Simultaneous submissions acceptable. Replies in 4 weeks. Catalog available. Send SASE.

WALKER AND COMPANY, 720 Fifth Ave., New York, NY 10019. (212) 265-3632. Founded in 1959. Elisabeth Wansbrough, Editor. Jeanne Gardner, submissions editor. Publishes 10 titles for ages 6 to 8; 30 titles for ages 9 to 12; and 5 teen titles each year, all hardcover.

☐An educational publisher, Walker issues curriculum-related and/or supplementary material for children: schools and public libraries are its primary markets. Acceptable nonfiction: science, biographies, history, recreation, music, drama, activities, and contemporary social issues; 27,000 words maximum. The editors also seek viable titles for their Breakthrough series for children, ages 12 and up. Walker occasionally publishes juvenile fiction: adventure, historical romance, westerns, science fiction, mystery, and romantic suspense; length varies. Successful titles: *The Windows of Forever* by John Morressy, *Bear Bryant* by E. Simpson Smith, and *A First Look at Bird Nests* by Millicent Selsam and Joyce Hunt.

☐Pays standard royalty (10% to 12% to 15%) on retail price; occasionally purchases manuscript outright. Offers advance of $500 to $3,000: half upon signature, half upon publication. Buys North American, first, or all rights.

Prefers to receive entire manuscript from unpublished writers; table of contents, synopsis, and sample chapter from published writers. Rarely interested in reprints. Simultaneous submissions acceptable. Replies in 8 weeks. Author guidelines and catalog available. Send SASE.

WATERFRONT BOOKS, 98 Brookes Ave., Burlington, VT 05401. (802) 658-7477. Founded 1983. Sherrill N. Musty, Publisher. Publishes 1 title for ages 2 to 5; 2 titles for ages 6 to 8; 2 titles for ages 9 to 12; 1 teen title; and 2 young-adult titles each year, 75% paperback.
☐Waterfront Books' primary focus is mental health, education, prevention, juvenile, and psycho-social topics for readers of all ages; length varies. Successful titles: *Playful Perception: Choosing How to Experience Your World,* by Herbert L. Leff, Ph.D.; and *The Divorce Workbook: A Guide for Kids and Families*, by Ives, Fassler & Lash.
☐"Waterfront books is open to considering all children's manuscripts," says Musty.
☐Pays 10% to 15% royalty; no advance. Buys all rights. Prefers to receive entire manuscript ("as we'll want to see it before a decision is made anyway"), but will consider outline/synopsis with sample chapter. Interested in reprints. No simultaneous submissions; photocopies acceptable. Replies in 6 weeks. SASE preferred.

ALBERT WHITMAN & COMPANY, 5747 W. Howard, Niles, IL 60648. (312) 647-1358. Founded 1919. Kathleen Tucker, Managing Editor. Abby Levine, Editor. Ann Fay, Senior Editor. Publishes a varying number of hardcovers each year, primarily for juvenile and teen readers.
☐Seeks a wide variety of material for children from infancy to age 12. The editors look for general nonfiction for existing "How To" and "Behind the Scenes" book series (average: 48 pages); riddle books (80 to 100 riddles); humorous picture books (32 pages); and easy-to-read biographies (48–79 pages) on a variety of subjects (recent titles dealt with the lives of Edmond Halley, Amelia Earhart, and a Revolutionary War heroine). Acceptable fiction: picture books and easy-to-read mysteries for children just "getting their wings as independent readers," as well as longer novels and mysteries for middle-grade readers. Maximum length for a novel: 110 manuscript pages. Successful titles: *Tink in a Tangle* by Dorothy Haas, *There Is No Such Thing as a Chanukah Bush* by Sandy Goldstein, and *Who Is a Stranger and What Should I Do?* by Linda Girard.
☐"We are especially interested in developing a line of 48-page easy-to-read biographies," comments Fay. "We are open to new ideas."
☐Pays both royalty and flat fee (amount varies); pays advance: half upon signature, half upon publication. Buys all rights. Prefers to receive query with outline and sample chapters (entire manuscript for picture books). Not interested in reprints. Simultaneous submissions acceptable if editor is so informed. Replies in 8 weeks. Author guidelines and catalog available. Send SASE.

WINGRA WOODS PRESS, PO Box 9601, Madison, WI 53715. (608) 256-2578. Founded 1981. Margarete Anders, Managing Editor. M.G. Mahoney, submissions editor. Publishes 3 titles for ages 2 to 5; 3 titles for ages 6 to 8; and 3 titles for ages 9 to 12, all paperback.
☐Primary focus is on nonfiction for children: general information,

biographies, and Americana; any length. The editors are also interested in books about animals and nature; 2,000 words and up. Wingra Woods issues very little fiction, so query first. Successful titles: *The Christmas Cat, America Talks,* and *Santa and the Mouse.*

□ Pays negotiable royalty; offers variable advance upon acceptance. Buys all rights. Prefers to receive query with outline/synopsis and sample chapter. Interested in reprints. Simultaneous submissions and photocopies acceptable. Replies in 8 weeks. Send SASE.

WORD BOOKS PUBLISHER, PO Box 1790, 4800 W. Waco Dr. Waco, TX 76703. (817) 772-7650. Al Bryant, Managing Editor. Patricia Wienandt, Senior Editor. Publishes a variable number of children's titles each year, 90% paperback.

□ A Christian publisher, Word Books publishes textbooks and fiction for juveniles, and is interested in reviewing all types of manuscripts, including church and Bible history, Christian lifestyle, romance, and science fiction; 150 to 300 pages, depending on the topic and readership. Suggestion: children's Christian fiction is just getting off the ground—a great opportunity if you know how to write for the religious market. Successful title: *Approaching Hoofbeats* by Billy Graham.

□ "All books, including fiction, must adhere to Christian principles," says Wienandt.

□ Pays up to 15% royalty on the retail price; offers average advance of $2,000, depending upon author's track record and marketability of the proposed book. Buys all rights. Prefers to receive query with outline, synopsis and sample chapters. Interested in reprints. Simultaneous submissions acceptable if editor is so informed. Replies in 6 weeks. Author guidelines and catalog available. Send SASE.

FIVE

PRODUCERS OF SCRIPTS AND SCREENPLAYS

A few authors possess the God-given talent of being able to watch—from start to finish—an entire story inside their heads, complete with full-color action and dialogue. If you happen to be one of these creative and blessed individuals, scriptwriting may be your forte.

The industry comprising television, movie, and commercial scriptwriting traditionally has maintained a very restrictive, closed-door policy to newcomers. With six-figure incomes available to those who succeed in this market, it's not difficult to understand why so many writers would like to enter it.

Before you can sell a script to most film companies, you must be a member of the Writers Guild of America (WGA). But to be considered for WGA membership, you must have sold two or more TV or film scripts. As if this Catch-22 scenario weren't discouraging enough, the WGA requires a $1,500 membership fee.

Obviously, there are ways to get around this obstacle course (there have to be; otherwise, how did so many writers make it to Hollywood?). Producing educational film scripts for children and students is perhaps the best-known, fastest way. This is not to suggest that children's scripts are easier to create or of lesser quality than others: in fact, they often are more creative (ever try to capture a child's attention for 60 minutes?).

Patiently selling a few scripts here and there to smaller educational film companies will give you the credentials you need to gain membership in WGA. After you pass this test, you are free to pursue the giants of filmland. To give yourself an edge, call the Market Update hotline, (213) 859-4858. Sponsored by the WGA, this 24-hour service has a recorded message describing the current script needs of major TV studios and lists contact names and phone numbers.

If you already have written a script and want to sell it, you can register it, for a nominal fee, with WGA's script registry service at 555 W. 57th St., New York, NY 10019 (212) 245-6180; or 8955 Beverly Blvd., Los Angeles, CA

90048 (213) 550-1000. This will provide you with proof of when your idea and/or script was first created (useful if you are ever unfortunate enough to be involved in a plagiarism suit).

This accomplished, your next step—assuming that you're unagented—is to request a release form from the studio or company to which you want to submit your script. A release form states terms agreeable to both parties. For example:

- The studio is not in any way obligated to buy or produce the script just because they read it.
- You are the script's owner and have the right to sell specific rights to it should the studio wish to buy them.
- The studio can't be held liable either for buying a similar script or for producing a related script that already exists in-house.
- Your script will be read within a reasonable period of time and returned with a decision on whether the studio wants to buy it.
- Perhaps most important: you retain the copyright to the script. (The script is your creation, isn't it? Keep it that way!)

If the studio does not make a standard release form available to you, write one yourself that contains the above conditions. If you feel uncomfortable about doing this, ask an attorney experienced in screen contracts to prepare one for you.

Once the release form has been signed by the studio (and a photocopy returned to you), mail your manuscript to the contact person via registered mail. This protects both you and the studio in case the package never reaches its destination. (It also documents your financial investment for tax purposes.)

To improve your manuscript's chances of acceptance, type it, single-spaced, with triple-spacing between the dialogue of two different characters. Use good paper (25% cotton content) that is *not* erasable, and do not send photocopies unless they are of excellent quality. Be as professional as possible in your approach; editors will remember and appreciate you for it.

Your accompanying cover letter should be one page long and should contain a summary of the story's plot in one or two sentences; an estimate of the screenplay's program length (one page is equivalent to one minute of film, except for 2-hour feature films, for which you can estimate 125 to 150 typed pages); an overview of the intended audience; and a brief profile of your writing/production background.

If and when a studio expresses an interest in your script, it's best to get the celebrating out of your system before officially responding to the offer. After all, you don't want excitement to interfere with your business decision.

Experienced screenwriters recommend that you refuse to work for a studio on speculation; you are a professional and deserve to be compensated accordingly for your talents and efforts.

If the firm or studio is unwilling to pay your full fee up front, suggest alternative payment schedules, including partial payment at various stages of production (e.g., 25% now, 25% when shooting begins, and 50% at the project's completion). Also request a kill fee at the WGA's suggested rate of at least 20% of your script's market value, to be paid to you within 6 months, should the project be cancelled.

For professional assistance with the legalities or the paperwork required by contract negotiations, don't hesitate to consult an attorney or an agent who is experienced in advising screenwriters.

ABS & ASSOCIATES, PO Box 5127, Evanston, IL 60204. (312) 982-1414. Founded 1973. Alan Soell, President. Produces 35mm, videotape, cassettes, filmstrips, slides, multimedia kits, and multi-image media. Buys 5 to 10 scripts each year for young adults and adults, ages 16 and up, on these topics: safety, management, customer service, and sales.
☐Seeks how-to series programs for general consumer use; film length varies from 10 to 30 minutes. Looks for "writing style, clarity, and brevity of message." Interested in producing low-budget films.
☐Pays negotiable fee, royalty, or outright purchase; no advance. Buys all rights and percentage rights. Prefers to receive sample of writing style and outline of proposed topic. Not interested in previously produced material. Simultaneous submissions acceptable. Replies in 8 weeks. No author guidelines or catalog available. SASE not required.

A/V CONCEPTS CORP., 30 Montauk Blvd., Oakdale, NY 11769. (516) 567-7227. Founded 1975. Philip J. Solimene, President. Contact: Kathryn L. Brennan, Editor. Buys 25 scripts each year for elementary, junior-high, high-school, and remedial students.
☐Remedial reading is the focus of A/V Concepts Corp., which produces 35mm films, filmstrips, teaching machine programs, and computer programs for the 48K-Apple computer (IIc and IIe). Film length varies with grade level; average 15 minutes. Seeks scripts on: language, short stories, science, and social studies. Interested in low-budget films as well as original reading and language-arts programs that can be adapted to the 48K-Apple computer. Successful titles: "Cloze Thinking," *The Classics* series, and *The Contained Reading* series.
☐"We are looking for well-written, interesting content that will motivate children to read," says Brennan. "Manuscripts must be written using our list of vocabulary words and meet our readability formula (FRY). Specific guidelines are devised for each level."
☐Purchases material outright ($100 minimum); no advance. Buys all rights. Prefers to receive query with writing samples and author resume, or entire manuscript. Not interested in previously produced material. No simultaneous submissions. Replies in 4 to 6 weeks. Author guidelines and catalog available. SASE preferred.

BARR FILMS, 3490 E. Foothill Blvd., Pasadena, CA 91107. (213) 681-6978. Founded 1946. Don Barr, President. Contact: George Holland, Vice-President, Product Development. Buys 20 to 30 scripts each year for elementary, junior-high, high-school students, and adults.
☐Produces 16mm films and videotapes in all curricula for children and teens, as well as management and training films for adults. Average length: 12 to 15 minutes. Looks for "imaginative treatment of clear ideas in all educational areas," and considers whether a script will make a good educational film or literary adaptation. The producers are interested in low-budget films. Successful titles: "You're Not Listening," "Driving Under The Influence," "All Things Animal," "Comet," "Write A Letter," and "Home Alone."
☐"Research our catalog and the market first," suggests Holland.

□Pays royalty of 2% to 3% or purchases material outright for $2,000 to $2,500; advance ranges from $1,000 to $1,500. Buys all rights. Prefers to receive short treatment, outline, or entire manuscript. Will consider previously produced material. Simultaneous submissions acceptable. Replies in 4 to 6 weeks. Catalog available. Send SASE.

BOARD OF JEWISH EDUCATION OF GREATER NEW YORK, 426 W. 58th St., New York, NY 10019. (212) 245–8200. Founded 1910. Mrs. Lilian Eisman, President. Contact: Yaakov Reshef, Director, Multimedia Services. Buys 5 to 10 scripts each year for elementary, junior-high, and high-school students.
□This educational publisher produces 16mm films, videotapes, cassettes, filmstrips, and slides for Jewish children and teens. Average film length: 15 to 20 minutes. The producers are interested in short, creative videotape projects, children's stories, and short plays. They look for interest and creativity. Interested in producing low-budget films. Successful titles: "The Empty Chair" and "Strangers."
□Pays 10% to 15% royalty on sales, or flat fee ($1,000 minimum); no advance. Buys all rights. Prefers to receive outline with samples or entire manuscript. Not interested in previously produced material. Simultaneous submissions acceptable. Replies in 4 weeks. Catalog available. SASE preferred.

THE CHAMBA ORGANIZATION, 230 W. 105th St., Suite 2A, New York, NY 10025. (212) 864–7350. Founded 1969. St. Clair Bourne, President. Produces 3 to 4 16mm films and videotapes for young adults each year.
□Specializes in producing PBS documentaries, drama, and network public affairs documentaries for contemporary, general, and special audiences (e.g., Black American, Youth). Occasionally produces "NBC White Paper" Specials. Chamba is looking for professionally written, "offbeat stories featuring minorities, youth, and women." No sexually exploitative or violent material. Successful title: "On the Boulevard."
□Pays negotiable flat fee (Writers Guild standards); offers advance upon signature. Buys screen rights. Prefers to receive synopsis and author resume. ("Send a letter and treatment;" suggests Bourne, "we will then respond.") Will consider previously published material. Simultaneous submissions acceptable. Reply period varies. No author guidelines or catalog available. SASE preferred.

CINE DESIGN FILMS, 255 Washington St., Denver, CO 80203. (303) 777–4222. Founded in 1973. Contact: Jon Husband. Produces 5 to 7 16mm and 35mm films each year, including 2 juvenile films.
□Seeks material "which can be produced in the West and scripts that will not exceed $1.5 million to produce." It also produces TV specials and documentaries.
□Pays negotiable royalty, commission, or flat fee (Writers Guild standards). Offers advance upon option of story. Buys varying rights. Prefers to receive outline with synopsis. Simultaneous submissions acceptable. Will consider previously produced material. Reply requires several months. Author guidelines available. Send SASE.

CINETUDES FILM PRODUCTIONS, LTD., 295 W. Fourth St., New York, NY 10014. (212) 924–0400. Founded 1976. Christine Jurzykowski, President.

Contact: Gale Goldberg, Vice-President/Executive Producer. Produces 1 16mm film each year for young adults, ages 14 to 18.

□Looking for human interest scripts, preferably with a New York locale. Does not consider exploitative material. Successful titles: "No Big Deal" (feature-length film for the cable market that was sold to HBO, Showtime, Disney, and WHT), and "Would You Settle For Improbable?"

□Pays negotiable flat fee or makes outright purchase (Writers Guild standards); advances one-fourth upon acceptance of first draft. Buys varying rights. Prefers to receive treatment (often from an existing book) with an accompanying script. Will consider previously produced material. Simultaneous submissions acceptable. Usually replies in 3 to 4 months. Author guidelines available. Send SASE.

CONTEMPORARY DRAMA SERVICE (Meriwether Publishing Ltd.), 880 Elkton Dr., Colorado Springs, CO 80907. (303) 594–4422. Founded 1960. Arthur L. Zapel, President/ Publisher/Editor. Buys 60 to 80 scripts for junior-high, high-school, and college students each year. (See also Meriwether Publishing Ltd. in Chapters 5 and 7.)

□A publisher that produces playkits, filmstrips, slides, and occasional videotapes on drama, speech, and religious education for teens and young adults. Average film length: 20 minutes. The producers are interested in 1-act plays for Christmas and Easter, scripts for filmstrips on theater and communication arts, scripts for their Reader's Theater, how-to manuscripts on any of the communication arts, and clown/mime scripts; length varies. Not interested in producing low-budget films. Successful filmstrips: "How Theater Began," "What Makes an Actor," and "The Techniques of Mime."

□Pays 10% royalty, flat fee, or makes outright purchase (negotiable); no advance. Buys all rights in the U.S. and United Kingdom. Prefers to receive query with synopsis and outline or entire manuscript and synopsis. Simultaneous submissions acceptable. Replies in 4 to 5 weeks. Author guidelines: SASE with $1 postage. Send SASE with all submissions.

CP FILMS INC., 4431 N. 60th Ave., Omaha, NE 68104. (402) 453–3200. Founded 1971. Gregory F. Pflaum, President. Buys 3 educational scripts each year for junior-high students, high-school students, and adults.

□Seeks scripts on English topics for videotapes and cassettes. Average film length: 60 minutes. The editors are interested in producing low-budget films. Successful titles: "The Christmas Letter," "Winter Rain," and "First Two Years of Marriage."

□"We follow the lines of book publishers," reports Pflaum. "We are looking for one-person plays on famous persons: historical (U.S.), composers (musicals), and religious. We also want rights to produce a show 'live.' "

□Pays 6% to 8% royalty on wholesale price of cassettes. Buys North American, video, and live-performance rights. Prefers to receive either entire manuscript (in stage form or as radio/story narrative) or "call to discuss your idea." Will consider previously produced material from another medium. Simultaneous submissions acceptable. Replies in 4 weeks. Catalog available. SASE not required.

NORM DREW ENTERTAINMENT FEATURES, 1600 Beach Ave., Suite 608–L, Laurier House, Vancouver, British Columbia V6G 1Y6, Canada. (604) 689–1948. Founded 1974. Norman G. Drew, President.

☐Produces 16mm, 35mm, videotapes, cassettes, filmstrips, slides, and multi-media kits for preschool, elementary, junior-high, high-school, and remedial students. Film length: 8 seconds to feature length. Not interested in producing low-budget films (but will consider "a series of 30-second to 5-minute, economical, animated gag films"). Drew also seeks innovative, heartwarming scripts for animated TV series and specials. Short, animated subject matter about contemporary world issues (e.g., environment, space, hunger, state of human condition) also is welcome. Scripts must use irony and humor that entertain and enlighten. Successful title: "Chika's Magic Sketch Book."

☐Pays 25% royalty on original concepts and characters co-scripted and developed by Drew; variable flat fee for commercial contract productions; makes outright purchase of material for its own cartoon character productions. Offers no advance. Buys all rights. Prefers to receive query with 25-word synopsis of the concept. ("Do not send full scripts cold," stresses Drew.) Does not consider previously produced materials. No simultaneous submissions. Replies in 2 weeks. Send SASE; use IRC, if sending from outside Canada.

EDUCATIONAL FILM CENTER (EFC, INC.), 5101–F Backlick Rd., Annandale, VA 22003. (703) 750–0560. Founded 1969. Stephen L. Rabin, President. Contact: Ruth Pollak, Vice-President, Script Development. Buys 3 to 25 scripts each year.

☐Produces videotapes, cassettes, and 16mm films for preschool, elementary, junior-high, and high-school students as well as for public television and commercial use. Areas of interest: history, health, science, economics, teen pregnancy, alcohol abuse, mental health, English classics, and general drama. Film length: 30, 60, or 90 minutes. The editors look for strong family and children's dramatic narratives to develop as afterschool specials for commercial, cable, and public TV. Criteria: strong character development and plotlines; published material samples; ability to integrate educational objects smoothly; ability to pace; non-predictability; fresh approach to material. Interested in producing low-budget films and family/youth dramas. Successful titles: "Powerhouse" (a 16-part childrens series for PBS), "Economics USA" (a 28-part PBS historic/documentary telecourse), and "Out of Time" (a 60-minute children's drama on NBC).

☐Pays either flat fee (Writers Guild minimum) or makes outright purchase (negotiable). Offers no advance. Buys all rights. Prefers to receive outline with story synopsis and outline ("Short 'pitch' document, with resume, followed by phone call"). Does not consider previously produced material. Simultaneous submissions acceptable. Replies in 2 to 4 weeks. Catalog available. Send SASE.

EDUCATIONAL IMAGES LTD., PO Box 3456, Westside Station, Elmira, NY 14905. (607) 732–1090. Founded 1969. Charles R. Belinky, Ph.D., Executive Director.

☐Issues educational videotapes, cassettes, filmstrips, slides, multimedia kits, and computer software. Areas of interest: mainly science; social studies; vocational education; and English subjects for elementary, junior-high, and high-school students, as well as colleges, national parks, and zoos. Average film length: 80 to 120 frames for filmstrips. Interested in low-budget films. The producers look for accurate, well-written scripts on the "hardcore sciences." Artwork and photos welcome. Successful titles: "Animal Kingdom: The Invertebrates," "Hazardous Chemicals: Handle with Care," and "To Know a Pond."

☐Payment, usually royalty, varies. Buys all rights. Prefers to receive cover letter with outline and photos or other artwork, if available. Does not consider previously produced material. Simultaneous submissions acceptable. Replies in 8 weeks. Author guidelines and catalog available. SASE not required.

EDUCATIONAL INSIGHTS, 19560 Rancho Way, Compton, CA 90220. (213) 637–2131. Founded 1962. Burt Cutler, President. Contact: Dennis J. Graham, Director of Development.

☐A producer of cassettes, records, teaching machine programs, books, and games, Educational Insights is interested in all curricula for preschool, elementary, junior-high, and remedial students as well as the home learning market. Film length varies with intended audience. The editors also are interested in producing educational records, plays for classrooms, and video lessons, and seek high-quality writing with strong market potential for all school subjects. Not interested in producing low-budget films. Successful titles: "Phonics," "Add and Subtract," and "Plays for the Classroom."

☐Pays flat fee (negotiable) and advance. Buys all rights. Prefers to receive outline with synopsis or entire manuscript; "send letter with details," suggests Graham. Will consider previously produced material. Sumultaneous submissions acceptable. Replies in 3 weeks. Send SASE.

FIRE PREVENTION THROUGH FILMS, INC., PO Box 11, Newton Highlands, MA 02161. (617) 965–4444. Founded 1970. Julian Olansky, President. Buys 1 to 3 16mm film and videotape scripts each year for children and teens.

☐Specializes in fire prevention and general safety films for preschool, elementary, junior-high, and high-school students. The producers look for new ideas and new approaches to fire prevention and general safety. Average film length: 20 minutes. The editors will consider low-budget films. Successful titles: "Safety Elements in Lab Practice; A, B, C, or D?" (use of portable fire extinguishers); and "Men, Women and Children" (fire prevention in the home).

☐Pays flat fee, $500 minimum; small advance possible. Buys all rights. Prefers to receive either phone query or written query with outline. Will consider previously produced material. Replies "as soon as possible." Catalog available. SASE not required.

FRIED PRODUCTIONS, INC., 768 Farmington Ave., Farmington, CT 06032. (203) 674–8221. Founded 1972. Joel Fried, President. Contact: Ms. Roy Shaw, Vice-President, Productions. Buys 20 to 60 scripts each year for children and teens.

☐Produces books; computer software; videotapes; cassettes; filmstrips; slides; records; multimedia kits; teaching machine programs; and multi-image media for preschool, elementary, junior-high, high-school, and remedial students. Areas of interest: early learning, reading, science, history, English, math, religion, social studies, and vocational. Average film length: 10 to 20 minutes. Interested in low-budget films. The producers seek original plots with good production work, and writers knowledgeable in the subject and intended audience of their scripts. Proposals for computer software (any format) are also welcome. Successful titles: "City and Country Opposites," "Inside-Outside Shapes," "The Marvelous Mystery," and "Animal Alphabet."

☐Pays $200 to $300 per educational script; no advance. Buys all rights. Prefers to receive written proposal, outline, or entire manuscript ("with samples of previous work"). Will consider some previously produced material, depending upon subject, length, and approach of the film. Simultaneous submissions acceptable. Replies in 2 to 4 weeks. Author guidelines available. SASE not required.

GESSLER PUBLISHING CO., INC., 900 Broadway, New York, NY 10003. (212) 673-3113. Founded 1930. Seth C. Levin, President. Buys 15 to 20 language arts scripts each year.
☐Produces videotapes, cassettes, filmstrips, slides, records, and multimedia kits for elementary, junior-high, and high-school students. Areas of interest: Spanish, French, German, Italian, Latin, and ESL. Filmstrips average 40 to 60 frames; videotapes average 60 minutes. The editors are not interested in producing low-budget films. Successful titles: "Bulletin Board Kit" (French and Spanish), "Bataille de Mots," and "ESL Picture Book."
☐Pays variable royalty; no advance. Buys all rights. Prefers to receive outline or "synopsis of the program and the media for which it is intended." Will consider previously produced material. Simultaneous submissions acceptable. Replies in 3 to 5 weeks. Catalog available. SASE preferred.

GOLDSHOLL ASSOCIATES, 420 Frontage Rd., Northfield, IL 60093. (312) 446-8300. Founded 1954. Morton Goldsholl, President. Produces 4 to 6 35mm films, 16mm films, and videotapes each year for entertainment and educational purposes.
☐Goldsholl plans to produce cassettes and television broadcasts of children's stories with limited animation and dramatic readings. The editors seek fantasy, wonder stories, and science fiction for children; no restrictions.
☐Pays flat fee (according to Writers Guild standards) after production begins, plus percentage of sales; will consider making outright purchase of material. No advance. Buys all rights. Prefers to receive synopsis only. Simultaneous submissions acceptable. Replies in 2 weeks. No author guidelines or catalog available. SASE not required.

HANNA-BARBERA PRODUCTIONS, INC., 3400 Cahuenga Blvd., Hollywood, CA 90068. (213) 851-5000. Founded 1957. Joseph Barbera, President. Contact: Sam Ewing, Vice-President, Development. Produces a variety of 35mm and 1-inch video films for young children and teenagers.
☐Hanna-Barbera, with many successful animated productions for TV networks (Saturday morning programming) and syndication, considers agent submissions only. Looks for character and story in a script. Successful titles: "The Smurfs," "Scooby-Do," "The Flintstones," and "The Jetsons."
☐Pays flat fee (according to Writers Guild standards); offers negotiable advance. Prefers to receive either manuscript or outline/synopsis with resume. Will consider previously published material. Simultaneous submissions acceptable. Reply period varies. Author guidelines available. SASE preferred.

IMPERIAL INTERNATIONAL LEARNING CORP., PO Box 548, Kankakee, IL 60901. (815) 933-7735. Founded 1969. Spencer Barnard, President. Contact: Patsy Gunnels, Editor. Buys 6 to 10 scripts each year.
☐Produces 35mm films, videotapes, cassettes, filmstrips, multimedia kits,

and microcomputer programs. Areas of interest: science, history, language arts, math, study skills, and life skills for preschool, elementary, junior-high, and high-school students. Average videotape length: 10 to 20 minutes. Interested in producing low-budget films. The producers look for thorough development of an educational concept, a topic supplemental to school curriculum, and clear writing, appropriate to the intended audience. Successful titles: "Math Story Solvers" (microcomputer), "Math Mystery Theater"(cassette and filmstrip), and "Formula 1" (math workbook and cassette).

□ "We're looking for microcomputer or videotape programs on social studies concepts, problem-solving strategies, logical thinking skills, reading comprehension, life-coping skills, and simulations requiring application of math, reading, and study skills," says Gunnels.

□Pays variable royalty or flat fee and advance. Buys all rights. Prefers to receive entire manuscript or completed computer program. ("Explain your idea in general terms and request a nondisclosure agreement before submitting your script or program," suggests Gunnels.) Will consider previously produced material. Simultaneous submissions acceptable. Replies in 4 weeks. Author guidelines and catalog available. SASE preferred.

KIMBO EDUCATIONAL, 10 N. Third Ave., Long Branch, NJ 07740. Founded 1962. Robert G. Kimble, President. Amy Laufer, Editor. James Kimble, Production Coordinator. Buys up to 10 scripts each year for children and teens.

□Primarily producing cassettes and records for young children, Kimbo also produces movement-oriented fitness programs for preschool, elementary, junior-high, and high-school students. The producers seek "programs that are fun yet educational." Successful titles: "My Teddy Bear and Me," "Toddlers on Parade," "Preschool Aerobic Fun," and "Songs for You and Me."

□ "Kimbo is always looking for new ideas that are sure to spark today's early-childhood market" says Laufer.

□Pays 5% to 7% royalty on lowest net price; no advance. Buys all rights. Prefers to receive query with detailed outline, or rough narrated cassette, including activities and songs. Does not consider previously produced material. Simultaneous submissions acceptable. Replies in 8 weeks. Author guidelines and catalog available. SASE preferred.

KOCH/MARSCHALL PRODUCTIONS, INC., 1718 N. Mohawk St., Chicago, IL 60614. (312) 664-6482. Founded 1979. Phillip Koch, President. Contact: Sally Marschall, Vice-President. Buys 1 to 5 scripts for teens each year.

□A producer of videotapes, 16mm, and 35mm files, Koch/Marschall seeks scripts for junior-high and high-school students on social studies, health education, sex education, fiction, and drama and comedy. Average film length: 30 to 90 minutes. Koch/Marschall solicits original stories suitable for such PBS shows as "American Playhouse" and "Wonderworks." Original screenplays for feature films intended for general audiences also are wanted. The editors will consider low-budget films. Successful titles: "Medusa Challenger," "Pink Nights," and "Growing Up Young."

□Pays 10% royalty or makes outright purchase ($500 to $2,500); offers advance. Buys all rights. Prefers to receive query with resume and brief outline. Does not consider previously produced material. Simultaneous submissions acceptable. Replies in 6 to 8 weeks. No author guidelines or catalog available. Send SASE.

LORIMAR PRODUCTIONS, 3970 Overland Ave., Culver City, CA 90230. (213) 202–2000. Founded 1969. Lee Rich, President. Lucy Johnson, Vice-President, Children's Programs. Eleanor Richman, Director of Development.
□Lorimar, which produces material for network TV, for syndication, and for the home video market, considers agent submissions only. Contact the Lorimar Motion Picture Division for current information about its feature motion picture needs.
□Payment is negotiated according to Writers Guild standards. Buys TV, film and allied dramatic rights. Prefers to receive story treatment. Will consider previously produced materials. Reply requires several months. Send SASE.

MARSHFILM ENTERPRISES, INC., PO Box 8082, Shawnee Mission, KS 66208. (816) 523–1059. Founded 1969. Joan K. Marsh, President. Buys 8 to 12 scripts each year for children and teens.
□Produces 35mm filmstrips with cassettes, and computer software (Apple) in the areas of health and guidance for elementary, junior-high, and high-school students. Average length: 10 to 15 minutes for films; 50 frames for filmstrips. Scripts should demonstrate that the author is adept at handling spoken dialogue. Not interested in producing low-budget films. Successful titles: "Latchkey" series and "Stress" series (filmstrips and cassettes), "Alcohol—The Party" (computer software), and "Alcohol and Tobacco" (computer software).
□Pays flat fee; no advance. Buys all rights. Prefers to receive resume, writing sample, and query "with outline of ideas you could develop." Does not consider previously produced material. Simultaneous submissions acceptable. Replies in 2 to 4 weeks. Catalog available. SASE not required.

NYSTROM/EYE GATE MEDIA, 333 N. Elston Ave., Chicago, IL 60618. (312) 463–1144. Founded 1903. John F. Heise, President. Contact: Darrell A. Coppock, Editorial Director.
□This producer issues cassettes, filmstrips, and multimedia kits for elementary, junior-high, and high-school students. Average film length: 10 minutes. The editors seek a wide range of scripts on diverse disciplines, including social studies, geography, and history. Reading level and content of scripts must be appropriate for their audiences.
□Payment information not available. Buys all rights. Prefers to receive query and outline with "specific title in mind." Simultaneous submissions acceptable if editor is so informed. Replies in several weeks. Catalog available. Send SASE.

PHOENIX FILMS, INC., 468 Park Ave. S., New York, NY 10016. (212) 684–5910. Founded 1973. Mr. Heinz Gelles, President. Barbara Bryant, Executive Producer/Executive Vice-President. Robert E. Dunlap, Editor. Buys 36 to 40 scripts each year.
□Produces 8mm films, 16mm films, and videotapes for preschool, junior-high, and high-school students, and other audiences. Areas of interest: science, history, English, and math; stories for children and young adults; and material about AIDS. Film length varies with audience and topic. The editors

will consider low-budget films. Successful titles: "Frog Goes to Dinner" and "Molly's Pilgrim."

☐Offers advances, but does not pay royalty or fees. Buys all rights. Prefers to receive either an outline or treatment. Will consider previously produced material. Simultaneous submissions acceptable. Reply period varies. Catalog available. Send SASE.

SCOTT RESOURCES, PO Box 2121, CO 80522. (303) 484–7445. Michael Hobbs, Vice-President of Operations.

☐Produces computer software for the Apple II series, primarily science and math programs for elementary, junior-high, and high-school students. The editors seek educational and instructional materials, laboratory guides for science, and software for the Apple II.

☐Pays negotiable royalty. Buys all rights. Prefers to receive entire manuscript. Does not consider previously produced material. Simultaneous submissions acceptable if editor is so informed. Replies in several weeks. No author guidelines or catalog available. Send SASE.

SPENCER PRODUCTIONS, INC., 234 Fifth Ave., New York, NY 10001. (212) 697–5895. Founded 1961. Bruce Spencer, President. Buys 6 to 10 scripts each year.

☐Spencer produces humorous and satiric 16mm films, 35mm films, videotapes, and cassettes for elementary, high-school, and college students. Average film length: 15, 30, or 90 minutes. The producers also are interested in low-budget films. Successful titles: "Young Opinions" (a half-hour program where 4th graders comment on world events); "Jester at Large" (two 1-hour TV specials featuring practical joker Ala Abel); and "The Story of the Doodle-Li-Boop" (a humorous narration with music for orchestra or band concerts for ages 2 to 12).

☐Pays 10% to 25% royalty or flat fee (negotiable); negotiable advance. Buys all rights. Prefers to receive query with detailed outline or synopsis. Will consider previously produced material. Simultaneous submissions acceptable. Replies in 2 to 4 weeks. Author guidelines available; catalog not available. SASE preferred.

TALCO PRODUCTIONS, 279 E. 44th St., New York, NY 10017. (212) 697–4015. Founded 1964. Alan Lawrence, President. Contact: Peter Yung or Marty Holberton. Commissions from 1 to 10 scripts each year.

☐Talco produces 16mm films, 35mm films, videotapes, cassettes, filmstrips, slides, and records for educational institutions and nonprofit organizations. Areas of interest: history, current events (of national interest), and social studies. Average film length: 15 to 60 minutes.

☐"All of our scripts are custom-written," reports Lawrence. "We do not accept unsolicited manuscripts."

☐Purchases scripts outright (negotiable); advance varies. Buys all rights. Prefers to receive query with resume. Does not consider previously produced material. No simultaneous submissions. Replies as soon as possible. No author guidelines or catalog available. Send SASE.

TEL-AIR INTERESTS, INC., 1755 Northeast 149th St., Miami, FL 33181. (305) 944–3268. Founded 1960. Grant H. Gravitt, President. Contact: Sara Jean Noll. Buys 10 educational scripts each year.

☐Produces 16mm films, 35mm films, and videotapes for TV and theatrical audiences of all ages. The editors are not interested in producing low-budget films.

☐Pays variable flat fee; no advance. Buys all rights. Prefers to receive query letter with detailed outline. Does not consider previously produced material. No simultaneous submissions. Replies in 3 weeks. No author guidelines or catalog available. SASE not required.

VIDEOCASSETTE MARKETING CORP., 323½ Richmond St., #803, El Segundo, CA 90245. (213) 322–1140. Founded 1981. James Spencer, President. Contact: Cindy Greisdorf. Buys 4 scripts each year.

☐This company creates videotapes for preschool, elementary, junior-high, and high-school students. Geography topics are of special interest. Average film length: 30 to 60 minutes. The company will consider producing low-budget films. The editors are looking for scripts with strong marketing potential for school and home-video markets. Successful titles: "Meet Your Animal Friends" and "VCR Passport—The Video Travel Game."

☐Pays 5% to 10% royalty; flat fee ($1,000 to $2,000); or makes outright purchase ($1,000 to $2,000); advances one-fourth of payment. Buys all rights. Prefers to receive written queries. Will consider previously produced materials. Simultaneous submissions acceptable. Replies in 2 weeks. SASE preferred.

SIX

PUBLISHERS AND PRODUCERS OF PLAYS

Playwriting offers perhaps the greatest challenge to children's writers. A play-wright must learn to write within a production budget (so that sets and costumes can be created with more imagination than money), keep the number of characters and locales manageable, and create strong, believable characters without sacrificing dialogue or action.

If you are new to playwriting, you can gain experience by becoming active in local school and community plays as a stagehand, actor, or director. Study successful plays: their dialogue, the scene designs, rhythm, and character development. After you've written a few scripts, take them to a college theater instructor for criticism and advice.

As you prepare a script for publication or production, ask yourself these questions:

- Are the characters and dialogue believable?
- Are there any specific staging problems?
- Is the story a good one?
- Is the pacing quick, or does it lag somewhere?
- Is it going to cost too much to produce?
- Will the intended audience understand it without being offended?
- Can I improve this play in any way?

Before you put your manuscript in the mail, solve any problems suggested by these questions.

In your query letter to the publisher or producer, describe your play: its plot, length, number of sets, number of male and female roles, and musical requirements. You also should include information about your production and writing experience and send a list of your writing and performance credits. This query will substantiate your knowledge of the industry and its unique needs, and will introduce you as a professional to the producer who reads it. Before you approach a major play publisher, try to have a script produced; it makes all the difference in helping you become established.

Your manuscript should be as readable as possible. Don't be afraid to leave lots of white space on each page of the script; unlike many published books of plays, which have as many words per page as possible, a manuscript must be typed so as to be as readable as possible. Single-space, but leave two lines of space to separate the narrative, and three lines of space to separate dialogue from the rest of the manuscript.

Once the script is completed, put it into a binder—a clasp binder, for example—and add a title page with your name, address and phone number. Of course, you should follow any submissions procedures outlined by a producer or playhouse.

A rejection of a script may be almost immediate, but an acceptance can take months. If you do not receive a response within a reasonable time, send a polite inquiry as to your script's status. If there still is no response, send a registered letter withdrawing your script from consideration.

As in all children's writing, it's important to remember that today's youth are intelligent, aware, concerned, and very anxious to be taken seriously. They have real fears, joys, and dreams—just like you. If you write down to them, the play's over.

As an aspiring playwright, you might consider becoming a member of The Dramatists Guild, 234 W. 44th Street, New York, NY 10036, (212) 398-0838. This organization offers a monthly publication with information about developments in the industry, contract negotiation, and marketing techniques for your script. Also in New York, the Theater Development Fund (1501 Broadway, Suite 2110, New York, NY 10036) helps playwrights obtain reduced-priced tickets to Broadway and off-Broadway performances.

The big word in playwriting is perseverance. Your script may be rejected time and time again, but this doesn't necessarily mean that your script is weak. In this industry, rejection is more likely to be the result of budget considerations, casting, or theater politics. So continue to circulate your script. If you persevere long enough, you'll be rewarded with applause.

ALLEY THEATER, 615 Texas Ave., Houston, TX 77002. (713) 228-9341. Founded 1947. Pat Brown, Executive Director. Contact: Robert Strane, Literary Manager. Produces 3 to 4 school plays for children and young adults each year: musical, comedy, storybook, and legends.
□Produces "good plays, preferably small cast," with "production requirements that would not hinder touring," and seeks scripts for musicals with excellent structure, characterization, book, and score. Typical length: 2 acts. Successful plays: *Finding Home* and *Pecos Bill Rides Again.*
□Pays negotiable fee for scripts. Buys varying rights. Prefers to receive synopsis, agent submission, or professional recommendation. Interested in previously produced material. Usually replies in 2 to 6 months. Send SASE.

BAKER'S PLAY PUBLISHING CO., 100 Chauncy St., Boston, MA 02111. (617) 482-1280. Founded 1845. M. Abbott Van Nostrand, President. Contact: John B. Welch, Editor. Produces 12 to 18 school and church plays for young adults each year: musical, comedy, tragedy, contemporary, and drama.
□Contemporary plays that deal with issues of importance to young adults are

a special interest of Baker's, especially plays in which young adults play themselves. The editors look for "real dialogue from honest characters in an interesting environment or situation." Typical length: 20 to 35 minutes for 1-act plays; 2 hours for 2-act plays.

□ "Baker's Plays has established a new division—Plays for Young Adults," reports Welch. "Since its beginning with the publication of Peter Dee's *Voices from the High School,* this division has grown enormously. Hence, we are now aware that the marketplace will support very contemporary plays dealing with today's difficult themes. We search for honest plays for today's teens."

□ Pays 50% to 80% in split royalties; rarely makes outright purchase; no advance. Buys stock and production rights, and first-class options. Prefers to receive entire manuscript. Interested in previously produced material. Simultaneous submissions acceptable. Usually replies in 4 months. Author guidelines and catalog available. Send SASE.

BLACK HAWK CHILDREN'S THEATER, PO Box 433, Waterloo, IA 50704. (319) 235–0367. Founded 1964. Jons Olson, President. Contact: Tom Ballmer, Director. Produces 4 to 6 community plays for young adults each year: musical, comedy, contemporary, drama, storybook, and history.

□ Interested in adaptations of classics to the stage (e.g., *Tom Sawyer, Charlotte's Web),* fairy tales, and musicals. Typical length: 1-act, continuous action.

□ "Usually our plays run from 45 minutes to 1 hour and 15 minutes." Recent plays: *Charlie and the Chocolate Factory* and *The Prince and the Pauper.*

□ Pays per performance (negotiable); no advance. Buys production rights. Prefers to receive entire manuscript. Interested in previously produced material. Simultaneous submissions acceptable. Usually replies in several months. Send SASE.

ELRIDGE PUBLISHING CO., 299 Hill Ave., PO Drawer 216, Franklin OH 45005. (513) 746–6531. Founded 1906. Nancy S. Vorhis, President. Produces 10 school, community, and church plays for young adults each year: musical, comedy, contemporary, drama, storybook, history, and legends.

□ The editors seek 1- to 3-act plays for their Christmas collection, as well as 1- and 2-people playlets, monologues and melodramas. Successful play: *Don't Rock the Boat* by Tim Kelly.

□ "All material must be in good taste. We've received material concerning artificial insemination and sexual frigidity, subjects which are too mature for our audiences," Vorhis says.

□ Pays a percentage of per-copy sales, royalty, or purchases scripts ($125 to $300); no advance. Buys all rights. Prefers to receive entire manuscript. Interested in previously produced material. Simultaneous submissions acceptable. Usually replies in 3 months. ("We wish it could be sooner," notes Vorhis, "but it really takes us that long to carefully read and consider all the manuscripts we receive.") Catalog available. SASE preferred.

SAMUEL FRENCH, INC., 45 West 25th St., New York, NY 10010. (212) 206–8990. Founded 1830. M. Abbott Van Nostrand, President. Contact: Lawrence R. Harbison, Editor. Publishes 2 to 3 school plays for juveniles and young adults each year: musical, comedy, contemporary, drama, storybook, history, and legends.

☐Seeks small-cast plays (with simple sets) and new myths; no public-domain story adaptations. Typical length: 1 act.

☐"The children's theater market is very small. We leave most of it to our smaller competitors, concentrating instead on the adult market," comments Harbison. "If we do pick up a play for the juvenile/young adult market, it is generally one with contemporary relevance to this market. For instance, our latest acquisition is a children's musical called *No More Secrets,* which deals with child abuse. We are not interested in adaptations of familiar fairy tales."

☐Pays 10% book royalties; 80% amateur production royalties; 90% professional production royalties. Offers varying advance. Buys stock, amateur, and production rights. Prefers to receive query. Interested in previously produced materials. Simultaneous submissions acceptable. Usually replies in 8 weeks minimum, 8 months maximum. Author guidelines: $3; catalog: $2. Send SASE.

HEUER PUBLISHING CO., 233 Dows Bldg., PO Box 248, Cedar Rapids, IA 52406. (319) 364–6311. Founded 1925. C. Emmett McMullen, President. Produces variable number of school plays for juveniles and young adults each year: comedy, contemporary, drama, mystery, and mystery comedy.

☐Interested in full-length plays, preferably comedy "with a large number of characters (16 to 24) suitable for the junior- and senior-high market, not depicting the so-called family scene." Typical length: 1 to 3 acts.

☐McMullen looks for plays that have "a theme within the intellectual and emotional range of students." Playwrights also should consider the scope of high-school production ability when writing a script.

☐Pays royalty or purchases material outright; no advance. Buys amateur rights only. Prefers to receive either a synopsis or entire manuscript. Interested in previously produced material. Simultaneous submissions acceptable. Usually replies in 5 to 6 weeks. Author guidelines and catalog available. Send SASE.

HONOLULU THEATRE FOR YOUTH, PO Box 3257, Honolulu, HI 96801. (808) 521–3487. Founded 1955. Contact: John Kauffman, Artistic Director. Produces 6 to 10 young-adult plays each year: comedy, tragedy, contemporary, drama, storybook, history, legends, and mime.

☐Scripts should have a cast of 6 to 8 actors and should run 60 to 90 minutes. Typical length: 1 act. Successful plays: *To Kill a Mockingbird; East of the Sun, West of the Moon;* and *Raven the Hungry.*

☐"We are especially interested in scripts that explore cultures of the Pacific basin," says Kauffman.

☐Pays flat fee, a per-performance fee, commission, or royalty (negotiable); offers negotiable advance. Buys production rights, first-class options, and percentage of future royalties on commissioned scripts. Prefers to receive entire manuscript. Interested in previously produced material. Simultaneous submissions acceptable. Usually replies in 4 months. No author guidelines or catalog available. Send SASE.

MERIWETHER PUBLISHING LTD./CONTEMPORARY DRAMA SERVICE, 885 Elkton Dr., Colorado Springs, CO 80907. (303) 594–4422. Founded 1970. Arthur L. Zapel, President. Buys 50 to 75 school and church plays for young adults each year: musical, comedy, contemporary, and mime.

☐A multifaceted publishing house for scripts, Meriwether is interested in easily-staged comedies, religious drama, short skits, and humorous monologues. Typical length: 1 act. Successful play: *Isn't This What Christmas Is All About?*

☐"One-act comedies should not exceed 35 typewritten pages," notes Zapel. "Playwrights should send an outline of 3-act plays or musicals."

☐Pays 10% royalty on playbook sales and 50% split on a royalty play. For non-royalty plays, publisher pays 10% of playkit sales up to a negotiated maximum or purchases material outright. Offers no advance. Buys amateur performance rights and publishing rights. Prefers to receive query with outline or synopsis; entire manuscript for 1-act plays only. Interested in previously produced material. Simultaneous submissions acceptable. Usually replies in 4 weeks. Author guidelines and catalog: $1. Send SASE.

NASHVILLE ACADEMY THEATER, 724 2nd Ave. South, Nashville, TN 37210. (615) 254–9103. Founded 1931. Contact: Scot E. Copeland, Artistic Director. Produces 4 professional plays for young adults each year: comedy, tragedy, contemporary, drama, storybook, history, and legends.

☐Interested in well-written dramatizations of classic stories. Plays should not run over 90 minutes (60 minutes preferred), or have more than 10 actors. Non-musicals preferred. Typical length: 50 to 90 minutes, all acts. When considering submissions, the producers weigh a play's literary merit, action, interest, and artistic integrity.

☐"We produce 2 plays each year for K to 4, 2 plays for grades 5 to 8, and 2 plays for our academy students, usually classically oriented," says Copeland. "We do not produce campy or cutesy material. We limit ourselves to quality; we plan eclectic seasons."

☐Payment negotiated on individual basis, usually royalty per performance based on prevailing rate for published work in the field. No advance. Buys production rights. Prefers to receive entire manuscript. Interested in previously produced material. Simultaneous submissions acceptable. Usually replies in 2 to 4 months, depending on time of year. SASE preferred.

PERFORMANCE PUBLISHING CO. (See entry for *Baker's Play Publishing Co.*, which has purchased Performance Publishing.)

PIONEER DRAMA SERVICE, PO Box 22555, 2172 S. Colorado Blvd., Denver, CO 80210. (303) 759–4297. Founded 1963. Shubert Fendrich, Publisher. Contact: Patrick Dorn, Assistant Editor. Publishes 10 to 12 young-adult school, community, and church plays each year: musical, comedy, contemporary, drama, storybook, religious, melodrama, farce, seasonal, and participation.

☐Seeking 1-act and full-length plays: religious dramas, mystery, contemporary children's plays, and participation theater. Considers a script's cross-market accessibility (i.e., suitability for schools, churches, and community theaters). Average length: 30 to 90 minutes. Successful plays: *Luann,* a musical by Eleanor Harder, and *Hurricane Smith,* a comedy by Tim Kelly.

☐"Scripts must be previously produced, with one set or simple staging area, be mostly written for female roles, and have a 1- or 2-act structure," says Dorn.

☐Purchases all rights. Prefers to receive "query letter describing play in terms of plot synopsis, duration, production history, number of sets, number of male and female roles. It it's a musical, please include cassette tape of the music." Interested in previously produced material. Simultaneous submissions acceptable. Usually replies in 4 weeks. Author guidelines and catalog available. SASE preferred.

PLAYERS PRESS, INC., PO Box 1132, Studio City, CA 91604. (818) 789–4980. Founded 1965. William Alan Landes, President. Contact: Robert W. Gordon, Editorial Vice-president. Publishes a variety of scripts.
☐Players Press is a full-service catalog for children's theater. It handles all rights for most authors, services motion picture, television, and theater, and publishes previously produced material as storybooks, cassettes, videotapes and films. Currently looking for comedy and children's scripts.
☐Pays either commission or buys scripts outright; negotiable. No advance. Buys stock and production rights, as well as first-class options and film/TV rights. Prefers to receive entire manuscript with author biography/resume and a copy of the flyer and program with production dates on it. ("No manuscript will be considered unless the play has been produced.") Simultaneous submissions acceptable. Usually replies in 3 to 4 months. Catalog available. Send SASE for the return on your manuscript and two #10 SASEs for correspondence.

SHAKESPEARE THEATER AT THE FOLGER LIBRARY, 301 E. Capitol St., S.E., Washington, D.C. 20010. (202) 547–3230. Founded 1970. Robert Linowes, President of the Board. Contact: Michael Kahn, Artistic Director; Sally Bailey, Assistant to the Artistic Producer. Produces a variable number of school and professional plays each year: comedy, tragedy, and history.
☐Seeks adaptations of plays by Shakespeare and other classical authors, from the Greeks to the early realists, in order to introduce young audiences to the classics. The producers prefer a small cast (4 to 6 actors) and simple settings for easy touring. Typical length: 2 to 3 acts. Successful play: *A Midsummer Night's Dream.*
☐"In the past, we have toured a special program, *Play Around Shakespeare,* which helped introduce young audiences to Shakespeare's works. We are open to any type of adaptations which might serve as an overview of a particular author's work or of a classical period."
☐Pays variable fee depending upon number of performances and size of performance space. Offers negotiable advance. Buys production rights. Prefers to receive entire manuscript. Interested in previously produced material. Simultaneous submissions acceptable. Usually replies in several months. SASE preferred.

THEATRE CALGARY, 220 9th Ave. S.E., Calgary, Alta. T2G 5C4, Canada. (403) 294–7440. Founded 1968. Martin Kinch, Artistic Director. Contact: Randee Loucks, Assistant to Artistic Director/Extensions Director. Produces 1 to 3 juvenile/young-adult plays for schools and community halls each year; type varies year to year.
☐Looks for youth theater scripts on a variety of topics. Average length: 1 hour or shorter; 1 to 2 acts. Successful plays: *The Little Prince* by Cummins and Scoullard, *In Search of the Spark* (a commissioned adaptation by Murray McRae), and *How I Wonder What You Are?* by Robert Morgan.

☐Pays a flat fee, a per-performance fee, commission, or royalty; variable advance. Usually buys production rights. Prefers to receive synopsis and sample scene for preliminary assessment, as well as an author's resume of other publications and productions. Interested in previously produced material. Simultaneous submissions acceptable. Usually replies in 2 to 3 months. Send SASE with Canadian postage or postage voucher with all submissions.

THEATER FOUNTAINHEAD, 1179A King St. West, Toronto, Ontario M5S 2Y2, Canada. (416) 537–3459. Contact: Michael Miller, Office Manager. Produces 1 young-adult school play each year: contemporary and legends.
☐Interested in scripts with a multicultural theme. Wants plays with a maximum of 5 characters and sets that aren't too complex for touring. Typical length: 45 minutes. Recent play: *Invisible Kids* by Dennis Foon.
☐Pays $600 to $1,000 flat fee. No advance. Buys production rights. Prefers to receive entire manuscript with letter of introduction listing author's writing credentials. Interested in previously produced material. Simultaneous submissions acceptable. Usually replies in several months. Catalog available. Send SASE.

YOUNG ACTORS PROGRAMME (Drama Studio London at Berkeley), 2325 Fourth St., Berkeley, CA 94710. (415) 549–2595. Bruce Ducat, Programme Director. Produces workshop productions only.
☐A professional training program for actors ages 8 to 18, the Young Actors Programme seeks challenging material that is nonsexist and nonracist, has structured characters and story lines, considers the audience's attention span, and is well-written. Also looks for scripts that don't patronize the audience, that provide decent roles for actresses, and that offer a challenge to young performers. No stories about "frogs, faeries, dragons or princesses."
☐"Don't forget that kids aren't stupid," says Ducat. "They are aware, bright, concerned, and dying to be heard and taken seriously. Talk to a lot of kids! Don't assume anything about them. Consider the world we've given them."
☐Does not buy scripts; no advance. Buys varying performance rights. Prefers to receive entire manuscript. Interested in previously produced material. Simultaneous submissions acceptable. Usually replies as soon as possible. Send SASE.

SEVEN

GREETING CARD MANUFACTURERS

Writing verse for greeting cards can pay well, especially if a royalty is paid on sales (think of the 230 million birthdays celebrated in the U.S. each year), and it's just as creative as writing fiction. The space limitations force you to choose your words very carefully. For example, try to write a fresh, one-line text of 30 characters to humorously congratulate a girl on her thirteenth birthday. Tough? You bet!

Most cards are two-lined: one for the cover, to attract interest; the other, often with a twist, for the inside. The verse doesn't have to rhyme; card companies look for a variety of verse, including traditional and free verse, both short and long. (Some cards have just one word!)

Before writing any verse, ask yourself, "Who is going to send this card, and why?" Remember, cards must communicate. Something about the card should remind potential buyers of someone they know. If you can prompt buyers to say to themselves, "Gee, this is something I wanted to say to _____," then you're on the right track.

The difficulty is to discover those key words and phrases of universal appeal: words and phrases that are appropriate to many situations (birthdays, baby showers, teenage love), yet appear to be specifically intended for buyers to give to another person. It takes a special writer to be able to find these words, especially for an audience of children and teens.

Most card companies prefer to receive samples of verse on 3" × 5" index cards. Many of these publishers use computers to store and catalog verse so that examples from specific categories (e.g., 3-line rhymed Christmas verse) can be quickly retrieved and reviewed. Include your name, address, and phone number on the back of each index card.

You may wonder, "Do I have to submit drawings for the card, too?" It depends. If you can, by all means provide a sketch or a drawing done to scale of the image you see in your mind. However, if you can't draw a straight line, don't bother, unless you have a friend who can supply a professional-looking sketch. One alternative is to write a brief description of the situation, but don't go into so much detail that you limit the creative ability of the artist to conceptualize a better scene; leave some flexibility.

If you submit ideas for mechanical cards such as pop-up cards, it's best to send a prototype, but be certain that it works.

In all cases, neatly type the words as you envision them appearing on the finished product. If you submit dummy cards, add your name, address, and phone number to the back of each one, as well as an identification number for reference purposes. At the same time, you should keep a filing system to record where and when cards are sent to publishers, and the results.

Professional verse writers usually submit verses and dummies to publishers in batches of 5 to 20, depending upon the company. Follow the submission procedures outlined by each card company on the next few pages: pay attention to the number of samples each company prefers to review as well as its specific needs. More important, note the lead time required: you'd be surprised by the number of greeting card publishers that strictly observe a one-year lead time. Scheduled print times are *not* flexible.

Finally, remember to place the copyright symbol on each verse sample you submit, but don't be surprised if publishers insist on buying all rights to your verses; that's a fairly common practice. An exception to this often occurs when you offer an entire concept (e.g., a character, verse, or theme) for a new series of cards; in these cases, the rights are almost always negotiated.

BRILLIANT ENTERPRISES, 117 Valerio St., Santa Barbara, CA 93101. Founded 1967. Ashleigh Brilliant, President. Markets cards for children, teens, and young adults: humorous, contemporary, cute, informal, inspirational, seasonal, and birthday.
☐Seeks cards of "a highly original nature, emphasizing subtlety, simplicity, insight, wit, profundity, beauty, and felicity of expression. Messages should be of universal appeal, capable of being appreciated by all types of people and of being easily translated into other languages." Any accompanying artwork should be either decorative or a commentary rather than purely illustrative of the verse. No puns, topics limited to American culture, or topical references. Recent verse: "Maybe I'm lucky to be going so slowly. . . . Because I may be going in the wrong direction."
☐"Since our line of cards is highly unconventional, it is essential that freelancers study it before submitting," stresses Brilliant.
☐Pays on acceptance: $40 outright purchase for complete word and picture design. Buys all rights. Prefers to receive samples with artwork on 3″ × 5″ sheets of paper; no more than 15 per batch. Limit of 17 words per card. Does not accept previously published material. Replies in 2 weeks. Catalog and samples: $2. Send SASE.

DRAWING BOARD GREETING CARDS, INC., 8200 Carpenter Freeway, Dallas, TX 75222. (214) 638–4800. Founded 1959. Selwin Belofsky, President. Contact: Richard Hunt, Creative Director, or Jimmie Fitzgerald, Editorial Director. Markets cards for preschoolers, juveniles, teens, and young adults: humorous, contemporary, conventional, cute, informal, inspirational, promotions, punch-out, seasonal, birthday, and visual.
☐Drawing Board is "looking for everyday promotion ideas: fresh, new, sendable, and short of words but long on feeling. We like funny material, and pro-

mos with animals. We also do photo promos." Does not handle cards with attachments, complicated folds, or pop-ups. The editors consider freshness and strength of ideas.

☐Pays on acceptance: $30 to $80 per verse outright purchase; no advance. Buys all rights. Prefers to receive verse samples. Submit 10 to 20 ideas; 20 preferred. Lead time is 1 year for seasonal material. Not interested in previously produced material. No simultaneous submissions. Usually replies in 2 weeks. Writer's guidelines available. Send SASE.

FRAN MAR, 587 Main St., New Rochelle, NY 10801. (914) 632–2232. Founded 1956. Stan Cohen, President. Markets cards for children, teens, and young adults: humorous, contemporary, informal. Also publishes risqué material.

☐Publishes invitations—general and special titles—(4″ × 6″ pads) that have copy on 1 side only; they do not open as a conventional card does. Novelty stationery (e.g., camp notes) printed on 1 side only is also wanted; 6″ × 8″. All verse must have a good punchline.

☐Pays on acceptance: $25 per verse, outright purchase. Offers no advance. Buys all rights. Prefers to receive concepts typed on 3″ × 5″ cards with descriptions of artwork or rough sketches. Submit 6 to 10 samples. Not interested in previously produced material. No simultaneous submissions. Usually replies in 2 weeks. Writer's guidelines available. Send SASE.

MAINE LINE CO., PO Box 418, Rockport, ME 04856. (207) 236–8536. Founded 1979. Perri Ardman and Joyce Boaz, Presidents. Contact: Marjorie MacClennen, Editor. Markets young-adult cards for contemporary women; humorous, contemporary, risqué, seasonal, and birthday.

☐"We are one of the leading alternative greeting card companies publishing non-traditional, innovative cards for the contemporary woman; many young adults and college-age people also buy our cards," reports MacClennen. "We will look at original and innovative copy that deals with all topics of female concern, with a focus on everyday events: friendship, love, marriage, divorce, career. Lines should be punchy and to the point. "We like our cards to have relevant messages people can relate to." No cute, mushy, flowery, or blunt material.

☐"Messages should be positive, humorous, and upbeat, not insulting or a put-down," MacClennen stresses. "Outside must be intriguing; inside can't be flat or predictable."

☐Pays on acceptance: variable royalty or outright purchase. Offers no advance. Buys exclusive card and related product rights. Prints author byline on back of card. Prefers to receive verse samples on index cards with mock-ups. Submit minimum of 5 samples, one line per card. (Note: "A copyright symbol next to your name protects your entry.")

☐Lead time is 1 year for seasonal material. Not interested in previously produced material. No simultaneous submissions. Usually replies in 6 to 8 weeks. Author guidelines (attach $.40 postage to SASE) and catalog available. Send SASE.

VAGABOND CREATIONS, INC., 2560 Lance Dr., Dayton, OH 45409. (513) 298–1124. Founded 1957. George F. Stanley Jr., President. Markets cards for teens and young adults: humorous, cute, informal, and visual.

☐Primarily issues illustrated stationery based upon themes (e.g., kittens, puppies, camping, word games). The editors also seek general subjects with short, 1-line messages (no verse), as well as seasonal and everyday cards (birthday, get well, anniversary). Does not consider novelty, risqué, mechanical, punch-out, rhyming, inspirational, or lengthy-versed cards.

☐Vagabond also looks for cute, humorous cards featuring illustrations of animals. Submissions should be typed on 3" × 5" cards, have general themes for the widest possible audience, and contain a short message tie-in with artwork. Recent message: Turtle saying to another turtle: "I'd stick my neck out for you anytime."

☐"We require copy for a line of greeting cards featuring illustrations only on the front cover, with a short, general, clever tie-in message on the inside page," says Stanley. "Follow our stated requirements; so many contributors ignore our guidelines and send types of material which can't be applied to the line."

☐Pays on acceptance: $10 to $15 outright purchase. No advance. Buys all rights. Prefers to receive verse samples; 5 minimum. Lead time is 4 to 5 months for seasonal material. Not interested in previously produced material. Simultaneous submissions acceptable. Usually replies in 2 weeks. Author guidelines available; no catalog available. Send SASE.

WARNER PRESS, INC., 1200 E. 5th Street, PO Box 2499, Anderson, IN 46012. (317) 644-7721. Donald Noffsinger, President. Cindy Grant, Product Editor. Markets cards for preschoolers, schoolchildren, teens and young adults: contemporary, cute, inspirational, seasonal, birthday, and softline.

☐Specializes in greeting cards, coloring books, puzzles, punch-outs, stickers, and plaques with a Christian emphasis for children. The editors are looking for everyday verse ("please, avoid use of 'I' or 'we' "); non-rhyming verse preferred; word length not to exceed 8 lines. No risqué verse or ideas. When reviewing submissions, the editors consider timing, specific needs, the number of submissions and their appearance, potential for additional use of the materials, and whether it's a new product. Successful verse: "Laughter, smiles and sunshine, too. . .May these be God's birthday gifts for you."

☐Pays on acceptance: $10 to $40 per verse, outright purchase. Buys all rights. Prefers to receive 10 to 30 verse samples; 20 preferred. Lead time is 6 to 8 months. Simultaneous submissions acceptable if editor is so informed. Usually replies in 4 to 6 weeks. Author guidelines and brochures available. Send SASE.

EIGHT

NEWSPAPER AND MAGAZINE SYNDICATES

At one time or another nearly every children's writer dreams of being syndicated and of being able to reach the hearts and minds of hundreds of thousands of children.

Yet syndication is a fickle friend. Simply because your column or feature is syndicated doesn't automatically spell success; the income and influence you derive depends upon which newspapers and magazines buy your material, and whether people are willing to buy these publications in order to read you. If the public interest isn't there, your column will be dropped by the syndicate. As Euripides observed, "Some men never find prosperity, for all their voyaging, while others find it with no voyaging."

This is not to suggest that you do not attempt to syndicate your works. By all means try, but be realistic. Remember, you are competing against thousands of other writers who are vying for acceptance by the same syndicates.

Before you submit your column or feature idea to a syndicate, you should consider:

- Is this an interesting concept?
- Is it original?
- Does it have wide readership appeal?
- Does it offer material that readers can't get elsewhere?
- Will the topic be popular for quite some time?
- Does the concept fit your writing style?
- Does it allow for creativity?
- Is the concept one that truly interests you?
- Would you be willing to commit yourself to writing a mechanically-correct column of so many words on a regular schedule?
- Can you generate enough material to keep the column in print for a long time?

If you answer yes to all these questions, you have a good candidate for syndication.

You'll need to write several samples of your proposed column; samples allow submissions editors to see your writing style, organizational skills, and creativity at work. The length of a newspaper column is usually 500 to 1,000 words, requiring that that you use the succinct style of newspaper writing. However, strive to develop your own writing style. Don't mimic other styles, especially those of successful syndicated writers; offer a unique and captivating voice that the editors will want to share with their readers.

Your material stands a better chance of acceptance if you can persuade a local newspaper, magazine, or radio station to publish or broadcast your column, even if you receive no payment; publication suggests readership appeal to a syndicate.

What exactly do syndicate editors look for? In general, they look for short, fast-paced, interesting material that will appeal to a wide readership: cartoons, games, puzzles, short fiction, humor, commentary, trivia, article series, book excerpts, feature articles, and radio scripts. In today's market, a first column usually focuses on one aspect of a subject (e.g., healthy desserts for beginning cooks) and is written by someone who knows the subject thoroughly.

Many editors recommend that writers seeking syndication should offer a service that other media, such as radio or TV, can't. The material should always be current in its awareness of readers' lifestyles and goals, in order to avoid becoming outdated. The easiest type of material to syndicate is the "how-to" feature; the most difficult, the first-person narrative and material that competes with successful, established columns. The editors I spoke with did admit to occasionally giving preference to journalists, authors, and editors, but only because these writers tend to know what kind of material can be syndicated.

Before querying a syndicate, check the listings that follow in this chapter. To make certain that your column or feature idea is not currently being syndicated, review a sampling of newspapers, large and small.

If your idea is viable, submit material to appropriate syndicates based upon their guidelines. If no guidelines are available, send the editor a query describing your column and its potential market. Accompanying this should be your resume (indicating your special expertise to write the column), column format requirements, and several writing samples (preferably clips of your column). If possible, you also should include a list of potential topics for future columns. (Ideally, you should always have a "bank" of completed columns: 12 weeklies or 6 monthlies.)

When your material is accepted, you can expect to receive either a commission (25% to 75%) on the gross sales of your material or a flat fee ($5 to $500), depending upon the syndicate, the media to which it sells, their circulation, and the potential readership of your column or feature. Occasionally, a syndicate will contract a writer for a yearly salary. It's important that you, your agent, or your attorney draw up a contract with the syndicate outlining payment policy and criteria regarding your submissions (e.g., deadline, length, topics).

If you would like to keep 100% of the commissions for your material, you can attempt self-syndication. This requires that you not only write the material, but also approach local and regional media, market your column, distribute it, handle related paperwork, and do all the promotions. Self-syndication is demanding—among its drawbacks is the fact that you may not be able to capitalize on all available markets for your material—and somewhat costly; think carefully before attempting it.

A syndicated writer needs to keep a finger on the public pulse. Be alert to the media (especially ads) for subtle signs that signal a new trend in lifestyles or technology. If the trend is significantly different, it might suggest material for a column.

Don't let anyone tell you that becoming a syndicated writer is easy. It requires good writing skills, hard work, insight, and a lot of luck; and sometimes even all that is not enough. So keep your sense of humor, for you never know when success will arrive. If and when it does, according to Robert Browning, "a minute's success pays the failure of years."

CONTINUUM BROADCASTING NETWORK/GENERATION NEWS, 345 W. 85th St., Suite 46, New York, NY 10024. (212) 580-9525. Stephen Vaughn, Editor. Buys 200 to 300 features for syndication to radio and newspapers each year.
□Syndicates contemporary feature material primarily of interest to young-adult and adult audiences: comedy, interviews of interesting or well-known people, music trends, fitness, travel, lifestyles, nostalgia, and trivia. The editors seek radio scripts, ranging from 90 to 150 seconds for shorts, and from 30 to 60 minutes for special features; acceptable newspaper column/feature length varies. Well-received syndicated material: "Getting It Together" (a lifestyle column for teens).
□Pays either flat fee (up to $200) or commission (25% to 50%), depending upon length. Buys all rights (negotiable). For newspapers, prefers to receive query summarizing proposed material along with clips of published work; for broadcast materials, send demo tape or full script. Simultaneous submissions acceptable if editor is so informed. Replies in 4 to 6 weeks. Author guidelines available. Send SASE.

KING FEATURES SYNDICATE (A Division of Hearst Corporation), 235 E. 45th St., New York, NY 10017. (212) 682-5600. James D. Head, Executive Editor. Mary Clark, Senior Editor. Bill Yates, Comics Editor.
□The largest syndicate in the United States, King Features syndicates comic strips, features, and more than 80 columns to newspapers worldwide. Looks for humor, self-help, how-to, and commentaries; 600 to 800 words. Editorial cartoons and comic strips also accepted. No advice or medical columns considered. Currently syndicating: Mr. Rogers, "Blondie," "Popeye," "Beatle Bailey," and "Betty Boop."
□"We're always looking for new and proven talent," says Clark. "An author should be on the cutting edge of what is commercial, and send us not just an idea, but as many samples as possible to show us that the idea is indeed viable and that he can follow through and execute it."
□Payment varies with contract. Buys first rights and reprint rights (negotiable). Prefers to receive queries with 12 to 15 samples of the proposed column or feature. Replies in 3 weeks. No author guidelines available. Send SASE.

MINORITY FEATURES SYNDICATE, PO Box 421, Farrell, PA 16146. (412) 962-2522. Sally Foglia, Editor.

☐Syndicates material primarily to newspapers and magazines. The editors look for feature-length articles (up to 2,500 words) and filler material of interest to young adults and adults. They also consider scripts for newspaper comic features and comic books printed by Bill Murray Productions; send for guidelines on specific needs. Well-received syndicated material: "The Candyman" (a newspaper comic feature for young adults).

☐Payment varies depending upon length and quality. Buys first North American serial rights (negotiable). Prefers to receive query with clips of published work. Interested in reprints. No simultaneous submissions. Replies in 6 weeks. Author guidelines available for 2 first-class stamps. Send SASE with all submissions.

NEWSPAPER ENTERPRISE ASSOCIATION, INC. (A Division of United Media, a Scripps–Howard Company), 200 Park Ave., New York, NY 10166. (212) 692-3700. D.L. Drake, Executive Editor. David Hendin, VP/Editorial Director. Sarah Gillespie, Director of Comic Art.

☐Syndicates to more than 700 small- and medium-sized newspapers. Interested in comic strips, columns, and feature articles; length varies. No first-person columns. Currently syndicates "Born Loser," "Alley Oop," and "Frank & Ernest."

☐Buys all rights (negotiable). Prefers to receive a copy of the proposed feature, the author's plan for the column, and a biographical sketch; provide 4 to 6 weeks of samples for comic strips. Replies in 6 weeks. Send SASE.

OCEANIC PRESS SERVICE, PO Box 6538, Buena Park, CA 90622. (714) 527-5650. John Taylor, Editor. Distributes syndicated material to about 320 print sources.

☐Syndicates articles and stories of universal readership appeal that are either timely or intriguing; readers' ages range from late teens to adult. The editors seek how-to and feature articles on family relations, concerns of youth, social issues, home care, the environment, fashion, and biographies of well-known men and women; length varies. Acceptable fiction: romance, gothic novels, mysteries, westerns, and science fiction; up to novel length. Oceanic serializes books for domestic and international readers; translation services offered free. Photos, B&W and color, welcome.

☐Editor's suggestion: approach with published works for reprint.

☐Pays 50% commission or purchases material outright (up to $3,000); negotiable. Buys all rights (not negotiable). Prefers to receive query with clips of published work. Interested in reprints. Simultaneous submission acceptable if editor is so notified. Replies in 4 weeks. Author guidelines available for $1. Send SASE with all submissions.

SINGER COMMUNICATIONS, INC., 3164 Tyler Ave., Anaheim, CA 92801. (714) 527-5650. Natalie Charlton, Executive Vice President. Licenses 300 books and 500 features each year.

☐Supplies articles and books to newspapers, magazines, and radio and TV stations worldwide. Interested in contemporary romance, jokes, fillers, magazine columns and features, newspaper articles and column topics of global interest, radio and TV material, and business-related topics; length varies. Currently syndicates Dr. Glenn Griffith (children's health column).

☐"We want material that doesn't just cater to the U.S. market," says

Charlton. "Focus your column and article topics so they have a universal appeal."

□Pays 50% commission or flat rate for columns and articles. Buys all rights. Prefers to receive a query with published clips. Reprints accepted for foreign sales only. Replies in 4 to 6 weeks. Author's guidelines: $1. Send SASE.

TEENAGE CORNER, 70-540 Gardenia Ct., Rancho Mirage, CA 92270. David J. Lavin, Executive Editor. Buys about 150 items for syndication each year.

□Specializes in syndicating newspaper features on a variety of topics and issues; 500 words. Suggestion: contact editor before submitting material to determine current interest and needs.

□Pays $25 minimum. All rights retained by author. Prefers to receive entire manuscript. No simultaneous submissions. Replies in 3 weeks. Author guidelines available. Send SASE.

UNITED CARTOONIST SYNDICATE, PO Box 7081, Corpus Christi, TX 78415. (512) 855-2480. Pedro Moreno, Editor.

□Syndicates comic strips, features, and one-time articles to newspapers, magazines, newsletters, and book publishers. Considers human-interest stories, science fiction, and the supernatural; length varies. Comic strips should be family entertainment.

□Pays 40% commission. Buys all rights (negotiable). Prefers to receive query with 6 samples; photocopies acceptable. Replies in 2 to 4 weeks. Author guidelines: $5. Send SASE.

UNITED FEATURE SYNDICATE (A Division of United Media, A Scripps-Howard Company), 200 Park Ave., New York, NY 10166. (212) 692-3700. D.L. Drake, Executive Editor. David Hendin, VP/Editorial Director. Sarah Gillespie, Director of Comic Art.

□Syndicates columns, features, puzzles, and comic strips to more than 1,700 newspapers worldwide. Currently syndicates "Peanuts," "Garfield," and "Marmaduke" comics.

□"Cartoon drawing is a very difficult field," says Gillespie. "Study the newspapers to see what is already being done. I look for someone who can draw well, write funny lines, and who has an original voice. Don't be concerned with the concept—develop the comic strip."

□Offers standard syndication contract for columns and comic strips. Buys all rights (negotiable). For columns, prefers to receive queries with 5 or 6 samples; for comic strips, send 4 to 6 weeks of samples. Replies in 6 weeks. Author guidelines available. Send SASE.

UNIVERSAL PRESS SYNDICATE, 4900 Main St., Kansas City, MO 64112. (816) 932-6600. Lee Salem, Editorial Director.

□Accepts features, serialized books, comic strips, and columns for daily newspapers. Interested in food, travel, self-help, humor, and how-to; length varies. No one-shot stories or articles. Currently syndicates Betty Debnam ("Mini-Page" for children), "Doonesbury," "Cathi," "For Better/For Worse," "Ziggy," and "The Far Side."

□"Most of our writers are contracted to produce material on a weekly or biweekly basis," say the editors. "We don't encourage one-time appearance

articles. If you have a good idea for a *continuing* column or comic strip, send us a query."
☐Payment varies with individual contract. Buys all rights (negotiable). Prefers to receive query with 6 column samples; 4 to 6 weeks of samples for comic strips. Photocopies acceptable. Replies in 4 to 6 weeks. Author guidelines available. Send SASE.

WEEKLY FEATURES SYNDICATE LTD., 126 S. 8th St., St. Joseph, MO 64501. (816) 364-2920. Linda Bennett, Editor.
☐A newly established syndicate, Weekly Features primarily sells fiction to U.S. and foreign print media: romance, westerns, mysteries, short stories; length varies. Nonfiction should have domestic theme (interior decoration, holiday home design).
☐Pays 75% commission; up to $100 for acceptable photos accompanying a manuscript. Buys all rights (negotiable). Prefers to receive manuscript that isn't represented by an agent. Simultaneous submissions acceptable if editor is so informed. Replies in 4 to 6 weeks. Author guidelines available for 9″ × 12″ SASE. Send SASE with all submissions.

NINE

LITERARY AGENTS

Many writers dream of the day when they can nonchalantly say to an editor, "I'll have my agent get in touch with you about that." There's just something about that phrase, *my agent,* that sounds so impressive and successful to an author. The Society of Authors' Representatives (SAR), estimates that there are more than 200 literary firms in the U.S. that specialize in representing writers to the publishing industry.

Your agent is someone who represents your best interests in marketing your work. Most serious writers reach a point in their careers when they must consider the merits of going to an agent, when the time spent writing prevents proper self-marketing. It has been my experience, however, to observe that one of two things commonly happens when this "agent syndrome" hits: either the authors don't pursue an agent simply because they don't know how to begin, or they approach an agency with misconceptions as to what an agency can do.

Here's what an agent *can do* for you:

- Find appropriate markets for your manuscripts
- Examine and negotiate a contract in your best interest
- Examine book-royalty statements
- Collect overdue payments from publishers
- Obtain manuscript copyrights in your name
- Check on the editing and production of your manuscript by a publisher
- Represent any complaints you might have to a publisher
- Negotiate the specific sale of certain rights
- Reserve certain rights for later option purposes.

In return for these services—among others—an agency will charge a commission of 10% to 15% of your earnings as a writer.

And here's what an agent *can't do* for you:

- Teach you how to write
- Sell material that isn't salable
- Edit your manuscript until it's salable
- Act as your secretary
- Act as your lawyer or accountant
- Act as a banker and give you loans
- See you after working hours (except by appointment)
- Resolve your personal problems.

If you are easily hurt by rejection slips; if you would like to market your manuscript agressively but are not certain how to do so; if you would like to be able to bounce an idea off someone who's qualified to respond; and if you prefer to avoid learning the intricacies of contracts and copyright law, you should probably seek a good literary agent to represent your work. But be aware that some of the most successful agencies are reluctant to accept unpublished writers.

If you would rather not share 10% to 15% of your earnings with an agent, and if you are willing to work directly with publishers, then by all means continue to market your material yourself. The chances are good, especially if you have already established yourself among a strong network of editors, that you'll do just fine as an unagented author.

If you do decide to seek an agency, the agency may require you to sign a contract. Although a simple handshake used to suffice, today the author-agent agreement is committed to paper. This is because authors and agents want to protect themselves from a litigious society. A contract simply outlines the terms and conditions of what each party expects. If you are asked to sign such a document, consult your attorney before you sign on the dotted line.

Most literary agents in the U.S. belong to either the Society of Authors' Representatives (SAR) or the Independent Literary Agents Association (ILAA), and abide by ethics and rules outlined by each. Don't hesitate to ask about an agency's affiliations; if it has none, you might then want to inquire about its policies. According to some of the more commonly accepted financial practices recognized by literary agencies, an agency:

- Maintains separate bank accounts so that author's payments aren't mixed with the agency funds
- Pays clients within 10 days of receiving publisher's check
- Provides clients with itemized statements of expenses (but doesn't charge clients for normal office expenses)
- Treats the client's financial affairs as confidential

Reputable agencies give adequate notice to the client should the agency decide to terminate representation. (This may happen if a writeE goes "dry" for a long period of time; remember, agents are in business to make money, too!)

The following section lists a sampling of literary agencies and tells whether they currently seek new writers, what their requirements are, and most importantly, how to properly approach them. Break a rule here and you may jeopardize your chances for success. But abide by their wishes and allow them to do their job effectively, and the doors of opportunity may swing open.

MARCIA AMSTERDAM AGENCY, 41 W. 82nd St., New York, NY 10024. (212) 873-4945. Founded 1969. Marcia Amsterdam, President. Represents about 20 authors, including Joyce Sweeney and Rose Blue. Interested in new clients, including new and unpublished authors. Looks for originality. Obtains writers through inquiries and recommendations of editors, publishers and current clients.
☐Marcia Amsterdam Agency typically handles fiction, novels, humor, romance, science, and science fiction for juveniles and young adults. No poetry. Juvenile book represented: *Center Line* by Joyce Sweeney.
☐Accepts entire manuscript but prefers either partial manuscript or query letter. No reading fee charged. Commission fees: 15% for U.S.; 15% for Canada and England; 15% for foreign sales. No other fees. Affiliated with the Writers Guild. Send SASE.

JOSEPH ANTHONY AGENCY, 530 Valley Rd., Montclair, NJ 07043. (201) 746-7489. Founded 1964. Joseph Castrovilla, President. Represents many authors, including Max Barrett and Ed Adair. Interested in new clients, including new and unpublished authors. Obtains writers through inquiries and recommendations of editors, publishers, and current clients.
☐Handles fiction, education, romance, and picture books. No juvenile books currently represented. Looks for "good writing and something to say: a new style of writing and good dialogue that moves the story line." Interested in material about the problems of today's youth. Not accepted: pornography, poetry, romance, and articles.
☐"I do not rewrite, edit or blue-pencil your script," comments Anthony. "I am an agent, and an agent is out to sell a script. I do not offer a literary service, as many do. You write; we sell, if salable."
☐Accepts unsolicited manuscripts and outlines, but prefers to receive a query. Charges a reading fee: $50-$75 for novels; $75 for screenplays; $50 for TV screenplays; $75 for 2-hour TV movies; $30 for TV pilots; $20 for short stories. Commission fees: 15% of U.S. and film sales; 20% of foreign sales. No other fees. Affiliated with the Authors Guild and Writers Guild. Send SASE.

SHIRLEY BURKE AGENCY, 370 E. 76th St., B-704, New York, NY 10021. (212) 861-2309. Founded 1948. Shirley Burke, President. Represents about 20 authors, including Steve Longstreet and Lucy Freeman. Interested in new and unpublished authors. Looks for good education and publishing credits. Obtains writers through blind submissions and recommendations of editors, publishers, and current clients.
☐Handles fiction, novels, and some short stories for juveniles, and prefers young-adult contemporary stories. No pornographic or religious material. Juvenile books represented: an illustrated book by Cecil Maedon published by Vanguard Press.
☐Acepts unsolicited manuscripts and outlines, but prefers to receive query with outline and 2 sample chapters. No reading fee charged. Commission fees: 15% of sales to U.S. and Canada; 20% of foreign sales. SASE required.

RUTH CANTOR AGENCY, Room 1133, 156 5th Ave., New York, NY 10010. (212) 243-3246. Founded 1952. Ruth Cantor, President. Represents many authors, including Richard Puntill. Interested in new clients, including new and unpublished authors. Obtains writers through blind submissions, solicitations, referrals, inquiries, and recommendations of editors, publishers, and current clients.

☐Handles fiction, novels, nonfiction books, romance, science, women's and biographical material. No poetry, TV scripts, plays, pornography, short stories, magazine articles, or picture books. Has represented "hundreds" of juvenile books. Cantor is looking for "just good, salable, professionally executed, on-target material."

☐Accepts unsolicited outlines, but prefers to receive query with brief resume of publishing record and a synopsis of works in hand. No reading fee charged. Commission fees: 10% of sales in U.S.; 20% of foreign sales. Send SASE.

ANN ELMO AGENCY, INC., 60 E. 42nd St., New York, NY 10165. (212) 661-2880. Founded 1940. Ann Elmo, President. Lettie Lee, Editor. Represents about 50 authors, including Marilyn Durham and Hillary Waugh. "We represent novelists and nonfiction writers in adult and juvenile fields as well as playwrights." Interested in future clients; but no unpublished or new authors. Obtains writers through inquiries and recommendations of editors, publishers, college professors, and current clients.

☐Handles fiction, novels, nonfiction books, humor, romance, historical, women's, sports, stage plays, biographical, and documentary material. Looks for education and publishing credits. No fantasy, poetry, science fiction or textbooks. Juvenile books represented: All Zoa Sherburue books, and *The Great Brain* series by John J. Fitzgerald.

☐Accepts unsolicited outlines, but prefers to receive a query with summary and biography. No reading fee charged. Commission fees: 15% of U.S. sales; 20% of foreign sales. Other fees: a flat handling charge for novel manuscripts. Affiliated with the SAR, Authors Guild, and Writers Guild. SASE required.

HEACOCK LITERARY AGENCY, INC., 1523 6th St., Suite 14, Santa Monica, CA 90401. (213) 393-6227. Founded 1978. James B. Heacock, President. Rosalie G. Heacock, Vice-President. Represents 60 authors, including Martha Lambert, Othello Bach, and Audrey and Don Wood. Interested in new clients. Obtains writers through inquiries, blind submissions, solicitations, and recommendations of editors, publishers, and current clients. "We pay particular attention to referrals from our present clientele."

☐Handles fiction (5%), and nonfiction books (95%: science, biographical, and limited juvenile material). No pornography, magazine articles, poetry, or short stories. Juvenile titles represented: *Napping House* and *King Bidgood's in the Bathtub.*

☐Does not accept unsolicited manuscripts or outlines: prefers to receive a 1-page query. No reading fee. Commission fees: 15% of sales in U.S. and Canada; 25% of foreign sales; 10% of other sales. Affiliated with ILAA, Directors Guild, Authors Guild, and Writers Guild. Send SASE.

HINTZ & FITZGERALD, INC., 207 E. Buffalo St., Suite 211, Milwaukee, WI 53202. (414) 273-0300. Founded 1978. Sandy Hintz, President. Represents about 20 authors, including Dr. Karl Slaiken and Sharyn McCrumb. Interested in new clients; published authors preferred. Obtains writers through inquiries and recommendations of editors and current clients.

☐Handles fiction, novels, science, historical, science fiction, and biographical juvenile material.

☐Looks for "solid ideas/plots, writing styles, publishing credits, character development, potential." No educational texts. Juvenile books represented: *NASA Anniversary Book* and *Mars and the Inner Planets.*

☐Accepts unsolicited outlines, but prefers to receive a professionally-written query with author's credits and proposal. "We may ask to see sample chapters and a complete outline." No reading fee charged. Commission fees not available for publication. ILAA affiliation pending. Send SASE.

KAMBRINA AGENCY, PO Box 16, Depoe Bay, OR 97341. (503) 764-3433. Founded 1978. Kam Kavanaugh, President. Represents 37 authors ("not all active"). Interested in new clients, including new and unpublished authors. Obtains writers through solicitations and recommendations of publishers and current clients.

☐Handles fiction, novels, nonfiction books, romance, paramilitary, science fiction, mainstream novels, and how-to juvenile material.

☐Looks for authors with an "ability to write and willing to put out a presentable manuscript." No short stories, poetry, or plays. Juvenile books represented: *Three Grains of Sand* and *Blow the Man Down.*

☐Accepts unsolicited manuscripts, but prefers to receive a query. No reading fee charged. Commission fees: 10% of U.S. sales; 15% of sales to Canada and England; foreign and film sales negotiable. Send SASE.

SCOTT MEREDITH LITERARY AGENCY, 845 Third Ave., New York, NY 10022. (212) 245-5500. Founded 1946. Scott Meredith, President. Jack Scovil, Editorial Director. Represents 2,000 authors, including the juvenile books of Syd Hoff, Eth Clifford, and Arthur C. Clarke. Interested in new clients, including new and unpublished authors. Obtains writers through blind submissions, solicitations, inquiries, and recommendations from editors, publishers, and current clients.

☐Handles all types of material for juveniles and young adults. Does not consider "material which is derogatory to any religion, race, or other group."

☐"Our sole concern is the author's ability and the salability of material. Education is much less important; some top authors have substantial education, others don't."

☐Accepts unsolicited manuscripts and outlines, but prefers to receive query and writing sample. Reading fee: $150 to $250 for magazine fiction and articles; $200 to $600 for books; $200 to $600 for critiques; $200 to $250 for juvenile fiction and nonfiction; $200 to $250 for poetry (50 poems); $200 to $250 for other materials. Commission fees: 10% of U.S. and film sales; 20% of foreign sales. Send SASE.

DENNIS MULLENIX LITERARY SERVICES, 4210 N. University St., Peoria, IL 61614. (309) 682-9208. Founded 1978. Dennis Mullenix, President. Represents about 30 authors, including Sandra Douglas and James Duncan. Interested in new clients, including new and unpublished authors. Obtains writers from client referrals, blind submissions, solicitations, and inquiries.

☐Handles fiction, magazine articles, novels, short stories, nonfiction books, humor, romance, science fiction, biographical, religious, and picture books.

☐"We're especially interested in juvenile novels and short stories, and children's picture books." No pornography or obscene material. Juvenile books represented: *The Rooster that Saw the World* and *The White Alligator.*

□Does not accept unsolicited manuscripts or outlines; prefers to receive query. Charges a reading fee: $35 one-time agency fee. Editorial and typing services offered for additional fee. Commission fee: 10% of sales in U.S. and Canada; 20% of foreign and film sales. Send SASE.

MULTIMEDIA PRODUCT DEVELOPMENT, INC., 410 S. Michigan Ave., Suite 725, Chicago, IL 60625. (312) 922-3063. Founded 1971. Jane Jordan Browne, President. Represents about 75 authors, including Helen Hooven Santmyer and Mark Taylor. Interested in new clients, including new and unpublished authors. Obtains writers through recommendations of editors, publishers, and current clients.
□Handles fiction, novels, nonfiction books, romance, science, science fiction, and sports.
□"We're looking for extremely well-written fiction and science books." Looks for "professionalism in all aspects." No poetry, plays, or short stories. Juvenile books represented: *There's No Such Thing as a Channuka Bush* by Sue Sussman, *The Comet and You* by E.C. Krupp, and *The Case of the Purloined Compass* by Mark Taylor.
□Does not accept unsolicited manuscripts or outlines; prefers to receive "an intelligent, informative, compellingly written query letter." No reading fee charged; authors are charged for photocopying expenses. Commission fees: 15% of U.S., Canadian and film sales; 20% of foreign sales. Affiliated with the ILAA. Send SASE.

EVELYN SINGER LITERARY AGENCY INC., PO Box 594, White Plains, NY 10602. (914) 949-1147, (212) 799-5203. Founded 1951. Evelyn Singer, President. Represents about 75 authors, including Mary Elting and William (Beechcroft) Hallstead. Interested in new writers, including new and unpublished authors. Obtains writers through recommendations only.
□Handles fiction, novels, nonfiction books, romance, science, historical, science fiction, women's, sports, and biographical material.
□Looks for "previous publications or literary background, and whether the writer is an authority in a particular area or of celebrity status." No textbooks, poetry, or preschool picture books "unless written and illustrated by an author with previous publications." Juvenile books represented: *The Answer Book* and *Mrs. Billy Graham's Christmas Story.*
□"I'm especially interested in books either about current situations young people are in, or that would help young people cope."
□Accepts unsolicited outlines, but prefers to receive query outlining credentials and literary background. No reading fee charged. Commission fees: 10% of sales to U.S. and Canada; 15% of film sales; 20% of foreign sales. Send SASE.

GUNTHER STUHLMANN, AUTHOR'S REPRESENTATIVE, PO Box 276, Becket, MA 01223. (413) 623-5170. Founded 1954. Gunther Stuhlmann, President. Barbara Ward, Associate. Represents numerous authors, including Maia Wojciechowska, Newbery Medal Winner. Interested in new clients "only if extremely talented." Obtains writers only through recommendations.
□Handles novels, nonfiction books, biographies, documentaries, and religious material. "Especially interested in contemporary, young-adult fiction and nonfiction."

☐Looks for "literary talent in fiction writers, solid research capability and command of the English language in nonfiction writers. No science fiction, poetry, cartoons, or cute ideas for picture books. Juvenile books represented: *Shadow of a Bull, A Single Light,* and *Dangerous Journey.*

☐Accepts unsolicited outlines, but prefers to receive query letter with sample chapter and brief biographical background. No reading fee charged. Commission fees: 10% of U.S., Canadian and film sales; 15% of English sales; 20% of other foreign sales. Send SASE.

THE GERRY B. WALLERSTEIN AGENCY, 2315 Powell Ave., Erie, PA 16506. (814) 833-5511. Founded 1984. Ms. Gerry B. Wallerstein, President. Represents 45 authors, including humorist/cartoonist Tom Stratton, novelist Jack D. Coombe, and cartoonist Joe Kohl. Interested in new clients, including new and unpublished authors. Obtains writers through referrals, blind submissions, and listings.

☐Handles fiction, education, novels, nonfiction books, textbooks, poetry books, humor, romance, science, historical, science fiction, women's, sports, biographical, religious, and picture books.

☐Looks for "experienced and new writers who have good writing skills, an area of expertise, and who can accept constructive comment and advice. For clients, I handle any works they wish me to handle, if I think they are marketable." Exceptions: no plays, scripts, individual poems, or songs.

☐Prefers to receive query letter. Charges a reading fee: $50 for up to 5,000 words; $100 for 5,000 to 20,000 words; $200 for 20,000 to 65,000 words; $250 for more than 65,000 words. (No reading fees are charged to writers who have published regularly in major periodicals or who have sold a book or script.) Commission fees: 15% of U.S., Canadian, and film sales; 20% of foreign sales. Affiliated with the Authors Guild and Society of Professional Journalists. Send SASE.

TEN

A SENSE
OF BELONGING:
AFFILIATIONS

An organization can provide you with contacts and materials that you could not otherwise obtain—press credentials and passes, brochures containing contact names at publishing houses, information about job openings for writers, reduced medical/life insurance rates, vacation packages, free or low-cost legal aid, contract negotiation reports, newsletters informing you of industry happenings, and more. Professional affiliations can also be valuable should you ever decide to apply for a grant or fellowship; foundations and colleges tend to take such credentials into account in their decision-making.

Most writer's organizations specialize in a particular writing genre (e.g., children's writing, science writing, and most have moderate-to-difficult membership requirements.

It is not unusual for an organization to require affiliation with other professional guilds as a condition of membership. In these cases, apply for membership (if you qualify) with the required groups; after an acceptable period of time, you can then approach your original target for membership. To support your candidacy, many organizations also require you to submit three letters of reference from professionals in your field who know of you and your work: writers, editors, teachers, or publishers. Those you ask to recommend you should be knowlegable about your professionalism, ethics, aspirations, and your writing ability and accomplishments.

If you have published a book, you are eligible to join the Authors Guild, which has done much to improve the rights of authors worldwide. Most editors I have talked with weigh this credential heavily in a writer's favor when approached with a book proposal. Mentioning affiliation with the Authors Guild in your query letter tells the submissions editor that you have proven yourself as a professional.

This section describes a variety of writers' organizations that might interest you. If some of these do pique your interest, send for their brochures and application forms. Simply being affiliated with a professional organization will not sell your manuscripts, but at the very least, the experience will allow you to share with other writers the fun and mystery of writing.

THE AMERICAN SOCIETY OF JOURNALISTS AND AUTHORS, INC. (ASJA), 1501 Broadway, Suite 1907, New York, NY 10036. (212) 997-0947. Founded 1948. Dodi Schultz, President. Contact: Alexandra Cantor, Executive Secretary. A national organization with 5 regional chapters. "Includes more than 700 freelance writers of magazine articles, books, and general-interest nonfiction writing who have met the ASJA's exacting standards of professional achievements."
☐Offers conferences, dinner meetings, writers' referral service, members' directory and monthly newsletter, and ASJA awards programs. Committees: Editor-Writer Relations; Professional Rights Committees.
☐Membership requirements: must be a freelance writer of nonfiction for at least two years prior to application. Must have published a minimum of 8 articles, 2 books, or a combination of both. Trade credits, brochures, videos, or scripts are not sufficient by themselves for qualification. Two letters of recommendation are required. Charges initiation fee and annual dues.

THE AUTHORS GUILD, INC., 234 W. 44th St., New York, NY 10036. (212) 398-0838. Founded 1912. Madeleine L'Engle, President. Contact: Jean Wynne, Membership Secretary. "Acts as a collective voice for 6,000 writers in matters of joint professional and business concerns."
☐Keeps members informed of market changes, advises members on individual professional problems, sponsors workshops and discussions with experts in publishing trends and editor/author relationships, offers an Author's Fund for writers in financial need, and provides members with contract guidelines, special reports, surveys, statistical bulletins and a quarterly publication.
☐Note: "The 6,000 members of the Authors Guild are automatically members of The Authors League of America, which forms a family with its two component organizations—The Dramatists Guild and The Authors Guild. Each corporation has its own province. The two guilds protect and promote the professional interests of their members. Both guilds act together through the league on matters of joint concern to over 13,000 authors and playwrights: copyright protection, taxation, legislation, freedom of expression."
☐Membership requirements: must have published either a book with an established American publisher within 7 years prior to application, or 3 works (fiction or nonfiction) by a magazine of general circulation within 18 months prior to application. Charges initiation fee and annual dues.

MYSTERY WRITERS OF AMERICA, INC. (MWA), 105 E. 19th St., New York, NY 10003. (212) 473-8020. Contact: Executive Secretary. Membership includes authors of crime, mystery and suspense material, as well as editors and publishers of mystery books and magazines.
☐Membership requirements: must have sold at least 1 mystery or suspense piece to an established magazine or book publisher. Charges initiation fee and annual dues.

NATIONAL ASSOCIATION OF SCIENCE WRITERS (NASW), PO Box 294, Greenlawn, NY 11740. (516) 757-5664. Cristine Russell, President. Contact: Administrative Secretary. An affiliation of 1,100 writers and professionals who communicate science information from the research field to the general public.

□Provides members with annual reports, brochures on a variety of topics, and a quarterly newsletter. Regional chapters meet frequently, offering continuing-education programs and contacts.

□Membership requirements: must be actively engaged in disseminating scientific information and have two or more years experience in this field. Sponsorship by current NASW for 25 years.

NATIONAL PRESS CLUB, 14th and F St., N.W., Washington, D.C. 20045. (202) 662–7500. Andrew Mollison, President. Tom Squitieri, Vice-President. Randy Allen, Secretary. The oldest, largest and most prestigious press club in Washington, representing hundreds of reporters, editors, publishers, photographers, cartoonists, and information personnel from print and broadcast media based throughout the U.S. and overseas.

□Offers members evening debates and seminars on newsworthy topics, a weekly newsletter (*The Record*), domestic and foreign trips, a job-search committee, and in-house computerized reference center, teleconference services, conference facilities, luncheon news programs, a fitness center, and more.

□Membership requirements: must be a working journalist residing within 50 miles of the club for Active Member status. Other membership categories: Provisional, Non-Active, Associate, Non-Resident, and Graduate Student. Candidacy must be sponsored by three active members. Charges an initiation fee and annual dues.

THE NATIONAL WRITERS CLUB (NWC), 1450 S. Havana, Aurora, CO 80012. (303) 751–7844. James L. Young, Executive Director. Founded 1937. A nonprofit organization that acts as a collective voice for 5,000 freelance writers from all writing genre.

□Provides general assistance to writers by advocating authors' rights, attempting to correct unsatisfactory publishing practices, and advising on copyright, contracts, plagiarism, and libel. Offers members free Writer Research Reports (70 in all), market surveys, confidential reports, car rental discounts, agent referrals, complaint services, contests, workshops, writing courses, monthly and bimonthly publications, and a low-cost manuscript criticism service ($5 for 5,000 words).

□Membership requirements: must be a freelance writer. Charges initiation fee and annual dues.

PEN American Center, 568 Broadway, New York, NY 10012. (212) 334–1660. Founded 1921. A tax-exempt, nonprofit world organization of 10,000 (including 1,800 American) writers, poets, playwrights, essayists, editors, and novelists; 80 centers worldwide.

□Offers members panel discussions, receptions for authors, conferences, a variety of publications and reports, a translation committee, contests and awards, international congresses, a quarterly newsletter, and assistance to writers in prison and to writers in need.

□Membership requirements: "You must have published two or more books of literary merit, or one book that is generally acclaimed to be of exceptional distinction." No application form. Can self-nominate or be nominated by a current PEN member. Inquiries about membership should be directed to the PEN Admissions Committee. Charges annual dues.

THE SOCIETY OF CHILDREN'S BOOK WRITERS (SCBW), PO Box 296, Mar Vista Station, Los Angeles, CA 90066. "The only national organization for those who write or share an interest in children's literature." Offers brochures and pamphlets to members only. Publications include market reports, guide to contracts, research tips, and a publishing guide. Charges initiation fee and annual dues.

WRITERS GUILD OF AMERICA (WGA), East: 555 W. 57th St., New York, NY 10019. (212) 245-6180. West: 899 Beverly Blvd., Los Angeles, CA 90048. (213) 550-1000. A labor organization that represents all writers for screen, TV, and radio. Establishes minimum payment rates and author's rights within these media.
□Membership requirements: must have had a minimum of two scripts sold and produced. Charges annual dues.

ELEVEN

RECOGNITION: CONTESTS AND AWARDS

Sometimes money just isn't enough to satisfy a writer's need for acknowledgment. Nothing better affirms your place as a writer—and nothing is more satisfying—than receiving a prize or an award for something you have written.

If you want to enter a contest or nominate your work for an award, contact the sponsor to request more information, as well as an entry form.

Some contests require that you grant—in advance—reprint rights to your article or submission if it wins. In this case, make certain, if you do not hold the copyright on your work, that you receive written permission from the copyright holder allowing you and the contest sponsor(s) to reprint the piece. (If you have questions, contact your attorney or agent before submitting your entry.)

Don't be too disappointed if you don't win; the number of qualified entries in most writing contests is simply overwhelming. Judges have a difficult time in selecting winners, and it's not unusual for them to review the semifinalists' submissions several times before reaching a consensus.

Whether you win or not, I suggest heeding the wise words of poet Donald Hall:

"Prizes are all very nice if you get them, but if you don't get them, it's no big deal. You have to try as a writer to take it easy about the public response. Not to be bitter or worry about things, and not to let it go to your head if you are one of the lucky ones. But, rather, to keep at the desk, and keep working. That's all that counts."

Another way to bring yourself before the public's eye (and one that is occasionally profitable as well), is to list your name, writing specialty, and accomplishments in a variety of directories. By doing so, you not only promote yourself, but you may be able to get writing assignments from publishers and agencies that use these directories to find new talent.

One of the better directories for children's writers is *Something About Authors,* published annually by Gale Research Company (Book Tower,

Detroit, MI 48226). This directory is similar in style and format to its better-known sister publication, *Contemporary Authors.* In *Something About Authors* is information on some 6,000 writers and illustrators of children's books. Accompanying the text are hundreds of color reproductions of children's illustrations, as well as photographs of the artisans represented in the volume. There is no fee to apply for listing, but you must have published a children's book.

Other directories in which you might list your accomplishments include *Who's What and Where,* which lists minority journalists (PO Box 921, Detroit, MI 48231); *Freelancers of North America,* which lists more than 5,000 U.S. and Canadian freelance editors and writers (Author Aid/Research Associates International, 340 E. 52nd St., New York, NY 10022); and *Literary Marketplace,* which provides valuable information on the publishing industry as well as editorial services available throughout the U.S. (R.R. Bowker Company, 205 E. 42nd St., New York, NY 10017).

St. Martin's Press (175 5th Ave., New York, NY 10010) publishes a host of directories that list noted writers: *Twentieth Century Children's Writers, Twentieth Century Science Fiction Writers, Contemporary Poets, Contemporary Novelists,* and *Twentieth Century Crime and Mystery Writers.*

Gale Research Company also publishes *Contemporary Authors,* which is well known for the thoroughness of its biographies. Some entries have included transcripts of interviews with authors, rare photographs, and excerpts from published works. This directory usually lists about 1,200 active writers (in all genres) within each volume. An index to the approximately 80,000 previous entries is published every other volume.

To be listed in any of these directories, first request the proper forms. Be prepared to submit anything from a resume to clippings of published works, to letters of reference, to photocopies of your credentials; such requests are not uncommon. Make certain that your application is neat, complete and does not contain misleading information; the review committee of each publication examines every application carefully.

By entering contests and submitting listings for publication in well-known directories, you improve your chances of recognition. You also may earn some money from your efforts. But even if you receive neither fame nor fortune, you will have the satisfaction of knowing that you made the effort, and that you struggled alongside the best of today's literary figures.

THE JANE ADDAMS CHILDREN'S BOOK AWARD, Jane Addams Peace Association, 5477 Cedonia Ave., Baltimore, MD 21206. (301) 488-6987. Founded 1953. Annual award for the children's book (preschool through high school) that promotes world peace and social justice. Contact: Annette C. Blank. Deadline: March 15.

AMERICAN ASSOCIATION OF UNIVERSITY WOMEN AWARD, c/o North Carolina Literary & Historical Association, 109 E. Jones St., Raleigh, NC 27611. (919) 733-7305. Annual award to a published work of juvenile fiction, nonfiction, or poetry by a North Carolina resident. Contestant must reside in North Carolina for at least 3 years prior to the end of the contest. Contact: Rebecca A. Myer. Deadline: July 15.

AMERICAN BOOK AWARDS, Association of American Publishers, 1 Park Ave., New York, NY 10016. Recognizes books of distinction and literary merit in 18 categories, including children's fiction, children's picture books, and children's nonfiction. Books must be written or translated by a U.S. citizen and published by a U.S. publisher during the preceding calendar year. Award: $1,000. Query for details.

AMERICAN MINORITY PLAYWRIGHT'S FESTIVAL, The Group Theater Company, 3940 Brooklyn Ave., N.E., Seattle, WA 98105. (206) 545-4969. Honors 1-act and full-length plays written by minority playwrights in America.

HANS CHRISTIAN ANDERSEN PRIZE, International Board on Books for Young People, The Children's Book Council, 300 Barksdale Rd., Newark, DE 19714. (302) 731-1600. Founded 1956. Two medals awarded biennially: one to an author, the other to an illustrator, for their complete works. An honor list recognizes top writings and cites outstanding translators of children's books. Contact: Alida Cutts.

ANNUAL DELACORTE PRESS PRIZE FOR OUTSTANDING FIRST YOUNG-ADULT NOVEL, Delacorte Books for Young Readers, 245 E. 47th St., New York, NY 10017. (212) 605-3555. Considers unpublished, contemporary novels for young-adult readers.

AVON/FLARE YOUNG-ADULT NOVEL COMPETITION. Avon Books, 1790 Broadway, New York, NY 10019. (212) 399-1384. A fiction contest open to young writers, ages 13 to 18. Novel manuscript should be between 30,000 to 50,000 words. Send SASE with all submissions. Winning entry is published by Avon/Flare for an advance of $2,500 against royalties. Send SASE for complete list of rules.

ALVINE BELISLE AWARD, Asted, Inc., 7243 St. Denis, Montreal, Quebec H2R 2E3, Canada. (514) 271-3349. Presented annually to the author of the best juvenile book published in French in Canada during the year prior. Award: $500. Query for details. Contact: Lise Brousseau, Executive Director.

THE IRMA SIMONTON BLACK AWARD, Bank Street College of Education, 610 W. 112th St., New York, NY 10025. Annual award for a children's book, suitable for ages 3 to 8, that is judged excellent in text and illustration. Poetry books considered. Contact: William Hooks. Deadline: January 15.

THE BOOK OF THE YEAR FOR CHILDREN MEDAL, Canadian Library Association, 151 Sparks St., Ottawa, Ontario K1P 5E3, Canada. (204) 985-6488. Founded 1947. Honors the most outstanding children's fiction or poetry book of the year written by either a Canadian or a resident of Canada. Deadline: December 31. Contact: Bessie C. Egan or Joan Tutton.

BOSTON GLOBE-HORN BOOK AWARD, The Boston Globe, Boston, MA 02107. (617) 929-2000. Award for the best children's trade books (fiction, nonfiction, picture book) published in America. Award: $200. Contact: Stephanie Loer. Deadline: April 1.

CALDECOTT MEDAL, American Library Association, 50 E. Huron, Chicago, IL 60611. (312) 944-6780. Presented to outstanding illustrators of children's books; one of the most respected awards in children's literature.

CANADA COUNCIL CHILDREN'S LITERATURE PRIZES, Canada Council, PO Box 1047, Ottawa, Ontario K1P 5V8, Canada. (613) 237-3400. Awards prizes to writers and illustrators of juvenile/young-adult books.

CHILDREN'S LITERATURE PRIZES, Canada Council, PO Box 1047, Ottawa, Ontario K1P 5V8, Canada. (613) 237-3400. Founded 1975. Annual $5,000 award to Canadian authors and illustrators of juvenile literature. Two awards are given for English titles; two for French titles. Contact: L. Rochon. Query for deadlines.

CHILDREN'S SCIENCE BOOK AWARDS, New York Academy of Sciences, 2 E. 63rd St., New York, NY 10021. (212) 838-0230. An annual $500 award to the best general or trade book on a science topic for children. Two divisions: books for children under age 10; books for children ages 10 to 16. Contact: Ann E. Collins. Deadline: November 30.

CHILDREN'S & YOUNG ADULTS' AWARDS, The Texas Institute of Letters, PO Box 8594, Waco, TX 76710. (817) 772-0095. A $400 prize awarded annually for the best book for children and young adults by a Texan. Deadline: January 15. Contact: John Weems.

CHRISTOPHER AWARDS, 12 E. 48th St., New York, NY 10017. (212) 759-4050. Founded 1949. Annual medallion for adult and juvenile fiction/nonfiction published during the calendar year. Contact: Peggy Flanagan. Deadline: December 31.

MARIE-LOUISE D'ESTERNAUX POETRY SCHOLARSHIP, The Brooklyn Poetry Circle, 61 Pierepont St., Brooklyn, NY 11201. (718) 875-8736. Founded 1965. A $50 award given for the best poem (24 lines or less) written by a student, age 16 to 21. Deadline: April 1. Contact: Gabrielle Lederer.

E.P. DUTTON ANIMAL BOOK AWARD, E.P. Dutton, 2 Park Ave., New York, NY 10016. (212) 725-1818. Offers an advance against royalty for an original book-length manuscript, fiction or nonfiction, about an animal or animals. Query for details.

DOROTHY CANFIELD FISHER CHILDREN'S BOOK AWARD, 138 Main St., Montpelier, VT 05601. (802) 658-0238. Founded 1956. Annual award for the best book for children ages 9 to 14 by an American author. Books must be submitted during year of publication. Winners determined by Vermont children. Deadline: December 31. Contact: Kathleen Campbell.

FRIENDS OF AMERICAN WRITERS JUVENILE BOOK AWARDS, Friends of American Writers, 400 E. Randolf St., Chicago, IL 60601. (312) 527-1715. Founded 1960. A monetary award for a book for children (toddlers through high-school age) that either has a Midwestern slant or is written by a native (or 5-year resident) of the Midwest. Books must be submitted by publishers. Query for details. Deadline: December 31. Contact: Jean Morrison.

GENERAL ELECTRIC FOUNDATION AWARDS FOR YOUNGER WRITERS, Coordinating Council of Literary Magazines, 666 Broadway, New York, NY 10012. (212) 481-5245. The awards recognize excellence in new writers while honoring the significant contribution of America's literary magazines. Considers poetry, essays, and fiction.

GOLDEN KITE AWARDS, Society of Children's Book Writers, PO Box 296, Mar Vista Station, Los Angeles, CA 90066. (818) 347-2849. Annually recognizes outstanding children's books in fiction, nonfiction, and picture books written and/or illustrated by members of the society. Contact: Sue Alexander. Query for deadline.

GOLDEN SPUR AWARD, Western Writers of America, 1052 Meridian Road, Victor, MT 59875. Annual award recognizing outstanding western literature published in the preceding calendar year; 7 categories, including Best Juvenile Western (fiction or nonfiction). Query for details. Deadline: December 31.

GOLD MEDALLION BOOK AWARDS, Evangelical Christian Publishers Association, PO Box 2439, Vista, CA 92083. (619) 941-1636. Founded 1977. Annual award recognizing outstanding religious books from the previous year in a variety of categories, including children's books, Christian education, textbooks, poetry, and marriage and family. Contact: C.E. Andrew, Director. Deadline: October 31.

GUIDEPOSTS MAGAZINE **YOUTH WRITING CONTEST,** *Guideposts Magazine,* 747 3rd Ave., New York, NY 10017. Contact: James McDermott, Editor. Considers unpublished first-person, true stories (1,200 words maximum) with a religious theme, written by high-school juniors or seniors. Deadline: November 27.

HIGHLIGHTS FOR CHILDREN **FICTION CONTEST,** *Highlights for Children,* 803 Church St., Honesdale, PA 18431. Contact: Fiction Contest Editor. An annual contest for children's writers. Specifications: 600 words maximum for beginner readers; 900 words maximum for readers aged 9 to 12. No entry fee or entry form required. Deadline: March 31.

AMELIA FRANCES HOWARD-GIBBON ILLUSTRATOR'S AWARD, Canadian Association of Children's Librarians, Canadian Library Association, 151 Sparks St., Ottawa, Ontario K1P 5E3, Canada. (613) 232-9625. Founded 1971. Gold medal awarded annually to the most outstanding illustration for a children's book published in Canada. The illustrator must be a Canadian citizen or resident. Query for details.

INTERNATIONAL READING ASSOCIATION CHILDREN'S BOOK AWARD, International Reading Association, PO Box 8139, 800 Barksdale Rd., Newark, DE 19714. (302) 731-1600. Founded 1975. An annual award of $1,000 to an author of promise for author's first or second work published the previous year. Fiction and nonfiction categories. Deadline: December 1. Contact: Drew Cassidy.

JUVENILE BOOK AWARDS, Friends of American Writers, PO Box 1051, Park Ridge, IL 60068. (312) 527-1715. Contact: Jean Morrison. Presents awards for published juvenile books, fiction and nonfiction.

THE CORETTA SCOTT KING AWARD, American Library Association (Social Responsibilities Round Table), 50 E. Huron St., Chicago, IL 60611. (312) 944-6780. Founded 1969. Annual awards given to a black author and a black illustrator for outstanding contributions which promote peace and world brotherhood. Contact: Henrietta M. Smith. Deadline: December 31.

MADEMOISELLE **MAGAZINE FICTION COMPETITION,** *Mademoiselle* Magazine, 350 Madison Ave., New York, NY 10017. (212) 880-8591. Publication of story and $1,000 awarded annually to best original fiction written by an unpublished writer, age 18 to 30. Story not to exceed 25 pages. Query for details. Deadline: March 15. Contact: Eileen A. Schnurr.

VICKY METCALF AWARD, Canadian Authors Association, 24 Ryerson Ave., Toronto, Ontario M5T 2P3, Canada. (416) 868-6916. Founded 1980. Recognizes a body of work (4 books or more), written by a Canadian author, that is inspiring to Canadian children. All submissions must be previously published. Query for details. Deadline: December 31. Contact: Virginia Sumodi, Executive Director.

MILNER AWARD, Friends of the Atlanta Public Library, 1 Margaret Mitchell Square N.W., Atlanta, GA 30303. (404) 688-4034. Founded 1982. Glass sculpture and $1,000 awarded annually to an American author of children's books. Winner determined by children of Atlanta. Deadline: 2nd week of November. Contact: Carol Phillips.

NATIONAL JEWISH BOOK AWARD, Jewish Book Council, 15 E. 26th St., New York, NY 10010. (212) 532-4949. Contact: Ruth Frank, Director. Honors authors and illustrators of children's books with Jewish themes.

NATIONAL PLAY AWARD, PO Box 71011, Los Angeles, CA 90071. (213) 629-3762. Contact: David Parrish, Literary Manager. Considers unpublished plays that have not been professionally produced.

NEWBERY MEDAL, American Library Association, 50 E. Huron St., Chicago, IL 60611. (312) 944-6780. Honors outstanding children's books; one of the most coveted awards in Children's Literature.

NEW YORK TIMES **BEST ILLUSTRATED CHILDREN'S BOOK AWARDS,** New York Times, Inc. Presents awards to notable illustrated children's books, fiction and nonfiction.

SCOTT O'DELL AWARD FOR HISTORICAL FICTION, c/o Bulletin of the Center for Children's Books, University of Chicago, 1100 E. 57th St., Chicago, IL 60637. (312) 962-8284. Founded 1981. Annual cash award for outstanding historical fiction for children. Deadline: December 31. Contact: Zena Sutherland.

PACIFIC NORTHWEST YOUNG READER'S CHOICE AWARD, Pacific Northwest Library Association, University of Washington, Graduate School of Library & Information Science, 133 Suzzallo Library, FM–30, Seattle, WA 98195. (206) 543–1794. Annual award recognizing the author of a book popular with children ages 9 to 14. Deadline: February 15. Contact: Mae Benne.

PIONEER DRAMA PLAYWRITING AWARD, Pioneer Drama Service, 2172 S. Colorado Blvd., PO Box 22555, Denver, CO 80222. (303) 759–4297. An annual award that recognizes an outstanding full-length, unpublished play (original or adaptation) intended as a drama, children's theater, comedy, or musical. All submissions must be produced prior to deadline. Winning plays are published. Query for details and deadline.

PLAYWRITING FOR CHILDREN AWARD, Community Children's Theater, 8021 E. 129th Terr., Grandview, MO 64030. (816) 761–5775. Awards prizes to unpublished plays intended for 1st- through 6th-grade students.

EDGAR ALLAN POE AWARDS, Mystery Writers of America, 150 Fifth Ave., New York, NY 10011. (212) 255–7005. Annual recognition of the best mysteries published in America, including best juvenile novel. Deadline: December 31. Query for details.

THE CARL SANDBURG LITERARY ARTS AWARDS, Given by Friends of the Chicago Public Library, 78 E. Washington St., Chicago, IL 60602. (312) 269–2922. Contact: CSLAA Director. Presents awards to Chicago writers of a variety of genres, including children's literature (fiction and nonfiction).

SEQUOYAH CHILDREN'S BOOK AWARD, Oklahoma Department of Libraries, 2500 N. Lincoln, Oklahoma City, OK 73105. (405) 521–2956. Founded 1959. Plaque awarded annually to an American author of children's literature. Winner determined by children in grades 3 to 6. Deadline: January. Query for details. Contact: Betty Riley.

SEVENTEEN **MAGAZINE SHORT STORY CONTEST,** *Seventeen* Magazine, 850 Third Ave., New York, NY 10022. (212) 759–8100. First prize of $500 awarded annually for best original fiction (1,500 to 3,000 words) written by a teenager. Deadline: July 1. Query for details. Contact: Bonni Price.

SYDNEY TAYLOR BODY-OF-WORK AWARD, Association of Jewish Libraries, c/o National Foundation for Jewish Culture, #1512, 122 E. 42nd St., New York, NY 10168. (212) 427–1000. Founded 1978. Scroll and $1,000 awarded annually to children's authors in recognition of their contributions to Judaica for children. Contact: Esther Nussbaum.

TEXAS BLUEBONNET AWARD, Texas Library Association, Texas Association of School Librarians & Children's Round Table, 3355 Bee Cave Rd., Suite 603, Austin, TX 78746. (409) 294–1150. Founded 1979. Medallion awarded to most popular children's book as determined by children in grades 3 to 6. Query for details. Contact: Janelle Paris.

WILLIAM ALLEN WHITE CHILDREN'S BOOK AWARD, Emporia State University Library, 1200 Commercial St., Emporia, KS 66801. (316) 343-1200. Founded 1952. Bronze medal awarded for the most popular children's book as determined by children in grades 3 to 6. Candidate selection: by committee. Query for details. Contact: Mary E. Bogan.

LAURA INGALLS WILDER MEDAL, Association for Library Service to Children, American Library Association, 50 E. Huron St., Chicago, IL 60611. (312) 944-6780. Founded 1954. Bronze medal awarded triennially to an author or illustrator whose books have made a lasting contribution to children's literature. Query for details. Contact: Ann Weeks, Director.

GLOSSARY

Advance. Money paid to an author prior to publication, representing an advance payment of a portion of royalties expected to be earned through the sale of the author's book.

Auction. The sale of a book to the highest bidder. An auction generally is initiated by a literary agent or publisher. This form of sale was invented some 20 years ago by literary agent Scott Meredith.

B&W. Black and white.

Bimonthly. Every other month (also, twice monthly).

Bio. Biography; a short paragraph about the writer. Bios are typically located at the end of a magazine article or on a contributor's page in the front of the magazine. For books, the bio is usually on the back flap.

Biweekly. Every other week (also, twice weekly).

Byline. The author's name, usually printed at the beginning of a story or article: "By J. Jones."

Caption. Description of a photograph; usually appears beneath or beside the published photo or illustration.

Chapbook. A small booklet, usually 25 to 50 pages, of poetry or short stories.

Clean copy. What every editor dreams of: manuscript with virtually no errors, smudges, dogged ears, wrinkles, or deletions.

Clips (also tearsheets). Samples—from a magazine or newspaper—of a writer's published work. (Send photocopies, never originals.)

Column inch. All the text contained in one vertical inch of a typeset newspaper column.

Concept. A very brief statement, usually one sentence or paragraph, that summarizes a play or script. A concept typically is done before an outline, synopsis, or treatment is begun. Many book and magazine writers include the concept in a query letter.

Contributor's copies. Free copies of the publication in which an author's work appears.

Copyedit. To edit a manuscript for style, subject, grammar, punctuation, and consistency. (*See also* Proofreading.)

El-hi. Elementary to high school.

Feature. An in-depth article or story.

Filler. Very short material used by editors to "fill" remaining space in their magazines and newspapers: jokes, cartoons, humorous stories, and poetry.

Flat Fee. A one-time payment.

Gagline. The "punch-line" of a joke; also appears with cartoons and greeting cards.

Glossy. A B&W photograph with a shiny, smooth finish, as opposed to a matte finish.

Gothic novel. The storyline generaly contains these elements: an attractive, young female protagonist; a handsome, strong male hero; a mansion/castle or medieval setting; and either a real or supernatural threat.

Guarantee. A nonreturnable, guaranteed, payment to an author.

Guidelines. A sheet provided to prospective contributors outlining the specific writing style, submission requirements, payment rates, and thematic needs of a publisher.

Illustration. Any form of artwork, including ink drawings, air-brush paintings, sketches, engravings, and cartoons. Photos are not considered illustration.

International reply coupon (IRC). Use these in place of an SASE when sending manuscripts to Canada and other foreign countries. The U.S. post office can determine the required number of IRCs for your manuscript.

Kill fee. A portion of the agreed payment for a manuscript is often paid the author when a manuscript is rejected for reasons beyond the writer's control. A percentage of 33% is the industry standard for kill fees.

Model release form. A permission form to be signed by the subject of a photograph. This form gives the photographer the subject's permission to use the photograph for the purposes stated in the release.

Morgue. A publisher's files of clips, photographs, manuscripts, and other materials, usually kept for up to 3 or 5 years before being destroyed.

Ms. Manuscript.

Mss. Manuscripts.

Multiple submission. A manuscript simultaneously sent to several publishers with non-overlapping markets. Not a good idea for larger magazines. If you are multiply submitting, always state the fact in your cover letter. Compare *Simultaneous Submission*.

Novelette. A short novel, generally 6,000 to 15,000 words.

Outline. A summary of a manuscript's contents, usually presented in a vertical format with chapter headings and short, descriptive sentences.

Package sale. Manuscript sold with photos or illustration.

Page rate. The amount paid for an article according to its length.

Payment on acceptance. Payment made as soon as a decision is made to publish a manuscript (the payment method preferred by authors).

Payment on publication. Payment made *only* after a manuscript has been published. Since many months may elapse between a publisher's decision to purchase the manuscript and the actual date the piece is published, payment on publication is not to the author's advantage.

Photo feature. A magazine or newspaper feature that has as its emphasis not the text, but the photographs.

Plagiarism. Using another's ideas or words without attribution.

Proofread. To edit a manuscript for punctuation rather than for style and content. (*See also* Copyedit.)

Public domain. Uncopyrighted.

Q&A. Question-and-answer text, printed verbatim.

Query. A 1- or 2-page letter written to pique an editor's interest in a manuscript or an idea. It typically describes the story's slant, its intended readership, its approximate length, the availability of photos/illustrations, and the author's credentials for writing such a manuscript.

Rebus. Illustrations or symbols used to replace a familiar word or phrase (e.g., a drawing of a cat as a substitute for the word "cat").

Response time. The average length of time it takes an editor to accept or reject a manuscript and inform you of the decision.

Royalty. A percentage of the earned income of a book that is paid the author. Example: 10% of the retail price for the first 10,000 copies sold; 12% for the next 5,000; and 15% on all other sales above 15,000 copies.

SASE. Self-Addressed, Stamped Envelope.

SAPC. Self-Addressed Post Card.

Serial comma. An optional comma inserted before the words "and" or "or" when listing two or more things in a sentence (e.g., I like cats, dogs, and birds).

Sidebar. A short article that accompanies a feature, and either: 1) focuses and expands on one aspect of the feature, or 2) provides captivating, human-interest information that parallels the feature's primary slant.

Simultaneous submission. The submission of a manuscript to a variety of publishers, often with overlapping markets, at the same time. Many publishers object to this, and it is best to query publishers before attempting simultaneous submissions. Compare Multiple submission.

Slides. Color transparencies.

Slush pile. *See* Unsolicited manuscripts.

Speculation. Written with no guarantee of purchase.

Subsidy publisher (also vanity press). A book publishing house that charges authors to produce, market, and distribute their books. Several well-known authors began their literary careers through subsidy publishing, including William R. Burroughs of *Tarzan* fame.

Synopsis. A 1- to 2-page summary of a book's contents or a script's plot.

Tearsheets. *See* Clips.

Teleplay. A drama written for television.

Transparencies. Positive color slides.

Treatment. A synopsis of a play, television, or film script; far more detailed than an outline.

Unsolicited manuscript. Material sent to an editor or publisher that has not been requested.

Vanity press. *See* Subsidy publisher.

INDEX

SUBJECT INDEX/MAGAZINES

PSYCHOLOGY

PUZZLES/JOKES/RIDDLES

RELIGION

SUBJECT INDEX/BOOK PUBLISHERS